VIRGINIA

American Historical Press
Sun Valley, California

VIRGINIA

A COMMONWEALTH COMES OF AGE

AN ILLUSTRATED HISTORY

LISA ANTONELLI BACON

Photos attributed to:

Roanoke Valley Chamber of Commerce, Courtesy Roanoke Regional Chamber of Commerce.

Printing Services, Archives, University of Virginia Library, Courtesy Prints File, Special Collections, University of Virginia Library.

Library of Congress Catalogue Card Number: 2004110806
ISBN: 1-892724-43-X

Bibliography: page 356
Includes Index

CONTENTS

"The Reward of Industry," a fitting slo-gan for the state of Virginia, was the motto adopted by tobacco manufacturers D.C. Mayo and Company in Richmond for this early label. Courtesy, Virginia State Library

ACKNOWLEDGMENTS

◆

There are many people who contributed their talents, ideas, and efforts to this book. I would like to thank the venerable Virginius Dabney for his suggestions, as well as for all his illuminative writings. Friends Lewis F. Powell III, Stuart Shelton, and Stephen Gill lent their professional support, and for this I would like to offer heartfelt appreciation. There are other folks—particularly Peter Galuszka, Jim Bacon, and the librarians of the Virginia State Library—without whom my research would have been much longer and more laborious. Special thanks to Amber Avines, a great rescuer and a kind editor. With thanks and dedication to all the Antonelli men—past, present, and future—and the few strong women who willingly put up with them, and to Brad and Bradley, who put the sparkle in my eyes.

Lisa Antonelli Bacon

This primitive method of taking tobacco to market in Virginia was employed in the early 1800s. Courtesy, Valentine Museum

INTRODUCTION

When this book was first published back in 1988, Northern Virginia was an up-and-coming technology center based mainly on federal contracting. It seems incredible, but companies like America Online and MCI didn't even rate a mention back then. Today, the region has broadened its technology leadership to include telecommunications, software, and the Internet. In what seemed a distant dream at the time, the tech community has diversified its customer base. Although federal spending still underpins the economy, an increasing number of companies, fueled by a vibrant venture capital sector, develop products and services for national, even global, markets. Indeed, technology now surpasses the federal government as the major employer in the Washington, D.C., metro area.

While Northern Virginia has established its clear dominance as a center of corporate activity and economic growth, the state's other regions have struggled to reinvent themselves for a globally integrated economy. The Richmond region has managed to match the growth of the national economy, generating enough new start-ups and high-growth companies to replace a slew of lost corporate and banking headquarters, the restructuring of its manufacturing sector, and the downsizing of the tobacco industry. But Hampton Roads, which enjoyed booming defense spending during the 1980s, has yet to define a new role for itself in an era of a downsized military. Meanwhile, foreign competition and outsourcing have decimated the economic underpinnings of Virginia's mill-town economies. Fortunately, bright spots can be found in Charlottesville, Blacksburg, and Harrisonburg, where universities nurture the growth of local technology and knowledge-based businesses.

An old maxim warns us that those who are ignorant of history are doomed to repeat it. In the 1988 edition, I argued that the admonition needed to be restated: Those who are ignorant of history may be tempted to deviate from it. Virginians, I contended, were doing something right and needed not—to borrow another adage—fix what was not broken. Despite the legacy of slavery, which hindered the modernization of the agricultural sector, Virginia was a leader in the commercial and industrial revolutions of the early nineteenth century. Although the Civil War and its aftermath destroyed 250 years of accumulated wealth and saddled the state with a debt burden reminiscent of a Third World country, the state's economy consistently outperformed the nation's for most of the twentieth century. By the mid-1980s, average per capita income in the Old Dominion moved well past the national average.

The certitudes of 1988, however, are cracking. Virginia's economy has continued to outperform national averages, but the aggregate figures obscure a troubling reality. There are two Virginias—the booming, confident, tech-savvy economy of Northern Virginia (NoVa), and the tentative, often-struggling economy of the Rest of Virginia (RoVa). RoVa communities continue to pursue the economic development strategies—recruitment of out-of-state manufacturing and back-office operations, primarily—that propelled Virginia's success during the second half of the twentieth century. But, as China emerges in the new millennium as the world's workshop and India as the world's back-office and fulfillment center, corporate expansions and relocations are increasingly scarce.

Northern Virginia has figured out what it wants to be when it grows up. Indeed, it *has* grown up. The cluster of information and telecommunications companies in the Washington suburbs south of the Potomac can credibly claim to be one of the leading centers of technological and business innovation in the world. High-tech companies from outside the state relocate to Fairfax, Arlington, or Alexandria on almost a weekly basis.

Despite the dot.com crash, the Washington area economy has boasted one of the strongest regional economies in the country since 1999, creating roughly 180,000 new jobs. Federal spending since 9/11 on military transformation and homeland security—highly information-intensive fields—undoubtedly gave the region a boost, but the breadth of new business formation suggests that federal spending is only one factor among many driving the region's growth.

Other regions are going through painful reappraisals. The Richmond region probably has given more *thought*, than any other area, to reinventing its approach to economic development in the Knowledge Economy. It has focused on recruiting and retaining members of the "creative class," those artistically, scientifically, and entrepreneurially gifted individuals who contribute disproportionately to economic growth. At this point, however, the new thinking has not yet translated into significant new priorities for investing finite community resources.

Meanwhile, Southside and Southwest Virginia communities are rethinking rural economic development without tobacco and textiles. Under the umbrella of the Virginia Tobacco Indemnification and Community Revitalization Commission, funded by the settlement with major tobacco companies, these communities are investing in broadband access and distance learning as tools to overcome their traditional rural isolation.

Among other positive signs, there is near-universal recognition among Virginia's political, business, and civic elite that the state must invest in its educational system if its citizens are to share in the fruits of a global economy. The 2004 session of the General Assembly marked a significant shift in state policy with the passage of the largest tax increase in state history and allocation of significant new funds to the K-12 education system. There appears to be a consensus that, as undesirable as higher taxes may be, a better educated workforce is an absolute prerequisite for continued growth.

Frustratingly, no consensus has congealed on the issue of transportation funding. Growing traffic congestion in the major metro areas and interstate corridors is creating a fiscal crisis; the Commonwealth needs to raise tens of billions over the next 20 years to fund the transportation projects that planners say are needed. But a major strain of public opinion is skeptical that raising taxes and building more roads will do anything more than subsidize urban sprawl. In 2003, voters rejected the taxes-for-roads formula in regional referenda in Northern Virginia and Hampton Roads.

Every state, of course, is confronting the issues of taxes, education, and transportation funding, and few can claim to have found the ideal solution. As Virginia muddles through these complex issues, it will continue to be well-served by its traditional strengths: a AAA bond rating and sound finances, one of the finest systems of public education in the country, one of the fastest-growing ports in the U.S., its status as a right-to-work state, a relative conservative judiciary, and a pro-business regulatory climate.

As global trade reshapes Virginia's economy—crippling some industries, giving rise to new ones—it is worthwhile to recall the birth of the colony as a plantation culture tied into the global economy of the seventeenth and eighteenth centuries. Dependent upon a single cash crop, tobacco, Virginia was far more vulnerable to the vicissitudes of overseas markets than it is today. Virginians, unlike their fellow Americans in many other states, are accustomed to seeing themselves as part of a larger international trading system. Most importantly, they are resilient, accepting both the necessity for change and the need to adapt.

James A. Bacon
Publisher
Bacon's Rebellion

A TIMELINE OF VIRGINIA HISTORY

1606

Three ships carrying 104 people set sail from England to find riches in the New World.

1607

British settlers arrived in Jamestown.

1610

Felled by illness and starvation, 44 settlers died.

1612

John Rolfe planted Virginia's first tobacco crop.

1614

John Rolfe married Pocahontas, ensuring peace between colonists and Indians.

1618

Peace ended with the death of Chief Powhatan, Pocahontas' father.

1619

The first African slaves arrived in Virginia.

1624

King James revoked charter of The London Company.

1625

Royal Proclamation banned Spanish tobacco shipments to England, giving Virginia tobacco farmers a captive market.

1634-1704

Two-thousand indentured servants arrived in Virginia.

1642

The practice of transporting felons from England to Virginia ended.

1651-1663

A series of Navigation Acts required colonial exports to be transported in English ships. Seeds of dissension took root in Virginia.

1665

The first play ever produced in the Colonies, *Ye Beare and Ye Cubb*, was enacted in Accomack County.

1676

Bacon's Rebellion.

1693

The College of William and Mary was founded in Williamsburg.

Visitors arrive at the Governor's Palace in Williamsburg aboard a horse-drawn carriage, circa 1948. Courtesy, The Library of Virginia

1699

Williamsburg became the capital of the colony.

1700

Virginia's population reached 63,000.

1713

The Warehouse Act created an inspection system to standardize tobacco grades.

1716

Alexander Spotswood explored the western territories.

1722

A peace treaty between Iroquois and settlers opened the way for westward expansion.

1726

Benjamin Harrison, a signer of the Declaration of Independence, was born at Berkeley Plantation. His son, William Henry Harrison, became the ninth U.S. President.

1727

Speculators took advantage of land grants settled in western territories.

1735

Miners found significant amounts of coal in Midlothian, west of Richmond.

1750

Westward expansion took hold and towns like Winchester, Stephensburg, Woodstock, and Lexington sprang up.

1763

The Proclamation of 1763 prohibited Virginians from staking claim to land beyond the Alleghanys.

1764

The British Stamp Act sparked Colonial unrest.

1775

Patrick Henry delivered his famous "Give me liberty or give me death" speech in St. John's Church in Richmond. The Third Constitutional Convention committed the colony to war.

1776

Richard Henry Lee declared to the Continental Congress that the colonies should be "free, independent states."

1780

Benedict Arnold marched on Richmond, destroying industry and confiscating tobacco.

1781

The British surrendered at Yorktown.

The Berkeley Plantation, birthplace of Benjamin Harrison, circa 1950. Courtesy, The Library of Virginia

1792

The colony's first bank, the Bank of Richmond, was chartered.

1795

The first leg of the James River Canal was completed, linking western farmers to eastern markets and ports.

1804

Bank of Virginia established headquarters in Richmond.

1808

The Potomac Company canal opened markets all the way to Rockingham County.

1813

A U. S. embargo froze trade after the War of 1812.

1819

The bottom dropped out of the real estate market with the Panic of 1819.

1834

The Richmond, Fredericksburg, & Potomac (RF&P) Railroad was chartered by the General Assembly.

1836

RF&P Railroad's first train left the Richmond depot.

1845

Tredegar Iron Works in Richmond produced massive ordnance for the Federal government.

1850

Railroad fever swept Virginia, with lines criss-crossing the state.

1860

Richmond led Virginia in grain production; Jefferson Davis, president of the Confederate States of America, declared Richmond the capital.

1861

Northwestern counties organized their own government.

1862

West Virginia became a state and joined the Union; Lincoln's Emancipation Proclamation freed the slaves.

1865

Richmond fell to the troops of General Ulysses S. Grant; General Lee surrendered at Appomattox.

1869

Hampton Institute, a college "for young people without distinction of color," was chartered.

1870

The Commonwealth of Virginia rejoined the Union.

1871

Public education was established in Richmond.

1872

RF&P Railroad connected with the Alexandria and Fredericksburg Railway, establishing the first all rail route to Washington and points south.

1881

Virginia Electric Lighting Company brought electricity to Richmond.

1882

The community of Big Lick was chartered and renamed Roanoke. Within a year, it grew into a boomtown with 63 merchants, 44 tobacco dealers, 17 liquor dealers, and 12 factories.

1886

Chesapeake Dry Dock and Construction Company, later to become Newport News Shipbuilding and Dry Dock Company, was chartered.

A trainload of pipe, headed from Radford Pipe Works to the Panama Canal, circa 1915. Courtesy, The Library of Virginia

1887
Richmond was the first city in the nation with centrally-powered streetcars.

1890
Virginia and North Carolina tobacco firms formed a tobacco trust that controlled 95 percent of the nation's industry.

1900
Richmond's coal and iron industries dropped sharply due to a shortage of local coal and iron ore.

1903
Maggie L. Walker established the nation's first black-owned bank.

1909
The Virginia lumber industry thrived with logging operations and large sawmills.

1916
Virginia instituted a statewide prohibition, three years before the 18th Amendment was added to the U. S. Constitution.

1917
America's entry into World War I boosted business at the ports of Norfolk and Portsmouth.

1920
Coal mining was the bedrock in Southwest Virginia's economy.

1929
E.I. du Pont de Nemours Company opened a plant in Ampthill.

1930
Virginia led the nation in production of artificial silk. Overcutting decimated its lumber industry.

1931
Depression caused Virginia's industrial output to plummet and unemployment to skyrocket.

1934
Air mail service was extended to Roanoke.

1938
Black-owned businesses thrived, with more than $5 million in net sales.

St. John's Church, site of Patrick Henry's famous speech, circa 1950. Courtesy, The Library of Virginia

1939
Virginia's textile industry soared, providing one-quarter of America's production of rayon, yarn, nylon, and cellophane.

1940
Replenished forests revived Virginia's lumbering industry. Virginia ranked eight in the U.S. in black population and third in number of black-owned businesses.

1952
The Virginia State Port Authority was created.

1954
The U.S. Supreme Court ruled against segregation.

1969
Richmond advertising firm The Martin Agency developed the slogan "Virginia Is For Lovers," which spawned spinoffs internationally.

1985
In Fairfax County, Software Productivity Consortium opened a research center where the nation's top aerospace companies shared research.

1987
NASA located its space station headquarters in Reston.

1989
Virginia elected L. Douglas Wilder as America's first black governor.

1996
The Telecom Act of 1996 broke the chokehold that the "Baby Bells" had on local telephone markets, opening the way for competitors.

1997
Motorola, the world's third largest chipmaker, announced plans for a $3 billion semiconductor plant near Richmond.

1998
When supply outstripped demand, Motorola shut down construction of its Richmond operation. Governor Jim Gilmore appointed Virginia's first secretary of technology.

2003
Virginia enacted a business trust law that gave businesses greater latitude in their organization and operation practices, making the state more attractive to investment. Meanwhile, Phillip Morris USA relocated its headquarters to Henrico County, generating 450 jobs and an annual payroll of $83 million.

L. Douglas Wilder was elected in 1990 as America's first black governor. Courtesy, The Library of Virginia

The wealth generated by tobacco grown
in the Virginia colony created a class of
prosperous planter merchants, wholly
dependent on slave labor for the preserva-
tion of its privileged lifestyle. Courtesy,
Virginia State Library

TRADERS AND GENTLEMEN FARMERS

◆

On December 20, 1606, three ships carrying 100 men and 4 boys set sail from England to seek riches in the New World. After a wearying four-month voyage, the band touched shore at Cape Henry, then sailed into the Chesapeake Bay and up the James River. Finding a well-guarded peninsula with a suitable anchorage, the adventurers built a stockade and began sowing wheat, laying out a garden, and planting fruits and vegetables. They named their outpost Jamestown in honor of James I, King of England. From this base Captains John Smith and Christopher Newport launched explorations in search of the Northwest Passage, the fabled sea route to Cathay.

Inspired by tales of the Spanish conquistadors, these English adventurers sought trade and plunder. They had not come to settle a new land, but to discover quick riches—and to repay the investors in the London Company, the corporation financing their expedition. But even a hardened soldier of fortune like Smith, who had escaped enslavement by the Ottoman Turks and had roamed the steppes of Muscovy, was struck by the land's unspoiled beauty. "Heaven and Earth never agreed better to frame a place for man's habitation," he wrote back to England.

Virginia was the name given this uncharted territory. As Smith and his companions sailed up the estuaries of the Chesapeake and pushed overland in search of gold, the appellation seemed ever more appropriate. The virgin land was a patchwork of meadows, marshes, and woodlands. Thick green forests rose from the moist, dark soil of lowlands. The trees were wide and tall, far more magnificent than anything in England. Groves of walnut, ash, beech, and oak sprouted amid seas of reedy grasses. Fields of flax, sorrel, and parsley grew wild. And the riverbanks, enriched by alluvial deposits, appeared most hospitable to farming.

The crops planted at Jamestown quickly took root and game was abundant. The woodlands were flush with deer, foxes, beavers, and raccoons. The marshes supported a multitude of swans, geese, and ducks. Wild turkeys, many as large as 40 pounds, dwelled in the woodlands. For a time it seemed the colonists would never go hungry.

But the illusion of a newfound paradise did not linger long. The would-be swashbucklers preferred searching for gold to toiling on the meager four-acre farm. Although the colonists built up their stores of maize by trading with the Indians, relations with the natives were often unfriendly. Damp, muggy vapors hovering over nearby marshes seemed laden with disease. The long voyage had taken its toll—16 lives had been

Captain John Smith was in the party that founded Jamestown, in the area that would become the state of Virginia. From Cirker, Dictionary of American Portraits, Dover, 1967

lost crossing the Atlantic—and by August, more began to die. Dysentery and malaria took some lives; Indian attacks claimed others. Too exhausted to farm or hunt, many simply starved. By November all but 38 had died.

The London Company rescued the colony from extinction by dispatching more ships with supplies. By late spring, 500 new settlers were boarding ships bound for Virginia. Beset by plagues, bad weather and travel hardships, 100 died en route. The survivors arrived in Jamestown too hungry and sick to work. Virginia's dry summers had stilted the crops. Crows had damaged the maize before it ripened. The colony's food supply was already low when the 400 arrived.

Pitching camp on the banks of the Elizabeth River and on the lower Powhatan, many settlers survived by eating from the oyster beds and scrounging berries, nuts, and roots. During what became known as the "Starving Time," a few were reduced to cannibalism. The hungriest of the community dug up the body of an Indian killed by settlers and ate it. Later one man was executed for killing, salting, and consuming his wife. By the spring of 1610, Virginia's population had dropped to 60.

Salvation came in the form of two more London Company ships. But within two weeks the new acting governor, Sir Thomas Gates, found the situation hopeless and decided to abandon Jamestown. The colonists had set sail for home when an approaching rowboat brought word that three more ships from England were carrying provisions and another 300 men. Once again the colony was saved. In late September 1611, 350 men led by Governor Sir Thomas Dale laid out a small fortified settlement 15 miles below the falls of the James River and named it Henrico, in honor of King James' eldest son Henry, the Prince of Wales. The English had planted themselves on American shores to stay.

The repeated expeditions were expensive, however, and the colony yielded nothing of value in its early years. For all its virtues Virginia had no silver deposits to mine, no Indian empires to plunder. Far from providing a trade route to the Orient, the Chesapeake proved to be a dead end. Jamestown was not the Elysian field the pamphleteers spoke of so glowingly back home.

Perennially short of cash, the London Company twice issued additional stock to resuscitate the venture. To counteract the perception in England that Virginia was a doomed colony, the company launched a campaign to entice more settlers. Pamphleteers—the mass media manipulators of the seventeenth century—extolled the wonders of the New World without mentioning such inconveniences as pestilence, starvation, and hostile natives. They wrote of natural abundance and of fortunes to be made. In London the popular play "Eastward Hoe" depicted Virginia as a paradise where gold was more plentiful than England's copper, and where natives plucked rubies and diamonds from the landscape.

Once across the Atlantic, the new colonists learned differently. There was no gold; there were no gems. Even pragmatic schemes, such as a plan to raise silk, failed to take hold: rats ate the silkworms sent to the New World. The soil was ill-suited to rice, and there was little demand in England for the sassafras, beads, and pitch that the colony did manage to export. French

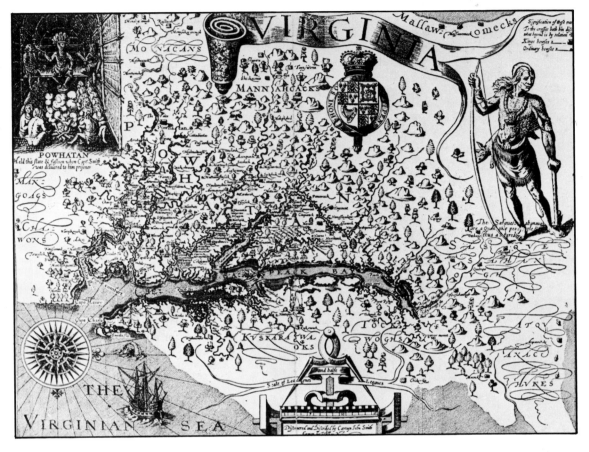

In May 1607, soon after landing at Jamestown, a party of colonists proceeded up the James River until its progress was halted by the falls at the future site of Richmond. One of Powhatan's villages was located nearby, and the inhabitants came down to the riverbank to greet the explorers. John Smith's 1608 map of Virginia, shown here, includes the "Falls" near the upper left corner. Courtesy, Maryland Historical Society

wine-dressers, recruited to cultivate vineyards in Virginia, boasted that the colony's grapes were large, plump, and superior to the product of their native Languedoc. But Virginia's first wine shipments arrived damaged in England and were poorly received.

Nothing could hide the fact that the London Company—the first financial venture associated with Virginia—was a financial disaster. The company had transplanted 5,000 colonists to the New World, but three-quarters of them had died. It had invested 200,000 pounds but failed to pay a single cash dividend. The company was broke and its investors demoralized. In 1624 King James revoked its charter.

Despite all its failures, the London Company had succeeded in planting a permanent settlement on a hostile foreign shore. While private investors were unwilling to put any more of their capital at risk, the English monarchy saw value in the colony. The small island nation looked with envy upon the Spaniards and the Portuguese, whose American empires spewed out gold, silver, pearls, sugar, and tobacco, making them

among the wealthiest nations in Europe. The English envisioned their own colonies producing valuable commodities that could be obtained only at great risk and expense from other nations.

The Crown saw another advantage to maintaining the Virginia colony: it would ease the pressure of excess population at home. In the early seventeenth century, England's ruling class sought a dumping ground for the island's human "refuse." The economy was growing, but not fast enough to accommodate the swelling ranks of England's poor. Peasants were being squeezed off communal land by the enclosure movement to make way for large herds of sheep. Thousands went jobless. A census of Sheffield in 1615 revealed that 775 of its 2,207 residents relied upon some form of charity.

A young man who owned no land and was not apprenticed in a trade or profession was destined to a life as an agricultural laborer. The annual wages of a rural worker in 1618 were eight pounds, eight shillings and nine pence; women made less as domestics. Even when both husband and wife were employed, they could

Governor Sir Thomas Dale, with a party of 350 men, founded the second settlement in Virginia, below the falls of the James River, and named it Henrico. Courtesy, Virginia Museum of Fine Arts, Richmond

barely afford to maintain a family; the cost of shelter, fuel, bread, meat, and clothing was reckoned at more than 20 pounds. Such was the plight of the working poor. Thousands of indigents roamed the countryside begging, stealing, or joining bands of highwaymen.

Even if Virginia yielded little in the way of riches, it could serve as England's social safety valve. At home the impoverished were a burden to the parish authorities and a menace to orderly society. In Virginia, with its abundant land, the same rabble might become a source of productivity and wealth.

It is somewhat ironic that James I, who launched the Virginia colony by chartering the London Company, was among the harshest critics of the commodity that would prove to be its salvation. A man of no mean literary talent, James is best known for commissioning a new translation of the Bible. But he also wrote a book on witchcraft—and a treatise denouncing the "filthy weed," tobacco.

The Spaniards had acquired a taste for smoking tobacco from the Indians, and the practice had spread to Europe. In the seven years before 1622, England imported an average of 60,000 pounds of West Indian tobacco annually; an equal amount may have been smuggled into the country. The first Virginia leaf, adopted from local Indians, was considered vastly inferior to the Spanish variety and sold for less than a third the price. But in 1612 John Rolfe introduced West Indian tobacco plants into the colony. Virginia tobacco soon gained a reputation as the equal of Spanish.

Tobacco's yield per acre was high, and when properly cured, it did not spoil in transit. Compared to other commodities, its shipping weight was low, therefore economical. Where grain fetched two shillings, six pence per bushel on the London market, Virginia tobacco brought three shillings per *pound*. No other product came close to generating the same return on investment, and it was not long before Virginians were devoting themselves utterly to the cultivation of the "sotweed." By 1619, the colony shipped home 20,000 pounds; by 1628, exports reached 500,000 pounds.

Efforts by the London Company and the Crown to diversify the economy through the production of wine, iron, and silk grass failed miserably. So passionate were the colonists in their cultivation of tobacco that they neglected to plant enough grain to feed themselves. To make sure the colony fed itself, the London Company demanded that land rents be paid in the form of grain for a common store: two and one-half bushels for every tenant and each of his servants. Governor Dale also prohibited farmers from planting tobacco in their private gardens until they had sown two acres of grain. Settlers even had to be prohibited from growing tobacco in the streets of Jamestown.

But tobacco gave the colony the economic base it had lacked. A small farmer could send tobacco valued at 100 pounds sterling to the English marketplace and bring back clothing for six agricultural servants, two guns, ammunition, various tools, and other merchandise. These he could trade profitably in Virginia for livestock, land, or other commodities. By the end of his second year, according to nineteenth-century historian Philip Alexander Bruce, such a planter would have an estate valued at 600 pounds sterling.

The profits from the tobacco cultivation enabled planters to expand production even more. Settlement extended rapidly as planters sought fresh soil—so rapidly that, in 1634, the General Assembly divided the colony into eight counties, each with its own administrative and judicial system. Springing up first in James City County near the Jamestown settlement, the tobacco culture spread along the waterways of the Chesapeake Bay and its tributaries. Between 1637 and 1640, tobacco shipments to England averaged 1.4 million pounds annually.

The emerging plantation economy discouraged urban development. Planters on riverfront estates rolled their tobacco in hogsheads down to river landings and loaded them directly onto sea-going ships. Merchant vessels plied their trade up and down the York, the James, the Rappahannock, the Appomattox, and the Potomac, stopping at each landing to drop off European goods in exchange for tobacco. Plantations became self-sufficient communities, and there was no need for ports or cities.

So addicted was Virginia to tobacco that the leaf became the colony's currency. Not only did colonists use it to transact business in England, they also employed it when settling accounts among themselves. Because coinage was in short supply, the authorities proclaimed a number of acts establishing a fixed ratio of tobacco to sterling in the payment of taxes, fees, quitrents, tavern rates, and ferry charges.

Tobacco brought a fragile prosperity, however. As production soared, prices plummeted. A royal proclamation banned Spanish shipments to England in 1625, in effect giving Virginia tobacco producers a captive market. And fearing the loss of revenues from duties and customs on the trade, the Crown even forbade cultivation in England. But prices kept falling. English merchants reexported the leaf to the Baltic countries,

and as prices slipped, England's less privileged classes began picking up the smoking habit as well. But increasing production far outpaced the growing demand.

For the next century and a half, prices would remain ruinously low, generally fluctuating between a halfpenny and three pence per pound. When harvests were bountiful, as they often were, prices plunged. When storms or Dutch warships sank the tobacco fleets, prices recovered. An occasional profitable year could not hide the reality, however, that tobacco had lost its appeal. In 1682 depressed prices sparked plant-cutting riots in New Kent, Gloucester, and Middlesex counties. Rioters managed to push up

Flowerdew Hundred Plantation, one of the earliest English settlements in the New World, is located on the south bank of the James River, 10 miles east of Hopewell, Virginia. Originally inhabited by Indians, Flowerdew was granted to Governor George Yeardley in 1618. The governor named the plantation for his wife's family, the Flowerdews of Norfolk, England. The settlement survived the Indian massacre of 1622 and became a thriving farm. According to records, a windmill was constructed on the plantation circa 1621. Courtesy, Virginia Division of Tourism

King James I launched the Virginia colony by chartering the London Company. Ironically, he disapproved of tobacco, the crop that would be the colony's salvation. Courtesy, Virginia State Library

transactions. A century later the legislature tried to prop up prices by mandating the destruction of inferior grades and restricting the last date of planting tobacco to curtail production.

Most of these measures were ineffectual. But Governor Alexander Spotswood did help in 1713 by establishing an inspection system to standardize the grades of tobacco. The Warehouse Act provided for public facilities where planters could take their tobacco for inspection and grading. Licensed inspectors enforced minimum standards by opening hogsheads and destroying inferior quality leaf. The class and grade of tobacco were marked on the hogshead.

By standardizing tobacco as a medium of exchange, the Warehouse Act gave Virginia planters and merchants a profound advantage over their Maryland competitors. Maryland brokers began moving to Virginia where they could buy better, more uniform tobacco, though at a higher price. In 1747, Maryland was forced to adopt similar measures.

Changing trading patterns in the 1700s made the Warehouse Act more practical to administer than it would have been a century earlier. As settlers pushed into the rolling hills of the Piedmont, they moved beyond the reach of the coastal merchant ships who served the Tidewater planters. Loading tobacco into carts or rolling them in hogsheads, Piedmont farmers transported their crop overland to the entrepots that sprang up at the fall lines of the major rivers. To handle the traffic between land-bound planters and seafaring merchantmen, markets, warehouses, loading docks, and customs houses arose at fall-line towns such as Petersburg, Richmond, and Fredericksburg.

While some government edicts benefited Virginia's trade, others crippled it. A series of Navigation Acts between 1651 and 1663 required that colonial cargo be carried in English ships. Certain "enumerated products," including tobacco, could be exported only to England, even if the final destination was another country. Finally, colonial imports had to originate in England or be transshipped from there. These measures augmented royal revenues and benefited

prices briefly by ravaging tobacco fields—even cutting their own plants—and smashing 10,000 hogsheads of tobacco, but the respite was only temporary.

Twenty-five years after the formation of the colony, the General Assembly embarked upon a series of futile price-fixing measures. A series of acts in 1632, 1639, and 1640 set a price level for tobacco and penalized its exchange at a lower rate. But the laws had little practical effect. With no central markets for the exchange of tobacco, there was no way to supervise the

English merchants at the expense of the Dutch, who generally offered lower shipping rates. But by driving up transportation costs and adding unnecessary middlemen, the Navigation Acts made Virginia exports less competitive in markets outside England and forced Virginians to pay higher freight rates, taxes, and commissions on imported goods.

Virginia was locked into a colonial economy, its interests subordinated to those of the mother country. Parliament discouraged manufacturing in the colonies, so that most exports were raw materials. Tobacco remained the major money-maker, though declining prices encouraged Virginians to diversify into grain, forestry products, iron, and furs. About 1740, for example, one merchant ship departed for Great Britain with 304 hogsheads of tobacco, 9,600 staves, 1,200 feet of plank, and 21 bales of deerskin. Virginians also supplied provisions to the sugar plantations of the West Indies. One typical cargo consisted of 764 bushels of corn, 60 barrels of pork, 10 of beef, 7 of tallow, and 3 of lard. Virginia conducted a smaller trade with the New England colonies, particularly Boston.

From the earliest times, Virginia's economy was tied into the world economy. Probing far into the interior, the Chesapeake Bay and its

Not only did the Indians teach the colonists how to grow corn to feed themselves, they also taught them how to cultivate tobacco. In 1612 John Rolfe followed their example and planted a crop at Varina, just below the future site of Richmond. Others followed suit, and the popularity of the "noxious weed" in England soon convinced the colonists that money grew, if not on trees, then on tobacco plants.

tributaries linked Virginia with the Atlantic Ocean and all the territories along its rim. Events on other continents reverberated with profound effects in Virginia: the increase in tobacco consumption in Europe, the creation of new markets in the West Indian sugar plantations, the growth of the African slave trade, the industrial revolution in England, and the wars with the Dutch and French.

Only toward the middle of the eighteenth century, as settlers pushed far inland, did a significant number of Virginians tear themselves away from the influence of the global marketplace.

An abundance of land and shortage of labor made living conditions for immigrants much better than back in Europe. Virginia offered small farmers and free laborers a chance to earn a better living and provided more political representation than the average person enjoyed almost anywhere else in the world. This remarkable society, however, was marred by the extensive use of slavery and the total disregard of the rights of blacks, both African-born and American-born.

The spread of tobacco cultivation created an insatiable demand for labor. Planting the seed, tending the crop, harvesting the leaves, and curing the tobacco were laborious tasks— ones that the sons of the English gentry who immigrated to Virginia in search of easy fortunes were hardly willing to undertake themselves. Unlike the Spanish conquistadors, however, Virginia planters could not turn to the indigenous population for labor. The Powhatan Confederacy was no Aztec or Inca empire; the Indians were few in number and unaccustomed to hard agricultural labor. Planters could, and did, pay the passage of Englishmen across the Atlantic in exchange for seven years of labor. But as soon as their commitments were fulfilled, the servants were lured to the frontier by the prospect of land.

In 1607 the colony's servants were indentured to the London Company. They received passage and sustenance while clearing and working the land for the company's profit. Once the servants had earned their freedom, the company allowed them to rent three acres of land in return

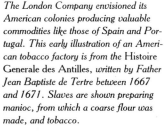

The London Company envisioned its American colonies producing valuable commodities like those of Spain and Portugal. This early illustration of an American tobacco factory is from the Histoire Generale des Antilles, *written by Father Jean Baptiste de Tertre between 1667 and 1671. Slaves are shown preparing manioc, from which a coarse flour was made, and tobacco.*

for a month's service every year and a donation of corn to the common store. In 1618 Sir Edwin Sandys, treasurer of the London Company, agreed to a superior inducement: an outright grant of 100 acres of uncleared land. To those who footed the bill for settlers to cross the Atlantic, he gave a 50-acre "head right" per immigrant. Seventeenth-century English reckoning associated land with wealth, and the offer enticed many to settle in Virginia.

The granting of head rights commenced a regular commerce in servants. Planters imported labor both to cultivate land and to acquire it. Traders sending ships to Virginia to pick up tobacco increased their profits by loading the bottoms with servants and selling them at the docks. Initially the London Company was discerning as to whom it admitted to the colony. But by 1621, as the need for labor grew, it became less discriminating. Overpopulated parishes in England happily sloughed off their charity cases, mostly young men over 15, for the cost of clothing and transportation to Virginia.

The Crown used the opportunity to dump convicts sentenced with the death penalty. These felons were not necessarily all thugs and murderers; some 300 crimes were punishable by death under British law at the time. One petitioner, for example, begged the authorities to release a certain John Throckmorton if she paid for his transport to Virginia. His crime: theft of a hat. Nonetheless, the colonials were none too happy about receiving criminals into their midst, and the practice of transporting felons to Virginia instead of to the gallows ended in 1642.

At times the commerce in servants degenerated into a sordid white slave trade. Perpetrators in seaport towns lured youngsters to their homes, altered the children's appearances, and sold them to sailors bound for Virginia. Even adults were shanghaied. In one such case, Robert Person, a Yorkshire drover visiting Smithfield, drank too much and was guided aboard a ship which, he was promised, would take him home. He awakened at sea. In another incident, Mary Cooper was told that she would

Tobacco even grew in the streets of Jamestown. From Heimann, Tobacco and Americans, *McGraw-Hill Book Company, 1960*

readily find work in Virginia which, she was assured, was a small town a few miles from the Thames. Another account tells of a guileless Elizabeth Smalridge accompanying a soldier on board and being sold into bondage on the spot.

Not all indentured servants were of humble origin. Many were like Adam Thoroughgood, who ignored his social connections in England and came to Virginia under indenture. Thoroughgood went on to acquire a great deal of

land in Princess Anne County and eventually rose to high office in the colony. Another indentured servant, Elias Nuthall, used part of his father's estate in England to buy his freedom.

Between 1634 and 1704, some 1,500 to 2,000 indentured servants arrived in Virginia annually. In 1671 Governor Sir William Berkeley reported that the roughly 6,000 servants in the colony accounted for about 13 percent of the population. Nearly all were male and worked as

Tobacco, an ideal crop for the young colony of Virginia, provided the economic base that was sorely needed there.

agricultural laborers; a few were apprentices learning marketable trades, and a handful were women who worked as domestics.

Indenture contracts, and later the law, provided servants some protection from abuse by their masters and guaranteed certain necessities. By custom, servants were allowed free time at night, part of Saturday, Sunday (the Sabbath), and all English holidays. Some beneficent planters allowed favored servants to grow their own

tobacco for sale. Often these servants invested profits in livestock or cash crops to build a base for their own farms when they received their freedom.

A standard contract provided that a servant be given a pair of shoes, three barrels of corn, and farming tools at the end of his indenture. Landowners often tailored the indenture contracts to suit their own needs and those of the servant. John Talbert's 1680 indenture, for instance, stipulated that his master teach him the shoemaking trade in exchange for an extra year's servitude. Other indentures forbade gambling, marriage, or fornication. As free persons, servants often became landowners themselves, sometimes hiring servants of their own. Many rose to prominence in colonial society. Seven of 44 burgesses in the 1629 General Assembly, for example, had been servants only a few years previously.

Freed indentured servants gave rise to a class of small landowners. By the time of Bacon's Rebellion in 1676, there were 4,000 farms. Unlike in England, land was not concentrated in the hands of a few earls and squires. The average land patent in Virginia was less than 500 acres; only a few estates were larger than 1,000 acres.

Planters acquired land in many ways. Governors were empowered to grant land to soldiers, colonial officials, and others for meritorious service. Sir Thomas Dale, for example, received lands worth 700 pounds sterling. The London Company also offered subpatents to private associations purchasing several shares. These associations transported families and servants to work as a unit to develop large tracts: Martin's Hundred and Smith's Hundred developed from the earliest-known subpatents.

In the seventeenth century the most common form of land grant was the "head right." Under this system, hundreds of landowners received grants for financing the transportation of settlers to the colonies or for completing their seven-year indentures. By 1619, records show, private planters had footed the bill for 660 of the 811 servants in the colony.

Governor Alexander Spotswood (1676-1740) established an inspection system in 1713 that standardized tobacco grades. From Cirker, Dictionary of American Portraits, *Dover, 1967*

Anyone paying the cost of transporting emigrants—about six pounds sterling—was granted 50 acres of land per head. Some planters created enormous tracts of land this way: between 1618 and 1623 the London Company granted 44 patents to colonists who had brought over 100 persons or more.

Given the abundance of land, most free persons settled quickly on their own farms. By the end of the seventeenth century, the number of indentured servants was dwindling. Indentures expired continually and land speculators were opening up vast frontier tracts, offering immigrants an alternative to servitude. Yet plantation acreage was expanding, and the demand for labor was greater than ever.

Desperate for labor, planters turned to slavery. Black African slaves were cheap to maintain. They ate mush, vegetables, and maize bread and did not require as much clothing as English servants. They adapted well to Virginia's hot, humid summer climate. And most important, once slavery was established, planters did not have to recruit a whole new work force every seven years. For slaves, servitude usually lasted a lifetime.

Blacks were first introduced to Virginia in 1619 when a Dutch ship arrived with 20 Africans. The evidence suggests that they were treated as indentured servants. Of the 300 blacks in Virginia three decades later, many had completed their terms of indentured service and were free persons. One of the earliest, Anthony Johnson, settled on the Eastern Shore, owned his own land, and was among the colony's early slaveholders. It was not until 1662 that the General Assembly mandated that all non-Christian servants be held as slaves for life.

There were only 2,000 blacks in Virginia by 1671, about 5 percent of the population. But English and Dutch traders landed slaves on Virginia shores in increasing numbers. Obtaining slaves became easier, too, as Virginia developed trade with the West Indian sugar plantations. The sugar planters paid for food and stores with rum, molasses, and slaves. Through imports and natural increase, the slave population increased to 23,000 by 1715. Compared to the harsh conditions of the West Indian sugar plantations and the South Carolina rice fields, working conditions in Virginia were relatively benign. Virginia planters took the view that slaves were valuable property.

Slaves participated in every aspect of the growing agricultural economy: dairy farming and animal husbandry, as well as planting and harvesting every crop. While female slaves had few occupational options outside domestic or agricultural labor, planters employed many male slaves as craftsmen or artisans. Some became skilled in the production of metal and wooden tools.

Although slavery inhibited the social and economic mobility of blacks, it did not preclude it. Some blacks were freed after serving lengthy terms of indenture, others after their masters died. Like white servants, many were allowed to cultivate small tracts for food or for profit; some even purchased their own freedom from their masters. There is evidence that hundreds of free blacks—either freed slaves or their offspring—prospered as small farmers.

But the white majority was uncomfortable with the idea of free blacks. In the mid-seven-

Deep-water ships moored at a Virginia plantation landing take on a cargo of cured tobacco. From Heimann, Tobacco and Americans, *McGraw-Hill Book Company, 1960*

teenth century, the General Assembly passed a number of laws defining slave status along racial lines and restricting the legal rights of blacks and slaves. In 1640 slaves lost the right to bear arms. In 1662 mulatto children of slave women were declared to be slaves by birth, the same as children born to black slave families. A later law provided that the slaves of owners who died intestate would be resold by the county courts.

Even when laws existed to protect slaves, they were often ignored. If a slave died from a beating, the murderer usually went unpunished. Authorities tolerated the killing of fugitive slaves and condoned harsh corporal punishment for minor offenses. Hog stealers, for example, were whipped for the first offense. Recidivists had their ears nailed to a pillory, then had them cut

from their heads. Tagged as rebels, earless slaves commanded a lower price on the market.

Understandably, planters feared slave rebellions. To prevent insurrections they passed ever stricter laws. In 1680 the General Assembly strengthened its earlier law prohibiting slaves from bearing arms or assaulting their masters. Slaves were forbidden to leave their plantations without a written certificate of permission. The plantation economy that had blossomed under a slave system was now a captive of the class tensions it produced.

In 1673 young William Byrd married Mary Horsmanden, the daughter of a Cavalier officer who had fled to Virginia during the Puritan regime of Oliver Cromwell. Byrd had inherited a rich estate near the fall line of the

Built in 1783 as a residence for the jailer, this building was converted into a prison for debtors in Accomac, Virginia, in 1824. During the early days of the colony, the Crown transported felons to Virginia instead of to the gallows. Courtesy, Virginia Division of Tourism

James, as well as a significant store of goods his uncle had used in trading with the Indians. In time Byrd would accumulate one of the greatest fortunes in colonial Virginia and establish a dynasty worthy of his native England. But he owed his success to more than a handsome inheritance and a well-chosen marriage.

Living on his plantation in the manner of an English lord, Byrd developed a trading network that extended from Virginia to London, Boston, the West Indies, and the Indian country of South

Carolina. Byrd bought and sold tobacco, differing from his fellow planters only in the tremendous scale of his transactions. He imported slaves and indentured servants, and supplied his neighboring planters with many of the English goods they desired. From New England merchants he acquired earthenware and Madeira wine. From Barbados he imported rum, slaves, and molasses. In a letter to an agent in the Indies, for instance, he ordered 4,000 gallons of rum, 5,000 pounds of muscovado (unrefined sugar), 6,000 pounds of sugar, and 10 tons of molasses. Byrd also made his plantation a center for commerce with the Indians. His traders traveled hundreds of miles south to the land of the Cherokee and the Catawba. In exchange for cloth, kettles, hatchets, guns, ammunition and, of course, demon rum, they brought back furs, deerskins, rare herbs, and minerals.

Byrd was the quintessential eighteenth-century Virginia aristocrat. He made money from working the land in the manner of the old English aristocracy, yet he did not disdain commerce. Like Byrd, members of the emergent Virginia aristocracy were far more concerned with a man's worldly success and his accomplishments than with his genealogy.

Noble birth and inheritance certainly did not hurt a settler's efforts to enter the ranks of the colonial elite. But breeding was no guarantee and a humble origin no barrier. Many of Virginia's leading citizens had commenced their New World careers as indentured servants; oth-

Despite his social connections in England, Captain Adam Thoroughgood came to the New World under indenture. He acquired a good deal of land in Princess Anne County, Virginia, and rose to high office in the colony. His house, built as early as 1636, still stands in Virginia Beach and is maintained by the Adam Thoroughgood House Foundation. Courtesy, Valentine Museum

"Westover," in Charles City County, was built about 1730 by William Byrd II, planter, author, and colonial official. An example of Georgian architecture, the house remained in the Byrd family until 1814. Courtesy, Virginia Division of Tourism

ers had been merchants in the Old World. Some merchant planters tapped their connections on both continents and set up stores on their plantations. These aristocratic retailers normally offered only necessities, but a few provided a variety of goods from cotton to calico, candlesticks to cowbells. One such merchant planter, Jonathan Newell, extended his trade over a four-county area as well as overseas.

Constant transatlantic travel was impractical in this era of sailing ships, so Virginia planters normally engaged English sales agents for their tobacco in London. Under this consignment system, planters relied on these agents to sell their produce for a profit and ship back clothing, foodstuffs, and other goods unavailable in Virginia. Although the system opened up trading opportunities abroad, it had its drawbacks. There was a 12- to 18-month lag time between a planter's purchase order and the delivery of goods. And the profitability of a planter's season was at the mercy of his agent's business acumen and personal taste in selecting trade goods to send back to Virginia.

Nontheless, by the beginning of the eighteenth century, the planter merchants straddled a vigorous, fast-growing society. In 1700 Virginia's population stood at 63,000. Although the number of inhabitants was no larger than that of a single large London parish, the colony spread over an area as vast as England. By midcentury, Virginia was home to nearly 250,000 people. Williamsburg, the capital since 1699, was a bustling town with a palace for the royal governor and one of the few colleges in the New World, William and Mary, named for King William III and Queen Mary.

By 1670, the Indians had ceased to be a threat, and planters no longer felt compelled to cluster together for self-defense. Free to settle anywhere, they spread out, each living upon a tract of land. Small farmers lived in isolation with a handful of servants or slaves. Although the wealthiest planters lived in baronial splendor, their resemblance to the lords of England was superficial at best. The old ties of feudal obligation and privilege had been replaced with a capitalist ethic. With the exception of slaves, who were treated as outright property, persons entered into free and voluntary agreements with one another.

Despite the multiplicity of laws, taxes, and tariffs designed to exploit the wealth of the colo-

nies for the benefit of the royal treasury and a few privileged English merchants, the Virginia planters enjoyed a rare prosperity. They lived in fine plantation houses filled with imported furniture and handsome prints. Silver, a symbol of wealth, was used liberally at social occasions. Orchards of apples, peaches, plums, pears, cherries, and figs surrounded the plantation houses; and many planters indulged in the aristocratic pursuit of gardening. The riverfront homes at Yorktown were so elegant that one British visitor compared them to those of London's exclusive St. James's district.

Left: Members of Virginia's planter class frequently assumed positions of responsibility in the government. This engraving of Patrick Henry by William S. Leney is based on the portrait of Henry by Thomas Sully. Henry served as governor of Virginia from July 6, 1776, to June 1, 1779. Courtesy, Valentine Museum

Below: "Tuckahoe," in Goochland County, was built about 1712 by Thomas Randolph, who had acquired the tract in 1710. It was the first plantation to be fully established above the falls. Courtesy, Valentine Museum

Above: "Berkeley," at Harrison's Landing on the James River, was built in 1726. It was the birthplace of Benjamin Harrison (1726-1791), a signer of the Declaration of Independence and governor of Virginia. His son, William Henry Harrison, was elected ninth president of the United States. Courtesy, Valentine Museum

The planter merchants adopted many mannerisms of the English ruling class. Often sending their children to England for schooling, the Virginia gentry placed great value on the Greek and Latin classics. They entertained one another with lavish parties, dinners, and dances. Horse races, usually informal affairs held on a cleared plantation field, offered another break from the routine of tobacco planting. Gambling was popular among the gentry, and Virginians were not picky about the sport: horse racing, cockfights, dicing, ninepins, cards. It was not unusual to bet tobacco by the ton. Those caught cheating were sentenced to time in the stocks.

Members of the Virginia gentry aspired to prominent office for reasons of prestige and self-aggrandizement. The colonists had been granted

considerable autonomy, and those with wealth routinely assumed positions of responsibility. The planter class dominated the government, holding seats in both the House of Burgesses and the Virginia Council, and the county courts. It was common for one individual to hold several positions. Richard Bland, for example, served on his county's court and in the House of Burgesses, and held the prestigious title of colonel in the militia.

Planters were only too happy to serve in administrative positions. The salaries provided a welcome source of income, and fringe benefits could be significant. As in Europe during this era, most people regarded appointment to government office as an opportunity for self-enrichment. For example, Alexander Spotswood, a royal governor admired for his efficient governance, did not hesitate to use the power of his office to pass legislation benefiting his interests in land speculation.

Yet these same Virginians exhibited far more concern for the common welfare than most ruling classes. Their attitudes toward individual rights and the need for countervailing powers in government set the tenor not only for Virginia, but also for an entire nation. It is incredible that an aristocracy so few in number could produce leaders and thinkers of the stature of George Washington, Thomas Jefferson, James Madison, Patrick Henry, and John Randolph. Built upon a traffic in " the filthy weed," eighteenth-century Virginia produced a golden age the likes of which has rarely graced the pages of history.

Left: The wheat harvest from "Berkeley" was shipped to Richmond, a booming industrial, commercial, and retail center early in the antebellum period. By the 1850s, Richmond had become the second largest flour producer in America. Courtesy, Valentine Museum

John Rolfe

The infant settlement of Jamestown had its share of bold, adventurous leaders. But John Rolfe more than anyone else deserves credit for saving the colony from an early demise. By marrying the daughter of an Indian chief, he ensured peace with the hostile natives. And by experimenting with tobacco, he discovered the commodity that would prove to be the colony's economic salvation.

The colony's first few years were precarious. The settlers had skirmished with the Indians, and war was an ever-present threat. Efforts to export silk, sassafras, glass beads, soap-ash, and pitch were miserable failures. Without a strong export commodity, Virginia seemed unable to generate any earnings for the London Company. Once the corporation ran out of cash and credit,

there would be an end to the ships replenishing the colony with provisions and eager new settlers.

The son of an old, wealthy English family, Rolfe had little experience in farming. He was, however, a heavy smoker, and he had an eye for opportunity. The colony's frequent warring with the tobacco-growing Indians disrupted what might have been a profitable

trade, so Rolfe decided to grow his own leaf. Indian-grown tobacco was strong and bitter—unpalatable to any English consumers but those transplanted to Virginia with no other source of smoke. The English preferred tobacco produced by the Spanish colonies in the Caribbean: the Orinoco, Trinidada, and Varinas varieties. Rolfe believed that it was possible to cultivate the same

high quality, pleasant-tasting tobacco in Virginia and sell it for high profit in England.

Through trading, Rolfe collected enough of the popular Spanish seed by late 1611 to begin experimenting the following year. He first planted the Trinidada seed. From the clearing of the land to the curing of the leaf, he produced the first crop entirely through his own labor.

As the tobacco grew taller, Rolfe became enchanted by an Indian princess held captive by Governor Sir Thomas Dale. The daughter of the powerful chief Powhatan, she was named Matoaka. But the charming Indian princess is better known by the nickname given her by the settlers: Pocahontas, meaning "playful person." Rolfe met her in the presence of a chaperone, and she counseled him in the Indian method of tobacco cultivation.

In the spring of 1614 Rolfe drafted a letter to Dale requesting permission to marry Pocahontas. In the letter he wrote that his request had no foundation in "carnall affection," but rather in "the good of this plantation, for the honour of our countrie, for the glory of God, for my owne salvation, and for the converting [the heathen Pocahontas] to the true knowledge of God." Dale granted permission, and the couple was married. Their union began a period of uninterrupted peace with the Indians that lasted until the death of Powhatan in 1618.

Of Rolfe's first tobacco harvest, a small amount spoiled. Of the remainder, Rolfe gave some to friends for testing, smoked his share, and shipped four hogsheads to a London merchant to sell on the market. Rolfe and his compatriots found that the tobacco smoked well and that it had a strong, sweet aroma. Still, Rolfe thought he could improve it. Before word of its reception

in England had reached Virginia, he secured some Orinoco seeds from Caracas, Venezuela, which he crossbred with the Trinidada seeds for a second planting.

Meanwhile, Rolfe received the news that his first shipment had fetched from five to eight shillings per pound on the market. Although less than the high price of Spanish tobacco, this signaled that Rolfe's was a competitive product. Rolfe continued his experiments in hopes of producing a superior tobacco, "one that thriveth so well that no doubt but after a little more trial and expense in the curing thereof, it will compare with the best in the West Indies."

His second shipment was small: 2,500 pounds. But by the next year, Virginia tobacco had caught on in the English market. Rolfe and Pocahontas had been invited to London on royal tour in 1616. Pocahontas never returned; she died of influenza at the age of 22. Rolfe returned alone to Virginia, leaving their young son to be raised in England. He eventually remarried and died in the early 1620s.

Rolfe laid the groundwork for Virginia's progression from a floundering quasi-military outpost on the edge of the New World to a vigorous agricultural community. Tobacco became Virginia's leading industry, providing the impetus to clear the wilderness and generate the wealth that created the colony's planter aristocracy. Through John Rolfe's efforts, Virginia's first successful commerce was established.

Left: The marriage of John Rolfe and Pocahontas. Courtesy, Valentine Museum

Incorporated in 1834, the Richmond, Fredericksburg, and Potomac Railroad sent its first train north from Richmond on February 13, 1836. The depot, shown here as it appeared in 1865, was located at Eighth and Broad streets. For many years there was no central depot for all the railroads converging on Richmond; passengers and freight had to be moved by foot or by wagon from one rail line to another many blocks away. From Harper's Weekly, *October 14, 1856*

CANALS, RAILROADS, AND IRONWORKS

◆

By 1700 Virginia had developed from a small military outpost into a vibrant provincial society. Representative governments in Williamsburg and the counties gave settlers a voice in their own destinies. The College of William and Mary instructed students in philosophy, mathematics, and Greek and Latin literatures. Even the arts had a place in the life-style of the aristocracy, which emulated the English ruling class in everything from fashions to sports. Indeed, the first play ever produced in the American colonies, *Ye Beare and Ye Cubb*, was enacted in Accomack County in 1665.

In the colony's first century, Virginians were reluctant to move beyond the lands of the Tidewater. Colonists were tied to the Chesapeake and its tributaries, which nourished an economy based on overseas trade. Having eliminated the threat of Indian attacks, they enjoyed a comfortable life-style within their own civilized boundaries. Settlement beyond the fall line, where Indians still roamed and where there were no expedient connections to the world marketplace, seemed a frightening prospect.

The first large-scale effort to settle west of the fall line inspired few to follow. About 1700, several hundred French Protestants seeking escape from Louis XIV's Catholic monarchy settled in Manakin, 20 miles above the falls of the James River. But the Huguenots were merchants and artisans, not farmers. They lacked the agricultural skills necessary to make their community self-sufficient. Many settlers moved to other communities where they could engage in the trades they knew.

But there were compelling economic and political reasons to expand to lands west of the fall line. Tobacco cultivation robbed the soil of nutrients necessary to yield a marketable product, forcing farmers to move on to fresh lands. As yields on the old lands declined, planters had no choice but to find virgin soil. Royal governors also were concerned about the intrusion by the French into the lands beyond the Allegheny Mountains—lands that the London Company charter of 1608 claimed for Virginia.

In 1671, as an expedition ordered by Governor Sir William Berkeley was preparing to explore the Great Lakes region in search of a passage to the Northwest, the French governor of Canada was making peace with the Indians near Lakes Superior and Huron in an effort to lay claim to their lands. Berkeley, like governors to come, believed that the British could win the

Concerned by the French settlement of lands beyond the Allegheny Mountains, Governor William Berkeley ordered an expedition to explore the Great Lakes region in search of a northwest passage. He encouraged Virginia colonists to move to the Piedmont, the valley and lands to the west of the Blue Ridge Mountains. Courtesy, Valentine Museum

tlements were not enough to guard against French interlopers.

With the double-barreled threat of French encroachment and agricultural disaster, Virginia's government liberalized the land grant system to stimulate westward expansion. In 1701 the General Assembly voted to disallow taxes on western lands to entice settlers to the new frontier. The next year the Virginia Council agreed to permit outright purchase of land at a price of five shillings per 50 acres.

Eastern farmers abandoned their homes in search of fresh, fertile soil, leaving the countryside dotted with rotting houses, weed-choked gardens, and fields overrun with wild growth. Anxious to beat the French to a stake of the western lands, Governor Alexander Spotswood persuaded the General Assembly to build a fort on the Meherrin, a branch of the Rapidan River. In 1714 he oversaw the settlement of a dozen German miners and their families there, and named the settlement Germanna in honor of the settlers' motherland and Queen Anne. It was the first major outpost in the Piedmont to thrive.

Two years later, Spotswood led a dozen men up the Rapidan from Germanna. In the course of their 400-mile expedition, the explorers discovered Swift Run Gap in the Blue Ridge, a byway through the mountains. When the group returned to Williamsburg, Spotswood launched a campaign to alert Virginians to the seductive lands of the west. With much fanfare he initiated the Order of the Golden Horseshoe, bestowing each of his fellow explorers with a gift of a small golden horseshoe embedded with precious stones.

Land speculation became a new avenue to wealth. Grasping the opportunity to claim as much property as possible, Spotswood acquired 3,000 acres around Germanna. Within a short time he owned so much land in the valley of the Rappahannock—25,000 acres—that he could not afford to pay the quitrents. At Spotswood's instigation the Assembly exempted western settlers from all taxes and asked the Crown to relieve landowners of all quitrents for ten years. When Brunswick and Spotsylvania counties

territorial struggle with the French if Virginia colonists moved to the Piedmont, the Valley, and the lands west of the mountains. It was the beginning of a bitter struggle that would culminate in the French and Indian War.

The only settlers in western Virginia were German and Scotch-Irish immigrants. Leaving Pennsylvania in search of religious freedom, they had trekked south, settling in the Shenandoah Valley. Among them were skilled tanners, potters, tinsmiths, and wagon makers. With their knowledge of agriculture—which included methods more advanced than those of the eastern planters, such as crop rotation, deep ploughing and use of fertilizer—they depended little on imported manufactured goods. But their small set-

were created out of these western lands in 1720, Spotswood had the boundaries drawn to include all the property on which he could not afford to pay quitrents. Confident that the King would indeed permit the exemption from quitrents, he quickly snapped up another 60,000 acres in the county named for him.

Land speculators made money by subdividing their properties and selling smaller tracts to settlers. In 1728 Governor Sir William Gooch appealed to the Board of Trade in England to grant large tracts to speculators who promised to settle western regions. Brunswick County, where few large grants had been made, was sparsely settled, he noted, while Spotsylvania with its expansive tracts was populous. Agreeing, the board relaxed the stipulations attached to land patents. Under the new system, landowners had only to settle one family per 1,000 acres over a period of years.

The liberalized system of grants and a peace treaty with the Iroquois in 1722 combined to spur western settlement. Speculators such as William Byrd II and Robert "King" Carter made tremendous profits by selling off tracts to eager farmers at reasonable prices. Settlers

Left: Governor Robert Dinwiddie (1693-1770) was active in the cause of westward expansion. From Cirker, Dictionary of American Portraits, Dover, 1967

snatched up land so quickly that the government permitted owners or their agents to transfer land titles on the spot, relieving purchasers of the need to travel to Williamsburg to handle the paper transactions.

In 1730 Carter obtained grants for approximately 63,000 acres in the Shenandoah Valley. In 1736 William Beverley was granted 118,491 acres near Staunton, which he called Beverley Manor. In dire need of money, Beverley hired Captain James Patton as his agent to attract buyers. Remembered as "the foremost man of the western section of the colony," Patton built his reputation on his involvement in the settling of that region.

Carter and Beverley also opened up to settlement land in the Northern Neck, a vast acreage stretching to the mountains, which became known as the Fairfax Proprietary. Acting as official agent for the sixth Lord Fairfax, Carter claimed certain lands in the northern Shenandoah Valley where settlers were beginning to stake out farms, arguing that the region was part of the Fairfax Proprietary, the boundaries of which had never been fixed.

A lordly brouhaha ensued. Lord Fairfax came to Virginia to claim his land, and the Brit-

Below left: Robert "King" Carter was an early land speculator in Virginia who made tremendous profits during the rush to settle the colony. From Cirker, Dictionary of American Portraits, Dover, 1967

ish Board of Trade appointed commissioners to survey it. Meanwhile, Pennsylvania settlers steered clear of the disputed zone, fearing that later adjudication would allow Fairfax to reclaim it. It took more than a decade and a half for the commissioners to reach a decision. In 1745 they confirmed that the contested land belonged to Fairfax, entitling him to collect quitrents on six million acres covering the entire Northern Neck and a swath of land stretching across the mountains into present-day West Virginia. Exempted from the Fairfax Proprietary were those lands granted to settlers by the government prior to the dispute.

While legal quarrels discouraged settlement of the Northern Neck, most of the Piedmont and the Valley was rapidly being populated. By 1749, settlers had pushed into what is now the Roanoke Valley and as far into Southwest Virginia as present-day Bristol. Adopting Spotswood's strategy, Governor Gooch encouraged Pennsylvania settlers to populate the Virginia frontier as a way to strengthen the buffer against the French in the Ohio Valley. Jacob Stover was notable among these settlers. A Swiss from Pennsylvania, Stover applied for a grant of 10,000 acres in the central Shenandoah Valley. Governor Gooch denied his request on the grounds that Stover offered no tangible assurance that he would be able to settle the land with the required number of families. Dissatisfied, Stover appealed directly to King George II, presenting a long list of names, all of whom he was sure he could settle on the land. King George approved Stover's land request, none the wiser that the list was composed of dogs, horses, livestock, and any breathing mammal to which Stover could ascribe a human name.

Two Pennsylvania Quakers, Alexander Ross and Morgan Bryan, acquired grants totaling 100,000 acres just north of Winchester. Under their auspices enough of their coreligionists settled in the northern Valley that, by 1738, Quaker meetings were a well-established feature of the area. Benjamin Borden, a New Jersey promoter, brought in more than 100 families in 1737, extending his title to a half-million acres

near Lexington. With the help of these Northern emigrants and others like them, Winchester was settled in 1730; Staunton in 1748; and Draper's Meadow (now Blacksburg) in 1750.

As Pennsylvania settlers moved south, prominent Virginians formed syndicates to acquire extensive tracts beyond the Blue Ridge and even the Alleghenies. As the frontier pushed west, they reasoned, they could sell their lands for significant profits. James Patton, John Buchanan, and John Preston formed the Woods River Company in 1745 and received a 100,000-acre grant near the New River, a tributary of the Ohio. Patton received a personal grant of 125,000 acres. By the end of the year, the area around present-day Blacksburg and Radford was filling with pioneers. The next year the Pulaski area had been surveyed and divided into tracts.

In 1749 a group of Northern Neck speculators, including Thomas Lee who had served as an agent for Lord Fairfax, formed the Ohio Company. In return for a 200,000-acre grant stretching across the Alleghenies, the company pledged to build a fort in the Ohio Valley to protect settlers from the French and Indians. The company further promised to win the Indians as allies by underselling competitive French fur traders.

On the very same day the Ohio Company received its grant, the Loyal Company, consisting of Albemarle County landowners including botanist and physician Thomas Walker, was granted 800,000 acres in Southwest Virginia on the condition that the company survey and settle it within four years. But the plans of both the Ohio Company and the Loyal Company would be thwarted by the outbreak of the French and Indian War.

When Governor Robert Dinwiddie arrived in 1751, he immediately became active in the cause of westward expansion. By the next year he had convinced the Ohio Indians to permit Virginians to build forts on the Ohio River. Dinwiddie then commenced to grant lands to settlers who promised to protect Virginia's ever-advancing frontier.

The French, too, were pushing into the Ohio Valley, first erecting a fort on the south side of Lake Erie, then marching overland to French Creek, a tributary of the Allegheny River, where they constructed Fort LeBoeuf. As the settlements of French and Virginians moved headlong towards one another, conflict was inevitable. Virginia, with some help from England and little from its sister colonies, undertook a war to force the French out of the Ohio Valley. After several less-than-glorious campaigns, the English captured the French stronghold at Fort Duquesne four years later.

After the last cinders of war had died, however, the treaty drove a wedge of resentment between Virginians and the mother country. When England wanted to keep the western lands from the French, she encouraged Virginia colonists to risk their money and their lives to settle there; once the French had been driven out, Virginia's interests were sublimated. Against Virginians' strong protests the Crown sealed a pact with France's former Indian allies—whose last-minute change of sides had made it possible to take Fort Duquesne. The Proclamation of 1763 officially prohibited Virginians from staking claim to land beyond the Alleghenies that they had fought to keep for the British.

In practice the proclamation had little binding force. Virginians who had settled the land more than a decade before were ordered to abandon their homes, but many stayed. Unable to obtain clear titles to the land west of the mountains, many new settlers ignored the paperwork and became squatters, moving across the mountains in violation of the act. Meanwhile, in order to protect their investments, land company speculators pressured government officials to extend the boundaries set by the 1763 agreement. With the Treaty of Fort Stanwix in 1768 and the Treaty of Lochaber two years later, lands were opened as far west as the Kentucky River and as far south as modern Bristol.

The compromises which overrode the Proclamation of 1763 were a short-acting balm. Having incurred an unprecedented public debt by the end of the "Great War for the Empire,"

On June 7, 1776, Virginian Richard Henry Lee declared to the Continental Congress that the colonies should be "free, independent states." From Cirker, Dictionary of American Portraits, Dover, 1967

England imposed a Stamp Tax on its colonies in 1765. The act aggravated a tension that had existed between the colonists and the mother country since the previous century, when Governor Berkeley's refusal to allow elections for a new House of Burgesses between 1660 and 1673 had inspired Bacon's Rebellion. The oppressive Navigation Acts were still in force, and Virginians had good cause to feel they had been shabbily treated after the French and Indian War. The colonists were tired of having their interests subordinated to the government in London.

A third Virginia Convention, held in Richmond from July 17 to August 26, 1775, committed the colony to war. In December 1775 Governor Lord Dunmore's forces were defeated at the Battle of the Great Bridge near Norfolk, and Dunmore fled to his ships. Although Dunmore would sail for England the following year, the British were to return to Hampton Roads several times before their final evacuation of Portsmouth in August 1781. Meanwhile, the burning of Norfolk in early January 1776 led to increased trade at Richmond and other river ports.

On June 7, 1776, Virginian Richard Henry Lee declared to the Continental Congress

Virginia statesman Thomas Jefferson was governor when Benedict Arnold's British contingent marched on Richmond late in the war. Jefferson and other officials barely escaped the city, which was set on fire. From Cirker, Dictionary of American Portraits, Dover, *1967*

that the colonies should be "free, independent states." Congress deliberated less than a month before passing Lee's motion on July 2. Two days later Thomas Jefferson's Declaration of Independence proclaimed the colonies' intentions to the world.

Until 1780, Virginia's direct contact with the war was largely through the troops she supplied for the Continental army. Suddenly, then, the war turned toward Richmond as the British sought to disrupt the tobacco trade and supply munitions depots. Marching from Westover, a British contingent led by Benedict Arnold set fire to the town's industry and confiscated its to-

bacco. Governor Thomas Jefferson and other officials barely escaped, and many state and county records were lost.

By May, Britain's General Lord Charles Cornwallis had reached Virginia from the Carolinas. He was unable, however, to defeat the American army in Virginia under Major General Marquis de Lafayette. On October 19, 1781, the British surrendered at Yorktown.

All elements of Virginia's population were affected by the war. Two blacks from Henrico County, Adam Armstrong and Humphrey Blaine, fought in the Continental army. James Armistead Lafayette, a slave from New Kent County, served as a spy; a forager for the British army, he frequented Cornwallis' headquarters. James Armistead Lafayette gained his freedom by legislative enactment in January 1787 and eventually was rewarded a small pension for his patriotic service.

Women also greatly aided the war effort. Besides making the soldiers' uniforms, some were employed at the Westham foundry, eight miles from Richmond. Anna Marie Lane of Richmond, who "in the garb and with courage of a soldier performed extraordinary military services and received a severe wound at the Battle of Bermantown," was granted a military pension after Yorktown.

Independence had its price. Although Virginia won freedom from Parliament's odious taxes and trade restrictions, the colony's economy was still bound closely to England. English mercantile firms were not about to forget the old debts that Virginia planters and merchants had accrued before the war. And Virginia's methods of combating postwar inflation proved troublesome. When the new Commonwealth called in paper money for exchange at one-thousandth of its face value, debtors were hard put to pay up. In some cases taxes had to be suspended; no one had the money to buy auctioned lands of delinquent taxpayers.

Agriculture, too, suffered after the war. Occupying troops had bought great quantities of wheat and bacon; when the soldiers left, the demand for these products plunged.

The former colonists also discovered the disadvantages of departing from the English mercantile system. They lost their privileged status as sole suppliers of tobacco to England and of flour and meat to the English colonies of the West Indies.

Invading troops had destroyed vast acreages of crops. Slaves had deserted their masters and joined the British, leaving plantations in-

hair piled high, and ornaments of feather and ribbon. Gentlemen replaced their wigs with powdered hair tied in braided pigtails. Knee breeches were still the style, and cocked hats had become quite the fancy.

In contrast, the wear of the west was that of the pioneer. Women's frocks were of the plainest homespun, woven from flax, wool, wild nettles, and buffalo hair, supplemented by the

The colonies won their independence when the British surrendered at Yorktown in 1781. Shown here is Yorktown's celebration of its centennial in 1881. Courtesy, Virginia State Library

sufficiently staffed. Many planters were forced to turn to wheat. Tobacco was still a viable commodity, but it would never again be King Tobacco.

Meanwhile, other changes confronted the Commonwealth. Virginia was dividing into two cultures, two ways of life.

In the 1750s eastern Virginians had enjoyed the blessings of civilization. The women followed London fashions: swishing hoop skirts,

occasional materials hauled overland at great expense. Fashionable accoutrements were expensive, unnecessary, and even a hindrance to the hardy workday life on the frontier.

There was no plantation economy west of the mountains. Working small tracts of land, settlers raised their own wheat, vegetables, and livestock. Wildlife was both manna and menace: elk and bears provided food and clothing; but wolves threatened the livestock that provided the

hides, milk, meat, and wool needed to survive. Trade with eastern communities was nearly impossible. The mountains created a natural barrier, and there was no money. Early settlers relied on a barter system, trading furs and skins for necessities brought in on horseback from the Tidewater. In the frontier society, settlers crafted what they needed for themselves, importing only a few necessities from the east, or went without.

As the eighteenth century progressed, towns arose around courthouses and trade centers. Acting as magnets for artisans, merchants, and businessmen, these towns became the seedbeds of new enterprises. Abundant salt, iron ore, coal, and timber supported several burgeoning industries. Farmers found new markets for their wool and wheat. In time the west lost its rough frontier edge and developed its own vibrant, self-sufficient economy—one that would find a firm foothold in the world marketplace once canals and railroads connected it to the eastern ports.

The western lands (including those now part of West Virginia) were rich in natural resources. Silica and clay supplies around Morgantown, Wheeling, and Wellsburg enabled local artisans and merchants to make a living in glassware and pottery.

Working small tracts of land, western settlers raised their own wheat, vegetables, and livestock for home consumption and nearby markets. This farmhouse in Goshen Pass, shown in 1922, is in sharp contrast with the plantation homes of eastern Virginia. Courtesy, Valentine Museum

Salt-making operations had begun in 1797 when Elisha Brooks erected a salt furnace at Malden on the Kanawha River. Salt, used both as a flavoring and a meat preservative, was a vital element of the local economy. The first facilities were crude contraptions that pumped brine from the earth through large hollow logs. Using this primitive method, Brooks produced about 150 bushels daily, which he sold for 8 to 10 cents per pound.

In the early 1800s David and Joseph Ruffner introduced iron drill bits and tubes of twine-wrapped wood strips to drive through rock. They extracted enough brine to produce 25

bushels—more than 1,200 pounds—of salt in a day. Adding the horse-powered mill, the brothers increased production even more.

Landowners up and down the Kanawha sank wells and built furnaces. By 1815 there were so many furnaces in the area—52—that it became known as the Kanawha Salines, churning out 2,300 to 3,000 bushels of salt a day. With other improvements, like steam power, the production of Kanawha Valley salt makers reached 3,200,000 bushels in 1846.

As well as providing a major source of employment, salt making sparked a demand for coal when salt makers began substituting it for

Isolated from the eastern regions of the Old Dominion, the settlers in the western and central Piedmont regions developed new markets for their produce. Western towns arose near courthouses and trade centers. Here farmers are shown bringing their tobacco crops to market at Drake's Branch in Charlotte County about 1890. Courtesy, Valentine Museum

By the early 1800s western settlers had shown they were self-sufficient. However, they had to reach larger markets if their enterprises were to prosper. Because the General Assembly did not support improvements to roads or river ports, and because the links between the James and the Kanawha and the Potomac and the Ohio seemed to take forever, a schism grew between the east and west. These buggies crossed the Jackson River on their way to Clifton Forge in western Virginia, circa 1880. Courtesy, Valentine Museum

wood. The Germans had been mining coal in western Virginia since Spotswood's settlement at Germanna, living off the demand of local markets. Drawing on the vast supply of iron ore, a multitude of ironworks sprang up in the Monongehela Valley around the turn of the century. Wheeling Iron Works would become an industry leader by 1835, producing 1,000 tons a year in bar, sheet, hoop, and boiler iron. These activities gave rise to other industries, which turned the iron into stoves, grates, nails, and other products.

By the early 1800s, settlers no longer had to create their own fabrics; they could buy them from local manufacturers. Farmers took wool to mills and had it processed; fulling and carding mills broke, carded, and wound wool into rolls.

One of the first factory owners, Robert Marshall, charged 10 cents a pound to process plain wools, 12 cents a pound for processing and dyeing. For every eight pounds he demanded a surcharge in butter or clean hog's fat.

As settlers built homes, the forests of the Alleghenies provided the timber. Wood fueled the iron furnaces, and when the byways to the east were opened, lumber became a major export. And as they raised crops, western farmers discovered the advantages of distilling spirits. Resourceful farmers used surplus corn and rye to make whiskey, their apples and peaches to make brandy.

Western settlers had proven that they could live independently of the east. But if their enterprises were to prosper, they had to reach larger markets. That meant they had to reduce the cost of overland transportation, which doubled the cost of imported goods and made the export of basic products almost prohibitive.

In the east, improved roads, bridges, and ferries made it relatively easy to transport produce to the James and other rivers. In the west, the river ports were distant, serviceable only by poor roads that were impassable in bad weather, dusty and bumpy in good weather. In essence, the government had supported the settlers in their move west, then left them stranded and isolated. In time this was one of the issues that would polarize the eastern and western counties of Virginia and inspire the western portion of the state to break away in 1863.

The schism between east and west first became evident in the war debt issue at the 1784 session of the General Assembly. Prior to the Revolution, Virginia planters had piled up debts totaling 2,300,000 pounds sterling by importing manufactured goods worth more than the tobacco they exported. Thomas Jefferson, for example, owed firms in Glasgow and London 10,000 pounds sterling. In the Treaty of Paris of 1783, negotiators for the American colonies accepted the responsibility of repaying these debts. But Virginians refused to cooperate.

Representing western Virginia, James Madison declared that Virginians should feel honor bound to repay the debts. Eastern representatives to the legislature, led by Patrick Henry, felt that repayment of the debt would be ruinous to Virginia's economy. Supporting Henry, a majority of legislators defeated Madison's resolution. The issue remained unsettled until the 1790s, when the United States assumed responsibility for the colonies' debts under the Jay Treaty. Virginians' debts accounted for almost half the total.

It was not the only time Madison and Henry would square off. Madison's faction objected to taxes which had to be paid in tobacco or in hard money. Western Virginians produced little tobacco, and they had little money. Valley delegates also opposed Henry's proposal to issue more paper currency on the grounds that it would

Virginian James Madison, who served in the state legislature between 1784 and 1786, led the faction that believed Virginia should repay England for debts accumulated before the war. Madison was later elected the fourth president of the United States. From Cirker, Dictionary of American Portraits, *Dover, 1967*

reduce their buying power in Maryland and Pennsylvania where many Valley Virginians traded. On this count, the westerners won.

But discontent continued to mount. In 1816 the western counties called for a convention in Staunton to discuss a lengthy list of grievances, some political, some economic. Although the white population west of the Blue Ridge exceeded that of the east, westerners formed a minority in the General Assembly. And although the General Assembly had created a separate fund for internal improvements and created a board of public works to assign money to worthy projects, trans-Allegheny Virginians claimed that the monies were not sufficient.

These issues were finally addressed in the Constitutional Convention of 1829-1830 held in the capitol in Richmond. The western Piedmont and the Shenandoah Valley were granted more seats in the legislature, although the trans-Allegheny region came away with less. Suffrage was extended to leaseholders and householders as well as landowners, and the eastern-dominated Privy Council was reduced in size, though it retained the right to appoint county sheriffs and justices of the peace. The General Assembly also held firm in its right to elect the governor rather than submitting the question to popular vote. Delegates representing the counties of modern-day Virginia voted to ratify the constitution; delegates from west of the Alleghenies voted solidly against it. The debate between east and west was far from over.

Efforts in the 1830s and 1840s to improve east-west transportation failed to meet the westerners' expectations. Improvements on the James and Potomac rivers moved goods cheaply downstream to market. But the promised links between the Potomac and the Ohio and between the James and the Kanawha seemed to take forever.

The census of 1840 incited westerners further by revealing that the white population of the trans-Allegheny region was 271,000—about 2,000 greater than the combined white populations of the Valley, the Piedmont, and the Tidewater. Yet the western counties had only 10 of the 29 members of the state senate and 56 of the 134 delegates. When the legislature of 1844-1845 refused to permit the Baltimore & Ohio Railroad to extend its line up the valley along the Kanawha—a measure that would have opened western Virginia to the port of Baltimore—angry representatives from 13 western counties coalesced to block any and all appropriations for transportation improvements in any other parts of the state.

Virginians called another Constitutional Convention in 1850 to address western grievances once more. The Constitution of 1851 granted suffrage to all whites and allowed the governor, judges, and county officers to be elected by popular vote. It abolished the Governor's Council, allocated money to establish a school system, and awarded seats in the House of Delegates on the basis of population. Regional tensions lingered, but the new constitution did buy 10 years of relative peace.

Realizing that a vigorous commerce benefited everyone, easterners were more willing to concede on issues of transportation. Without convenient access to Virginia's eastern ports, the trade in western wheat, iron, and salt might be diverted to New Orleans via the Mississippi. The advantages of transportation improvements were evident as early as 1784, when George Washington wrote to Governor Benjamin Harrison after a visit to the tramontane region. Virginia, he advised, should bring the rich region between the Great Lakes and the Ohio River into its economic sphere by taking immediate action "to preclude western inhabitants from being seduced into trade" with other regions. A growing commerce would compensate the Commonwealth "for any trouble and expense we may encounter to effect it."

Early the next year the General Assembly chartered the Potomac Company and the James River Company; George Washington was made president of both. The Potomac Company assumed the task of improving navigation on the Potomac and connecting it, by waterway, to the Ohio River. The James River Company was to build a canal from Richmond along the banks of the James to the river's headwaters to the west.

Two years later the General Assembly approved the creation of the Dismal Swamp Canal in conjunction with a similar act passed by North Carolina. The canal would enable North Carolina farmers to ship lumber and agricultural products from the Elizabeth River through Albemarle Sound to Hampton Roads 50 miles away. Tied in with improvements to the Roanoke River in 1826, the project made it possible for Southside farmers to send tobacco and grain from the Roanoke River area to Norfolk.

By 1795 the first leg of the James River Canal was complete. Improvements on the main bed of the James enabled farmers as far west as Lynchburg to float their products downriver to Richmond. Disappointed with the James River Company's slow westward progress, however, the state took it over in 1820, ultimately extending the canal to Buchanan at the foot of the Alleghenies, 196 miles from Richmond. Here construction was abandoned; funds, supplied by the state and the cities of Lynchburg and Richmond, had petered out. Nevertheless, the canal was an immense success. Freight barges carried coal, lime, iron, and grain downriver to Richmond.

On the journey back west they took flour, tobacco products, and manufactured goods. By 1841, 110,000 tons of freight moved along the James River Canal.

The Potomac Company had a slower start, completing its first canal around the Great Falls of the Potomac in 1802. By 1808 the canal had opened up markets as far inland as Port Republic in Rockingham County. The company eventually relinquished its charter to the Chesapeake and Ohio Company—a joint project of the U.S., Maryland and Virginia governments—to qualify for an injection of federal funds. But the project failed to benefit producers in the tramontane region, and Virginians lost interest as construction began inching towards Cumberland, Maryland.

Fifty-foot-long canal boats, pulled by horses or mules trudging along a parallel towpath, plied both the James and the Potomac rivers. While stagecoach lines offered transport between Alexandria, Richmond, and Petersburg, and well-kept turnpikes connected various parts of the state, many travelers in the 1840s preferred the smooth, leisurely ride of the packet boat. On the 36-hour trip from Richmond to Lynchburg, passengers could dine and sleep on board. After dinner, men clustered on deck to enjoy smoking, conversation, and spitting into the river without having to aim for a spittoon. Ladies read, played backgammon, or chatted before retiring to sleeping compartments separate from the men's. The 1845 fare: $5.27.

Before Virginia's canal system was complete, railroad fever swept the state. The Commonwealth issued some $37 million worth of bonds for internal improvements during the pre-Civil War era; more than $18 million was invested in railroad stock, half of that in the single decade of the 1850s.

This woodcut from an Anderson and Company photograph shows a canal boat being pulled by mules along the parallel towpath. The James River and Kanawha Canal system successfully opened transportation westward from Richmond to Buchanan in the Allegheny Mountains. Richmond in 1870, with its many churches, mills, and factories, is in the background. Courtesy, Valentine Museum

Left: In 1787 Virginia's General Assembly, in conjunction with North Carolina, approved the construction of the Dismal Swamp Canal. Courtesy, Valentine Museum

Below left: North Carolina and Virginia farmers used the Dismal Swamp Canal to transport their lumber and agricultural products along the Elizabeth River through the Albemarle Sound to Hampton Roads. Courtesy, Valentine Museum

Facing page: The Great Dismal Swamp is neither a swamp nor dismal; it is actually a 102,000-acre peat bog located in the Tidewater region of Virginia and North Carolina. Discovered in 1650 by William Drummond, the Dismal Swamp supports a wide variety of unique plant and animal life. A large part of the refuge was owned by George Washington, Patrick Henry, and other prominent Virginians. Courtesy, Virginia Division of Tourism

For all the millions it spent, Virginia failed to construct a unified rail system. New York, Pennsylvania, and Maryland developed long railroads linking eastern metropolises with emerging commercial centers in the west. In Virginia a rail system connecting Hampton Roads with major inland cities might have made Norfolk the greatest seaport on the Atlantic seaboard. But the fall-line cities—Richmond, Alexandria, Petersburg—stood in the way of a comprehensive system. As each city strove to carve out inland markets, the state ended up with a profusion of short railroads.

The Richmond, Fredericksburg & Potomac Railroad—still in operation and the only U.S. railroad to operate more than a century under its own name—was chartered to build a rail line between Richmond and Washington. Construction was plodding. The line reached Fredericksburg in 1837. Interrupted by war, the line did not reach Washington until 35 years later.

Construction proceeded at a much more heated pace to the southeast. To siphon off some of the traffic developed by the Dismal Swamp Canal, the Petersburg Railroad Company built a rail link to Weldon, North Carolina, in the 1830s. Concerned by this peril to their port, Norfolk merchants put their money behind the Portsmouth & Roanoke Railroad Company, also bound for a Weldon terminus. With a significant head start, the Petersburg Railroad Company developed the market first; revenues in 1839 amounted to $131,000. A perennial laggard, the Norfolk company logged only $73,000 the same year. Plagued by poor construction and high maintenance costs, the Portsmouth & Roanoke eventually folded.

In the 1840s some Norfolk investors applied for a charter to build a rail line from Norfolk to Petersburg. Fearing the loss of waterborne commerce, the river port staved off approval, but the legislature approved the charter the next year. Under the leadership of young William Mahone, the Norfolk & Petersburg line was completed in 1858. Mahone pushed Norfolk ahead in the fight for port trade by coordinating rail schedules with steamship lines running from Norfolk to Baltimore, Philadelphia, and New York. He ensured west-east freight traffic by coordinating his railway's schedule with those of the Southside Railroad and the Virginia & Tennessee lines.

Similarly, rivalries between cities slowed the development of the Richmond & Danville Railroad. Chartered in 1838, the company took almost 10 years to raise the necessary capital. Promoters tried to stimulate interest in Richmond, but merchants were afraid that the railroad company might select a different eastern terminus or that a railroad might harm the James River Canal trade. Overriding the objections, the Richmond City Council bought 2,000 shares. Two months later the state government purchased 1,800 shares.

The city of Petersburg tried to derail the project by refusing to allow the Richmond & Danville to lay tracks beneath one of the Petersburg line bridges. Forced to tunnel under the bridge, the company encountered additional expense and delay. Construction was not quite complete by the Civil War. Even so, the Richmond & Danville would serve as one of three lifelines to the capital of the Confederacy, carrying troops, food, and supplies.

While hindering everyone else's railroads, Petersburg had developed three of its own by the 1850s and was working on a fourth. For years, however, the city refused to allow the railroads to connect. Instead, each railroad maintained separate stations. To switch lines, freight had to be unloaded and carted across town to a different station. The crosstown traffic generated a lot of business for Petersburg merchants.

Rivalry with Baltimore spurred Alexandria to join the railroad competition. Reaching inland with the Baltimore & Ohio Railroad, the much larger Maryland city threatened to infringe upon Alexandria's traditional markets. Scraping up capital, Alexandria merchants chartered the Alexandria & Harper's Ferry Railroad in 1847. The plan was to open much of western Virginia by linking up with the independent Winchester and Potomac at Harper's Ferry.

But after 20 years of petitioning the General Assembly, the Baltimore & Ohio received permission to extend its tracks across Virginia territory. Not only did the railroad siphon off the western trade that Alexandria had hoped to tap, it also snatched up the Winchester & Potomac in 1848. The Alexandria to Harper's Ferry project collapsed without the first shovel ever being put to the earth. But other projects—the Southside Railroad, and the Virginia & Tennessee—succeeded. By the time of the Civil War, Virginia could boast 1,800 miles of track.

Blessed by river transportation and abundant natural resources, Virginia entered the industrial era as early as the 1790s. The west parlayed salt, iron ore, and coal into lucrative industries; the east did the same with tobacco, iron, and its own coal. Norfolk shipbuilders used Allegheny timber to craft tall masts for sailing ships. Richmond processed wheat and tobacco

from the Piedmont and points west, creating valuable export products. The union of east-west commerce proved profitable to the entire state.

Although tobacco no longer ruled the agricultural economy, it provided a cornerstone for the state's industrial development. By the 1820s, Virginia factories were processing one-third of all U.S.-grown tobacco, exporting leaf products to Europe as well as to Northern states. By 1860, Virginia was the country's number one tobacco manufacturer, with 252 tobacco factories centered mostly in Richmond, Petersburg, and Lynchburg.

Flour, with its higher value, surpassed tobacco as the state's leading product. By 1861, 1,383 Virginia mills, representing a capital investment of around $6 million, ground grain from several states. Richmond was the largest producer, but Petersburg and Alexandria had significant industries as well. Before the war

Iron manufacturing, begun in 1622, grew in response to the need for large and small machinery. Iron works such as Tredegar, established by Joseph Reid Anderson, made Richmond the South's only important antebellum manufacturing center. Courtesy, Library of Congress

Mills such as the Rexrode Grist Mill near Blue Grass, Virginia, were built along major waterways. Located on the south branch of the Potomac River's south fork, the mill, owned by Ray Rexrode, is 100 years old. By the 1860s, flour surpassed tobacco as the state's leading export. In 1861, 1,383 Virginia mills were grinding the grain. Courtesy, Virginia Division of Tourism

Jewish immigrants, fleeing the German Revolution of 1848, rose to prominence in Richmond as retailers and merchants. They built a synagogue on Eleventh Street near Marshall Street in 1848; Beth Ahaba, pictured here, was built on the same site in 1880. Courtesy, Valentine Museum

Virginians exported flour as far away as South America.

Settlers had found numerous iron deposits in the state. By 1856, Virginia had 88 charcoal furnaces for smelting iron and 60 forges for molding it into nails, tools, and other utensils. Virginia led the Southern states in iron manufacture. Iron working created a demand for the coal mined at the Chesterfield pits south of the James River. By 1860, Virginia also was one of the South's leading coal-mining states, producing the fuel for the local iron industry and for gas manufacture throughout the Atlantic seaboard.

Cessation of trade with England during the War of 1812 encouraged domestic manufacturers to replace imported goods. Twenty-two cotton mills arose around Petersburg, Richmond, Wheeling, and Lynchburg. Eighteen textile factories—many in western Virginia where merino sheep were raised—produced carpets and other woolen textiles. Smaller industries included paper mills, potteries, and furniture plants which made use of the state's great abundance of pine, oak, walnut, and maple trees.

Petersburg and Alexandria were prosperous cities by any standard, but nothing could compare to Richmond, one of the most affluent cities in the nation. It led the state in flour milling and tobacco manufacture. Its iron foundries ranked among the greatest in the country, and coal mining in its outlying districts made Virginia a leader in coal production.

Richmond stood at the economic center of the state, the beneficiary of superb transportation facilities, cheap waterpower, and accessible natural resources. At the fall line of the James, Richmond was an oceangoing port; at the terminus of the James River Canal, its commerce reached deep into the interior. By the mid-nineteenth century, the city was a major railroad center as well. Tapping the waterpower of the James, Richmond was a natural location for textile and flour mills. With coal mined in its suburbs and iron in its hinterlands, the city possessed the resources to support a vigorous iron industry. Few communities could boast of such a propitious combination of geography and natural resources.

Entrepreneurial talent migrated to Richmond, a city of opportunity. Among the developers of Richmond's flour mills were industrialists from Spain and Scotland. An influx of Northern capitalists joined the foreigners, adding to the reservoir of business talent. Newspapers heralded the arrival of several transplanted Northern businesses, such as a "looking glass manufactory" from New York and a hat manufacturer from Baltimore. The city also attracted a number of Jewish immigrants, who rose to prominence as local retailers and merchants.

Richmond expanded rapidly along the riverfront as droves of people arrived in packet boats, stagecoaches, and private carriages. Taverns with names like Hogg's, The Swan, and The Bird in Hand served politicians, doctors, clerks, and the ever-present tradesmen. Developers paved streets and laid sidewalks. Merchants erected stores and warehouses. Pioneer industrialists and their families built great brick mansions and fine churches.

The municipal authorities were hard pressed to keep up. One out-of-state visitor wrote that Richmond was dirty and that its streets were "narrow as well as crooked ...full of hogs and mud." But to Richmonders enthralled by the prospect of imminent wealth and success,

the conditions were like the emperor's new clothes: no one seemed to notice. A half-dozen years after assuming the distinction of state capital, Richmond sprawled across an area of two square miles. Eighteen hundred people, half of them slaves, inhabited 280 houses. Within four years the population doubled.

As houses and factories sprang up, real estate values climbed daily; by some accounts, prices matched those of New York. Land-hungry speculators swept through the town, marking cornfields and thickets for streets and lots. Samuel Mordecai, an eyewitness, described the frenzy this way: "Not one buyer in 20 purchased with the intention of building or even of holding longer than until the second or third installment should fall due, when, according to the auctioneer's assurance, he would double his money."

With the Panic of 1819, the bottom dropped out of the real estate market. Everyone dumped their property; everyone, that is, but those cool-headed capitalists with the nerve to purchase land while prices were in free fall and the patience to wait for economic growth to resume. At the bottom of the market, many speculators and small-scale entrepreneurs went out of business. The collapse blew away the speculative froth, but Richmond was a city of substance. Those who held out were amply rewarded.

Industry suffered little in the panic. Richmond's tobacco, iron, coal, and flour businesses had taken firm hold. The canal fed Richmond's port trade, drawing cargo from Virginia's interior for transloading onto vessels bound for ports around the world. Extensions of the canal in the 1830s and 1840s and the construction of railroads kept Richmond's docks in a state of constant activity.

Richmond had few peers as a manufacturing center. The city produced ceramics, beer, musical instruments, coaches, soap, and candles. And Richmond industrialists took the lead in transforming the tobacco industry. Traditionally, people had smoked tobacco; in the early 1800s, plug, or chewing tobacco, was all the rage.

Marketed under such charming brand names as Darling Fanny Pan Cake, Little Swan Rough and Ready, and the ever-popular Negro Head, plug enjoyed a booming popularity. One foreign visitor suggested that the national emblem should be the spittoon rather than the eagle.

The production of plug involved a lengthy process of stemming, flavoring with licorice, moistening with olive oil, and curing for 30 days. The stems were used in snuff, so there was little

waste. By 1819, 11 tobacco manufacturing plants in Richmond were turning out plug tobacco and snuff as well as the kind used for smoking. Eventually, Richmond would employ 2,000 workers in some 52 tobacco factories, processing five million pounds of leaf a year.

Coal mining put Richmond at the forefront of another industry vital to America's industrial revolution. Coal had been mined commercially in nearby Midlothian, just west of Richmond, since

Rocketts Landing was the waterfront extension of Richmond east along the James River. A depot area for steamboats and other sailing vessels, Rocketts was the point of arrival and departure for many travelers to and from Virginia. Courtesy, Valentine Museum

1735. The region's bituminous coal, prized for its purity, produced heat, and gas for lights; it fired iron forges and powered locomotives.

Coal deposits were found on both sides of the James. Seams on the southern banks were reported to be extraordinarily ample in places: 25- to 50-feet thick. Seams on the northern bank, a mere seven- to eight-feet thick, were generous by any other measure. By 1822, Richmond was exporting 42,000 tons a year of coal produced in Chesterfield, Henrico, and Goochland counties. By 1826, the volume of Richmond-mined coal had increased to 79,000 tons. Exports peaked in 1833 when the Chesterfield Railroad began hauling coal. Although Pennsylvania soon surged ahead as the nation's leading producer, Richmond's industry continued to thrive.

The coal industry greatly stimulated the local economy. "At the Chesterfield coal mines, a space less than a quarter of a mile square yields

Following the Revolutionary War, Richmond expanded rapidly. Northern capitalists and foreign industrialists built warehouses and stores, elegant houses and churches. St. Peter's Catholic Church was built in 1834 at the corner of Eighth and G (now Grace) streets. Courtesy, Valentine Museum

annually about a fourth of a million dollars," observed a visitor in a letter to the *Richmond Enquirer*. Industrialists made significant profits from their mining operations. Landowners pocketed profits from their royalties. Hundreds of workers found employment in the mining camps a few miles outside the city. Furthermore, the mines generated revenues for local railroads, and supported an industry geared to manufacturing steam engines and rail cars.

Most significantly, the abundance of coal stoked the fires of a vigorous iron industry. David Ross, a Scottish immigrant, pioneered the iron industry with his mill across the river from the capitol. In 1809 Philip Haxall built his own ironworks on the site. Haxall's operation included a nail factory, as well as a rolling and slitting mill. Four other ironworks were quickly established, the most prominent of them being the Belle Isle Rolling and Slitting Mill and the Nail Manufactory.

These foundries all would be eclipsed in the 1830s by the famous Tredegar Iron Works. Joseph R. Anderson, a West Point graduate, commenced his business career as a commercial agent and ended it as owner of Tredegar, the largest ironworks in the South by the 1850s. Tredegar produced locomotives, rails, and later, cannons used by the Confederate army.

Two families dominated Richmond's powerful flour-milling industry: the Gallegos and the Haxalls. By 1831, Philip Haxall ran a conglomerate of businesses, including an iron mill, a plaster-grinding mill, a sawmill, a blacksmith shop, and a corn and gristmill. Two years later his gristmill was grinding out 200,000 bushels of wheat a year. Haxall's mills were gutted by fire twice before the Civil War. Meanwhile, the Gallego flour had gained an international reputation. The nine-story building dominated Richmond's business district, grinding 300,000 bushels a year until it burned in 1830. Both Haxall's and Gallego's would be rebuilt to become even bigger producers than before.

In the 1850s Richmond mills drew from the wheat fields of Virginia, Georgia, Ten-

nessee, and North Carolina. Producing a half million barrels a year, Richmond industrialists supplied markets as far away as California and South America. Until Minneapolis took the lead in later years, Richmond was considered the flour-milling capital of the country.

Although Virginia was never a major cotton-producing state or a leader in the textile industry, Richmond did support several wool and cotton mills. In 1833 P.J. Chevallie's Richmond Woolen Manufactory turned out 9,000 yards of flannel per week until destroyed by fire in 1853; the Virginia Woolen Mills, located two blocks away, picked up its business. The Richmond Cotton Manufactory was born during the embargo of 1808 when it was deemed patriotic to buy homemade goods. The company was reor-

With the extension of the James River and Kanawha Canal westward along the James in the 1830s and 1840s, and the building of the railroads at the same time, wheat shipments poured into Richmond from the western sections of Virginia. Philip Haxall built his mill along the canal, and from 1809 until 1894 the property passed from father to son. This engraving of the Haxall Mills was published in 1888. Courtesy, Valentine Museum

In existence from 1798 to 1924, Gallego Mills helped to make Richmond one of the world's greatest flour centers in the antebellum era. The large brick building housing the mills was located on the east end of the turning basin of the James River and Kanawha Canal. Courtesy, Valentine Museum

This panoramic lithograph of Richmond was made shortly before the Civil War, in 1852. Courtesy, Valentine Museum

ganized in 1838 as the Richmond Cotton Manufacturing Company. Under new management it employed nearly 200 laborers to run its 3,776 spindles and 80 looms, which digested 1,500 pounds of raw cotton a day.

After the Civil War, Richmond would be tainted by its reputation as the capital of the Confederacy, a bastion of masters and slaves, moonlight, and magnolias. The reality could not have been more different. Richmond was in fact one of the most dynamic centers of industrial capitalism in America. As the city transformed the economic landscape of Virginia, it also added a few new twists to the "peculiar institution," slavery.

In search of labor, Richmond's industrialists did not hesitate to use slaves to supplement their white work force. Although tobacco manufacture was prospering, the old plantation system was on the decline and slaveholders only too happy to find a more remunerative employment for their property. Some landowners trekked with their slaves to the cotton fields of Alabama

and Mississippi. Others moved to Richmond. In an industrial setting the traditional relationship of master and slave broke down.

A handful of industrialists purchased slaves outright, but most hired slaves under contract from their owners. As factory workers, slaves enjoyed unprecedented freedom. Some received room and board with their factory jobs, giving them an opportunity to live free from their masters. Some simply made their own housing arrangements. As city laborers, factory slaves had the opportunity to earn extra money by working overtime, enabling some to buy their freedom.

Richmond was a melting pot of immigrants and natives: free and slave; Catholic, Protestant, and Jew. This bustling city on the James was a center of commerce and manufacture—and finance. Once, tobacco had been the only currency of the land; as industry grew, so did banks. The first, the Bank of Richmond, was chartered in 1792 but never became firmly established. In 1804 the Bank of Virginia set up headquarters

in Richmond. With $1.5 million in equity capital, it grew to the point where it established branches in nine cities.

By 1860, Richmond was a golden town. Five years later it would be a blackened ruin. As the eighteenth century progressed, several towns appeared in the western districts, usually centering around the county courthouse. Winchester was established in 1752. Within three years a small cabin was erected to serve as the courthouse, a necessity in a town where German and Scotch-Irish inhabitants didn't always mix well. As historian Samuel Kercheval notes, the Germans taunted the Irish on St. Patrick's Day by parading the effigy of the saint and his wife with strings of Irish potatoes around their necks. On St. Michael's Day the Irish returned the honor, exhibiting a mock St. Michael bedecked with sauerkraut. Riots often followed.

With the approval of the General Assembly, Stephensburg officially became a town in 1758, with Lewis Stephens, son of the founder, acting as surveyor. Four years later Jacob Sto-

ver's son Peter laid out Strasburg. Settled principally by Germans, their language was commonly used in those towns until the nineteenth century. Staunton, established in 1761, was settled primarily by the Scotch-Irish.

That same year, the General Assembly established Woodstock, the first large town in the west. Woodstock was settled—also by Germans—on 1,200 acres, 96 of which were divided into half-acre building lots. Streets and five-acre "out-lots" took up the rest of the area. In 1762 Mecklenburg, later called Shepherdstown for its surveyor, Captain Thomas Shepherd, was settled primarily by German mechanics, which proved to be somewhat prophetic: 22 years later James Rumsey would construct his first steamboat there.

Lexington was established in 1778, on a tiny chunk of land only 1,300 feet long and 900 feet wide, to give the new county of Rockbridge a place to hold its courts. Over the next three decades, more than a dozen towns would be established in the west.

On Saturday, April 2, 1865, while the Confederate army prepared to evacuate Richmond, military authorities set fire to warehouses over the objections of the city's civilian leaders. During the night, the fire spread through the city's business district, destroying flour mills, woolen mills, and the armory. This Currier & Ives lithograph shows the Confederate army and civilians fleeing the city south across the Mayo Bridge.

THE WAR BETWEEN THE STATES

In the words of Abraham Lincoln, the United States in the antebellum era was truly "a house divided." As the federal government exercised its powers to the advantage of Northern states, Southerners grew restive. They protested the use of federal funds to build canals and roads, which primarily benefited Northern capitalists and farmers. They were outraged by the "protective" tariff of 1828 which fed the North's industrial economy by eliminating foreign competition and threatened the overseas trade that buttressed the South's agricultural economy.

Overriding all other concerns was the issue of slavery. Although the debate took place on a lofty moral plane, the abolition of the "peculiar institution" would have profound economic consequences for the Southern states. First, it would wipe out millions of dollars in capital: in 1850 the average male slave was worth between $800 and $1,200 on the market. Second, abolition would undermine the plantation-based agricultural system which was built around gangs of slave labor. Without slaves the large plantations would be nothing but unwieldy chunks of land.

The North, where an industrial economy had no need of slavery, had grown increasingly intolerant of the institution. Sympathizers initiated the underground railroad in defiance of a federal law which demanded that fugitive slaves be returned to their owners. Tensions increased when Northern states refused to accept the U.S. Supreme Court's Dred Scott decision, which declared that slaves could be carried into non-slave states as property. *New York Tribune* editor Horace Greeley articulated the abolitionist sentiment when he wrote that the court decision deserved "as much moral weight as would be the judgment of a majority of those congregated in any Washington barroom." As Northerners continued to attack slavery and slaveowners, Southerners dug in their heels in the belief that it was each state's right to accept or reject slavery.

Virginia was a microcosm of the national miasma. Divided by sectional differences, the state engaged in debate over internal improvements and slavery, as well as free schools and political representation. Like the industrial Northeast, western Virginia's small-farm economy needed no slave labor. While 55 percent of the state's white population lived west of the Blue Ridge, only 13 percent of its slaves did. In the east, slaveowners held a majority in state government. A year before the war, 75 percent of the state legislators were slaveowners.

As early as the 1840s, western Virginians discussed the gradual abolition of slavery west of the Blue Ridge, and even of dividing the state. State-funded internal improvements, westerners

argued, had mainly benefited the eastern counties. Virginia's Constitutional Convention of 1850-1851 did little to soothe sectional strife. In return for concessions to the west on such issues as the franchise and legislative representation, the east exacted a provision barring the General Assembly from enacting an emancipation law. Although this act effectively closed the slavery debate, westerners remained dissatisfied. The institution of slavery had come to be directly equated with the east's political dominance.

Westerners, politically aligned with the North in their antipathy towards slavery, had become economically allied to the North through trade with Pennsylvania and Ohio. Major roads such as the Northwestern Turnpike, the Staunton and Parkersburg Pike, and the James River and Kanawha Turnpike connected western towns to Ohio River ports. By 1861, goods

in western Virginia were being shipped to Maryland markets via the Northwestern Virginia Railroad, terminating in Parkersburg, and the Baltimore & Ohio, extending to Wheeling. Promised improvements on the Kanawha, which would have facilitated east-west trade, were never made.

Tied by rivers, roads, and railroads to the North, western Virginians felt a greater sense of community with the cities of Pittsburgh and Cincinnati than with their brethren to the east. Virginians living on the far western fringes of the state resided closer to seven other state capitals than to their own. Given the difficulties in transportation, Richmond might as well have been on another continent.

Divided between Unionist and Secessionist parties, Virginia steadfastly straddled the fence as the United States careened toward Civil

War. Strong antislavery sentiment in the west precluded Virginia from siding immediately with the newly formed Confederate States of America. In February 1861 Virginia called for a peace convention in Washington. Northern states sent delegates with instructions to make no compromises on the issue of permitting slavery into the territories. The Confederate states sent no delegates at all.

Disheartened Virginians called for a special convention of distinguished citizens to determine the state's position. Virginians east of the Blue Ridge expressed secessionist sympathies; the people of the Valley supported a states' rights platform that tilted them moderately in favor of secession. Trans-Allegheny Virginia, however, was so strongly in favor of the Union that some western Virginians supported splitting

Settlers living in the far western regions of Virginia were tied by roads, rivers, and railroads to the North. Isolated from the eastern part of the state by mountains and inadequate transportation, they developed markets to the north and west. This photograph demonstrates the transportation problems faced by those western settlers. Courtesy, Valentine Museum

the state if the eastern counties insisted upon seceding. A newspaper article in the *Western Virginia Guard* urged readers to consider forming their own state. A writer for the *Parkersburg News* noted that "western Virginia, from its geographical position, must ultimately unite with the states in the Valley of the Mississippi," while an article in the *Wellsburg Herald* forecasted that the region would eventually become part of Pennsylvania. On April 4, after two months' debate, delegates voted 88 to 45 against secession, providing that the president refrained from using force to bring the Confederate states back into the Union.

As the Virginia debate drew to a close, South Carolina was preparing to take Federally held Fort Sumter by force. President Lincoln called for 75,000 volunteers, including three

regiments from Virginia, to subdue the rebellious state. To Virginians the call signaled clearly that the president would fight to force the Confederate states back into the Union. On April 17, 88 delegates voted to secede, and 55 voted against secession. Virginia became the eighth Confederate state.

One week later antisecessionist John S. Carlisle began garnering support for a convention. On May 13, 436 delegates from 27 counties met in Wheeling to discuss the future of Virginia's pro-Union western region. By 1862, the northwestern counties had organized a separate government. On June 20, 1863, the state of West Virginia was admitted to the Union.

As the Union and Confederacy commenced hostilities, the North appeared to have an immense advantage in population and indus-

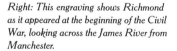

Right: This engraving shows Richmond as it appeared at the beginning of the Civil War, looking across the James River from Manchester.

try. The Union had 23 million people; the 11 Confederate states were inhabited by only 9 million, of whom 3.5 million were slaves who could hardly be counted upon to support the secessionist cause. Although the South had a predominantly rural economy, the North was far more capable of feeding itself. Southern acreage was tied up in cash crops, especially tobacco and cotton. So lucrative was the cultivation of cotton that the Deep South states actually imported grain from the North. Finally, the Northern states were far more industrialized. They possessed the economic base to manufacture the armaments of war and to keep some of the largest armies the world had yet known in the field.

General Winfield Scott, the recently retired commander of the Union's armed forces, believed that the best way to force the South to

Left: General Winfield Scott conceived a strategy which would force the South into submission by depriving it of much-needed supplies. From Cirker, Dictionary of American Portraits, *Dover, 1967*

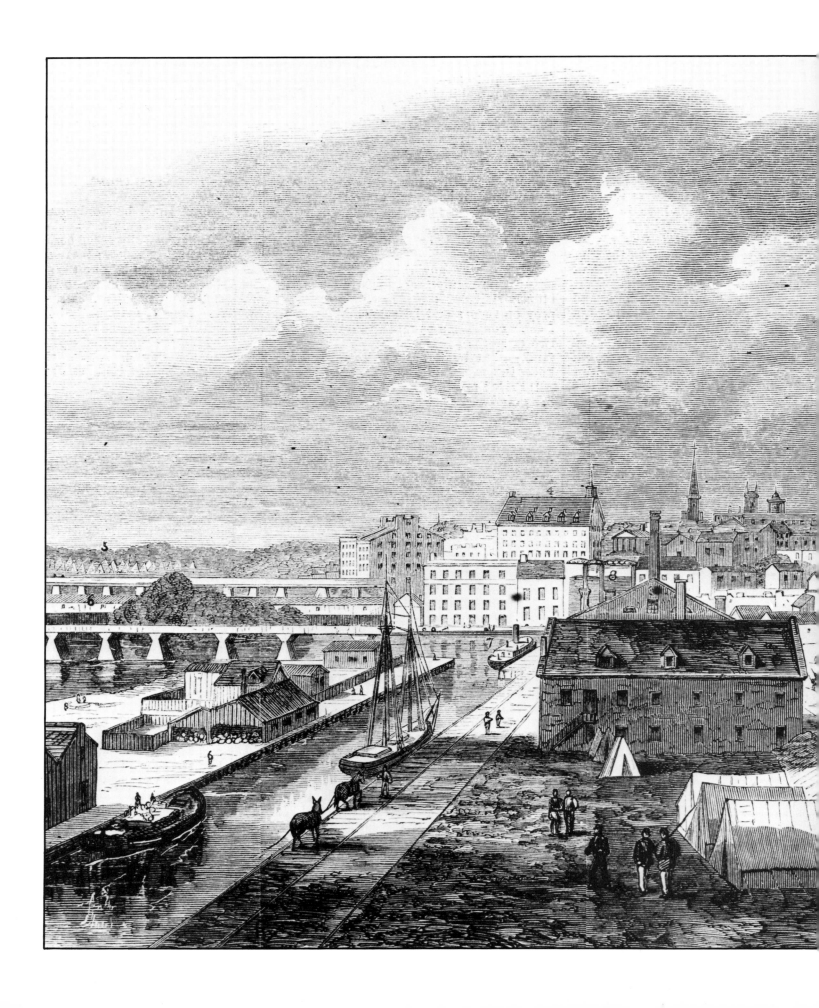

submission was to deprive it. By blockading the ports, the Union would cut the Confederacy's cotton and tobacco exports to Europe, prevent it from buying English and French armaments, and thwart efforts to import food. By controlling the Mississippi, the Federals also would cut off the main body of the South from supplies of Texas beef and grain. The strategy, designed to provoke hunger, hardship and, eventually, rebellion against the Confederacy, became known as Scott's Anaconda; like the powerful snake, it would squeeze the life out of the secessionists.

Although Scott's grand vision guided Union strategy in the long run, hot-blooded Union generals lacked the patience to wait for the South to slowly starve. They identified other targets that if captured would hasten the end of the war. Virginia was the one state in the Confederacy with an economy capable of sustaining the demands of mid-nineteenth century armies with their voracious appetites for supplies and their dependence upon railroads. Not surprisingly, Richmond was the premier target.

Not only was the city on the James the capital of the Confederacy, it was the South's only industrial center of importance. Richmond's

ARMORY.

ironworks, textile plants, and flour mills were vital to any enduring war effort. Not only were arms forged in Richmond, but niter, necessary to the manufacture of gunpowder, was also produced there. Additionally, with five railroad lines and a deepwater terminal on the James, Richmond was a major depot for supplies. Without Richmond as a base of operations, the South would have been hard pressed to field an army of sufficient size to oppose the North's massive Army of the Potomac.

A succession of Northern generals repeatedly struck at Richmond; Robert E. Lee repeatedly risked the destruction of the Army of Northern Virginia to prevent the city's fall. Many of the bloodiest battles in the Civil War—Fredericksburg, the Wilderness, Spottsylvania, Cold Harbor, Seven Pines, Petersburg, and the

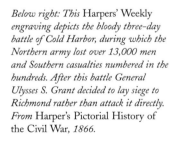

Below right: This Harpers' Weekly *engraving depicts the bloody three-day battle of Cold Harbor, during which the Northern army lost over 13,000 men and Southern casualties numbered in the hundreds. After this battle General Ulysses S. Grant decided to lay siege to Richmond rather than attack it directly. From* Harper's Pictorial History of the Civil War, *1866.*

Peninsula Campaign—were fought on the approaches to Richmond. When the city fell in 1865, the surrender of Lee's mauled army at Appomattox that same year was a mere afterthought.

Virginia offered many other tempting targets. Under the guns of the Union army in Washington, the port city of Alexandria was occupied early in the war. Norfolk fell soon afterwards, captured in a bloodless encounter by a contingent commanded by Abraham Lincoln himself. With Yankee ships patrolling the mouth of the Chesapeake Bay and soldiers occupying two of its major ports, Virginia was the first state to feel the squeeze of Scott's Anaconda.

Equally vital to the South's war effort was a reliable supply of salt. Without salt the South could not preserve the meat needed to feed the Confederate troops. Without salt livestock was vulnerable to a variety of diseases. Without salt Southern industry could not convert hides to the leather used in boots, horse tack, and shoes. Although some states set up their own works to extract the mineral from ocean water, mines near the southwestern Virginia town aptly named Saltville were the Confederacy's major source of

Above: General Thomas "Stonewall" Jackson saved the breadbasket of Virginia in his famous Valley Campaign. From Cirker, Dictionary of American Portraits, *Dover, 1967*

Facing page: On the morning of April 3, 1865, the capital of the Confederacy was a smoldering ruin. Its business and financial center had been torched as the Union forces approached Richmond. Gallego Mills, in the background, was back in operation within a year, but Virginia's economy would take years to rebuild following the war. Courtesy, Valentine Museum

Below: The White House of the Confederacy, designed by Robert Mills for Dr. John Brokenbrough, was occupied by Jefferson Davis and his family during the Civil War. Located at the southwest corner of Twelfth and Clay streets, the house also served as the headquarters for the commander of the First Military district after the Civil War. Courtesy, Valentine Museum

supply. Mining activity boomed in the mountain town, and loggers were kept busy for miles around supplying the wood used to dry out the blocks of salt. Recognizing the town's economic importance, Union forces launched sporadic raids against Saltville; the Confederates were equally determined to defend it. Saltville was so far from the major theaters of war, however, that it never became the site of a major battle.

The burden of feeding the Army of Northern Virginia fell largely upon Virginia, which had the most diversified agricultural economy of any Southern state. In 1863 the state legislature restricted the cultivation of tobacco in an effort to stimulate the production of corn and wheat. The

production of grain crops did increase substantially, but stores were pillaged by invading armies.

Yielding a great bounty of wheat, oats, and livestock, the Shenandoah Valley had considerable strategic value over and above its importance in protecting Richmond's western flank. General Thomas "Stonewall" Jackson saved the breadbasket of Virginia in his famous Valley Campaign. Southern armies in the Valley seemed to lead a charmed existence; in the Battle of New Market, young cadets from the Virginia Military Institute helped to rout a far larger Yankee force. But the North with its greater numbers eventually prevailed. Commanding an army

J. Becker sketched the surrender of the Confederate army at the Burkesville Station, Virginia, for Frank Leslie's Illustrated Newspaper. Many of the war's bloodiest battles were fought on Virginia's soil; the despair of the men and the devastation of the land is apparent.

of 35,000, Union General Philip Sheridan obliterated the Valley's economic usefulness by meting out the same treatment that General Sherman made famous in his march through Georgia. "I have destroyed over 2,000 barns filled with wheat, hay, and farming implements, over 70 mills filled with flour and wheat," Sheridan wrote. "I have driven in front of the army over 4,000 head of stock and have killed and issued to the troops not less than 3,000 sheep."

As invading forces ravaged Virginia's farm economy, Lee's army depended increasingly on the Carolinas and Georgia for food stores. But the line of supply was precarious. After years of warfare Virginia's railroad system was breaking down. Northern troops had torn up track, twisted rail, demolished bridges, wrecked the rolling stock, and burned stations at every opportunity. Unable to bring in sufficient

supplies from the south, Lee had to divert troops to eastern North Carolina and southwestern Virginia to forage for food.

The strains of war showed in the civilian economy as well. Runaway inflation inspired accusations of profiteering. A barrel of flour in October 1863 cost Richmonders an appalling $70; six months later the price had risen to $250 a barrel. Corn was $50 a barrel; sugar, $10 a pound; calico, $30 a yard. By February 1865, a dozen eggs cost $6. Confederate money lost its value as the government printed more and more notes without gold or silver backing.

Food, clothing, and medicine were so scarce that women took to the streets in protest. The most dangerous demonstration, known as the Bread Riots, broke out in Richmond in April 1863 when a band of 60 women shouting "Blood or bread!" stormed stores for bacon, flour, shoes, and other staples. Similar riots followed across the South.

With the blockade securely in place and half of the Confederacy subdued, only Richmond stood between the North and victory. On Saturday, April 1, 1865, Richmonders could hear gunfire from the south where the armies were clashing in the Battle of Five Forks. By 9:30 that night, Lee ordered his battered army to pull back from Petersburg, leaving Richmond wide open. As Union troops drew closer, Lee wired Confederate President Jefferson Davis

that there was no way to hold back the advancing army. Lee advised Davis to evacuate.

Richmond's bridges swayed under the weight of Confederate troops as they evacuated the city. The canal was brimming with packet boats loaded with fleeing townspeople. Trains heading for Danville—one car containing President Davis and his cabinet—were jammed to capacity.

By the morning of April 3, Richmond, once the South's most vibrant industrial and political center, was a smoldering ruin. Lee's

Lincoln's triumphal procession through the fallen Confederate capital of Richmond on April 4, 1865, was not greeted with universal enthusiasm; however, many inhabitants of the city were probably relieved to see the end of the long, bloody war. From Frank Leslie's Illustrated History of the Civil War, *1861-1865*

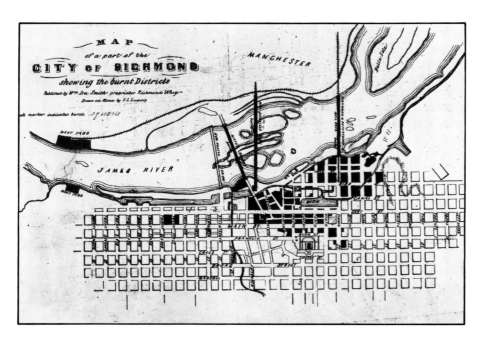

Most of Richmond's financial and manufacturing district was destroyed in the evacuation fire. This map shows the areas burned in some detail. From the Richmond Whig, 1865

surrender at Appomattox was only six days away.

The Civil War spread its devastation throughout the South, but nowhere else except Virginia had two mighty armies been locked in prolonged and destructive combat for four continuous years. Nowhere else had the economic underpinnings been so systematically destroyed. Invading armies had torn up railroads, turnpikes, and bridges. They had burned the cities and savaged the farms.

Virginia was picked clean. Troops had conscripted all the horses, burned the barns, stripped away the fences for firewood, foraged the hay, and slaughtered the cows, pigs, and sheep. Those few beasts not eaten on the spot were left to wander off through unfenced fields or to trample unguarded crops. An Augusta County resident described the area from Harper's Ferry to New Market:

There were no fences ... no cattle, hogs, sheep, or horses, or anything else ... fences were all gone ... barns were all burned; a great many of the private dwellings were burned; chimneys standing without houses, and houses standing without roof, or door, or window; a most desolate state of affairs; bridges all destroyed, roads badly cut up.

The wholesale devastation of the war was exceeded only by the economic calamity of the

Emancipation Proclamation. For all its evils, slavery had been the cornerstone of Virginia's plantation economy. Thousands of slaves ran to freedom during the war, leaving farms and plantations to founder. Although some slaves remained loyal to their former masters, Virginia's plantation economy was doomed. Until landowners could find a way to tap the labor of their former black servants, agricultural production would remain depressed.

Emancipation did far more than disrupt the plantation economy; it obliterated a significant portion of Virginia's capital stock. Where the North had invested in labor-saving machinery, the South had invested in slaves. Although slaves were in one sense a form of labor, they also represented a significant accumulation of capital. Planters could sell them for cash to the cotton barons along the Mississippi River or lease them

to labor-hungry industrialists in Richmond. By disposing of their slaves, Virginia capitalists could raise the money to forsake their moribund tobacco crops in favor of railroads and factories. But President Lincoln made that impossible with a stroke of his pen in 1863. Furthermore, emancipation undermined Virginia's tax base; much of the state's taxable wealth had been reckoned in the form of slave property.

Rebuilding Virginia's agriculture would be difficult enough without slaves. The decimation of the white work force made it nearly impossible. The war had wiped out an entire generation of men. Fifteen thousand Virginians had died; countless survivors were maimed.

Virginia would never recover the wealth and economic leadership of the antebellum years. Defeated, decimated, demoralized, and deprived of capital, the survivors had little with

which to rebuild. Even as the soldiers drifted home, the economy continued its downward slide. The wheat crop of 1865 failed miserably; the following year the yield was not much better. Tobacco cultivation withered. Confederate currency had lost all value. Confederate government war bonds were worthless, and even Virginia state bonds sold at a fraction of their face value. Land, the last vestige of wealth, plunged in price. Tracts that had brought $150 an acre before the war sold for $2.

Where war had stimulated the North's economy, it had devastated the South's. By one historian's calculation, the North's total wealth increased by 50 percent in the decade of the 1860s. In the South total wealth decreased by 60 percent. Virginia, once the most prosperous of states, would spend the next 120 years regaining the ground it had lost.

This scene, depicting the rebel soldiers taking an oath of allegiance to the Union in the State Capitol Senate Chamber in Richmond following Lee's surrender at Appomattox, was sketched by A.R. Ward. From Harper's Weekly, *June 17, 1865*

Joseph R. Anderson

Many years before people began talking about the "New South"—a land of industrial might where blacks and whites shared in economic progress—there was the Tredegar Iron Works. Under the leadership of Joseph R. Anderson, Tredegar put Virginia in the forefront of America's industrial revolution. Valuing economic efficiency over racial stereotypes, Anderson stood up to those who believed that blacks belonged in chains by giving skilled factory jobs to slaves. Later, during the Civil War, Tredegar produced the most sophisticated armaments of the mid-nineteenth century, enabling an overwhelmingly rural Confederacy to hold off the industrialized Union for four years.

Formed in 1836, Tredegar nearly failed at first. The Panic of 1837 and ensuing depression plunged the fledgling foundry into debt. In a desperate effort to save their investment, company directors recruited young Anderson to act as their commercial agent.

A West Point graduate and former army officer, Anderson had acquired a basic knowledge of ironwork in his native Rockbridge County before working as an engineer on the Valley Turnpike between Winchester and Staunton in 1836. When he joined Tredegar in 1841, he sought new markets. The depression had derailed railroad construction, so Anderson solicited the business of the federal government. Within a year the government had bought almost $90,000 worth of Tredegar iron in the form of chain cable, shot, and shell.

The next year proved more difficult. The navy blocked an order for 100 cannons when five pieces in the first delivery burst during test firings. As Anderson tried to persuade the government to continue its business with Tredegar, company officials became

meddlesome—unduly so in Anderson's appraisal—in the company's technical and business affairs. Chafing under their restraints the ambitious young agent proposed to lease the entire plant from the stockholders for five years at an annual rent of $8,000. The directors accepted the offer. Unencumbered,

Anderson continued rebuilding the business.

By December 1844, Anderson had regained the confidence of his federal customers and won new contracts. Soon Tredegar was back in full swing, turning out engines and boilers for navy frigates, heavy guns for the army, and the cannon upon which the reputation of Tredegar Iron Works would be built.

At the end of the five-year lease, Anderson bought Tredegar from the stockholders for $125,000; payments were to be staggered over six years. It looked like a solid venture. Virginia was back in the railroad business— eight railroads were chartered between 1846 and 1853—and it needed rail chairs, spikes, rolling stock, and locomotives. But Anderson had not anticipated competition from low-cost Northern and British rail manufacturers. He abandoned rail products and directed Tredegar's energies toward rolling merchant bar iron and rail chairs.

Narrow profit margins on the rolling mill operations made it difficult for Anderson to make his purchase payments. In 1853 he was forced to take in a partner; within two years he sold a three-fourths interest in the rolling mill and paid off the Tredegar owners. But through a series of financial combinations, Anderson reunited the Tredegar empire. By 1859—with the consolidation of the entire plant, including the rolling mill, and the formation of a partnership with the neighboring armory rolling mill—the Tredegar facilities became the South's largest ironworks, spreading over five acres along the James River.

Like several large factories of the times, Tredegar employed a great number of slaves. By letting slaves work in skilled jobs, Anderson undermined the slaveholders' contention that blacks were racially inferior. Fearful of where such innovations might lead and uneasy about the way Tredegar slaves came and went without overseers, newspaper editors fulminated about the threat to established society. Yet Anderson held firm. In 1847, when he assigned experienced blacks to work new furnaces, a

large contingent of Tredegar's white employees staged the first major strike in Virginia's industrial history.

On May 23 Tredegar's white workers refused to work unless slaves were removed from skilled jobs. Anderson responded in a letter addressed "to my late workmen at the Tredegar Iron Works" in which he declared that the workers had just fired themselves. He ordered the strikers to leave the factories and their company-owned homes and then took them to court, charging that they had "formed an illegal combination in uniting to exclude slaves" from his factory. The case was dismissed, but the strikers were not rehired; in many cases slaves replaced them.

But it was Anderson's government liaisons, not his slave work force, that made Tredegar an industry leader. Between 1844 and 1860, the Tredegar works delivered more than 880 pieces of ordnance to the federal government. In 1861, as the Civil War heated up, Tredegar's contracts with the federal government were still in force; weapons cast for both the federal government and the Southern states lay side by side in the Tredegar foundries.

As the conflict escalated into full-scale war, Anderson chose his side. "Will make anything you want," he telegraphed the Confederate government, "work night and day if necessary, and ship by rail." Tredegar's 1,000-man labor force produced cannons, shells, gun carriages, naval machinery, experimental submersible vessels, and equipment for other arsenals. Notably, it also produced the armor that covered the CSS *Virginia* to stand against the USS *Monitor* in the first battle of the ironclads in 1862.

While the war effort and Tredegar fed each other, Anderson's factories were devastated by fire in

1863. Tredegar's machine shops were crippled and restoration took several months. Anderson swore that his factories would never be the victim of arson again.

As Federal troops advanced on Richmond in April 1865, Confederate troops were ordered to move through the city, setting fire to warehouses of tobacco and cotton and blowing up munitions arsenals and the powder magazine. Anderson called out his Tredegar Battalion to defend the ironworks. Armed with muskets, the militia held back the arsonists until they retreated. As Richmond burned to the ground all around, Tredegar stood ready to continue its work.

Anderson died in 1892, but Tredegar survived to serve armies to come. It made ammunition for the United States in the Spanish-American War, both World Wars, and the Korean conflict. The company also thrived in peacetime; before his death Anderson had rebuilt his ironworks into a profitable operation supplying the local market. Although the operation was moved from downtown Richmond to Chesterfield County in 1957, Tredegar—run by Anderson's descendants—continued producing metal products until it closed in 1987 after 150 years of service.

Facing page: Joseph Reid Anderson. Courtesy, Valentine Museum

*Although Virginia's economy was se-
verely damaged by the war, the market in
Richmond seemed to be bustling on this
day in 1868. The old First Market was
located at Seventeenth and Main streets.
From* Harper's Weekly, *November 7,
1868*

A TIME TO REBUILD

◆

As the veterans trudged home from Appomattox, they faced the challenge of rebuilding a shattered economy. The odds must have seemed every bit as daunting as that of holding off the Union army. One-seventh of the white male population had been killed or maimed, while most of the blacks had fled their plantations. Farms were gutted, cities burned. Money was worthless, and the state government was hobbled with debt. Perhaps most galling of all, Northern capitalists, flush with profits from a successful war, descended upon Virginia to buy up the state's patrimony. Although capital from the North and abroad (principally England) would help finance the monumental task of rebuilding, Northerners did not hesitate to use their financial clout and political influence in the General Assembly to subjugate Virginia's interests to their own.

The war had reduced Virginia's once-proud yeomanry and aristocracy to an economic underclass. Confederate and Virginia Treasury notes were no longer legal tender; wealthy Virginians, having loyally invested their savings in now-worthless Confederate bonds, were penniless. By one historian's estimate, the monetary losses of Virginians from the beginning of the war until the end of Reconstruction totaled nearly a half-billion dollars.

The economy was frustratingly slow in reviving. After Appomattox deathly deflation replaced runaway inflation. U.S. greenbacks were slow to replace the worthless Confederate currency. "It seems to be an established fact that nobody has got any money," recorded one *Richmond Times* writer, "and, therefore, if business is to go on we see no alternative but resorting to an exchange of commodities."

The state government was as poverty stricken as its citizens. With a mounting debt, Virginia had no money to rebuild the railroad tracks that had been ripped up or canal banks that had caved in. Although West Virginia had absorbed one-third of the state's land and 300,000 of its residents, it refused to assume any part of the prewar debt it had helped accrue, leaving a population of 700,000 destitute whites and 500,000 penniless black ex-slaves to shoulder the full financial burden.

For five years following the war, Virginia's agricultural economy, which provided sustenance to the majority of the population, was at a standstill. Emancipation had reduced the black labor force on white farms by two-thirds across the South. With no money to buy labor, tools, seed, or fertilizer, Virginia landowners were forced to take up the plow and till what little land they could on their own; the rest they left to grow wild. As their work force of former slaves sought opportunities elsewhere, the labor-intensive plantations shrank in size and number: between 1860 and 1870, the number of Virginia farms

larger than 1,000 acres dropped from 641 to 317.

As if the war's devastation were not handicap enough, successive droughts hindered the recovery of successful farming. Those with farm products to sell were equally disheartened to find their chickens might bring 25 cents apiece; their eggs, 8 cents a dozen. The total value of the state's farm produce declined each year betwen 1866 and 1869.

After reigning for two centuries, Virginia tobacco lost its preeminence in the marketplace. Cut off from their markets in the North and in

Europe during the Civil War, Virginia tobacco growers had lost ground to their competitors. Without sufficient labor after the war, farmers were reluctant to plant the crop. In 1860 one-third of the nation's tobacco had been produced in Virginia; five years after the war the state supplied only one-sixth. Kentucky planters were raising a new leaf, white burley, that appealed to tobacco chewers because of its capacity to absorb flavoring. White burley was cheaper to produce; it didn't need fertilizer and it could be air-cured, a less-costly method than the fire-cure used to process the dark Virginia leaf. By 1870,

Kentucky was producing three times Virginia's output.

Manufacturing also had sustained staggering blows. Abingdon, Wytheville, Bristol, and Richmond had been burned. Factories in Fredericksburg and Petersburg had been silenced by bombardments. Northern Virginia had become a blistered wasteland. A scarcity of capital made it difficult to rebuild; even if the factories had been running, Virginia's economy was too impoverished to provide much of a market. By 1870, factory output had still failed to reach prewar levels.

But not all was bleak. Banks quickly reopened their doors. Within two weeks of Richmond's great fire, First National Bank, headed by Hamilton G. Fant of Washington, D.C., was chartered and providing currency. Robert E. Lee was one of the bank's first customers. National Bank of Virginia and National Exchange Bank opened shortly thereafter. Within six months of Appomattox, 16 new banks had begun operations in Virginia.

The livestock trade was one of the first industries to revive, thanks to the rising demand for beef in urban centers around the country. Imme-

diately after the war, livestock was needed on the farms as well as for food, leaving little surplus for breeding. Responding to the growing demand, however, farmers in the northern Piedmont counties and the Southwest turned increasingly to raising livestock. By 1880, the number of cattle equaled prewar levels, and Southwest and Valley farmers were exporting beef to Europe. Horse breeding took hold even faster. Shortly after the war, Virginia ranked second only to Kentucky in turning out fine racers and hunters.

Wheat revived as the chief crop in the Southwest and in the Valley. As those regions prospered, producing 55 percent of Virginia's wheat crop, compared to 30 percent before the war, the number of farms and their cash values began to rise.

With the establishment of far-reaching rail transportation in the 1880s, farmers no longer had to limit production for home consumption and nearby markets. Rapid transit and cooled

cars allowed farmers to ship produce to Northern markets and coastal ports for export. Blue Ridge farmers turned to fruit. The eastern slopes in Albemarle County became known for their peaches. Frederick and Clarke counties were the center of Virginia's burgeoning apple industry, which was generating revenues in excess of $1.4 million by 1899.

While the Southside's tobacco crop suffered from competition with North Carolina, farms around Suffolk grew such large quantities of peanuts that the small town became known as the "peanut capital of the world." Farmers on the Eastern Shore and along the western and southern borders of the Chesapeake Bay cultivated a wide variety of vegetables—potatoes, lettuce, spinach—for early sale in Northern markets. With the construction of the New York, Philadelphia & Norfolk Railroad in the 1880s, eastern Virginia produce could reach New York stands within 12 hours. Truck farms boomed in

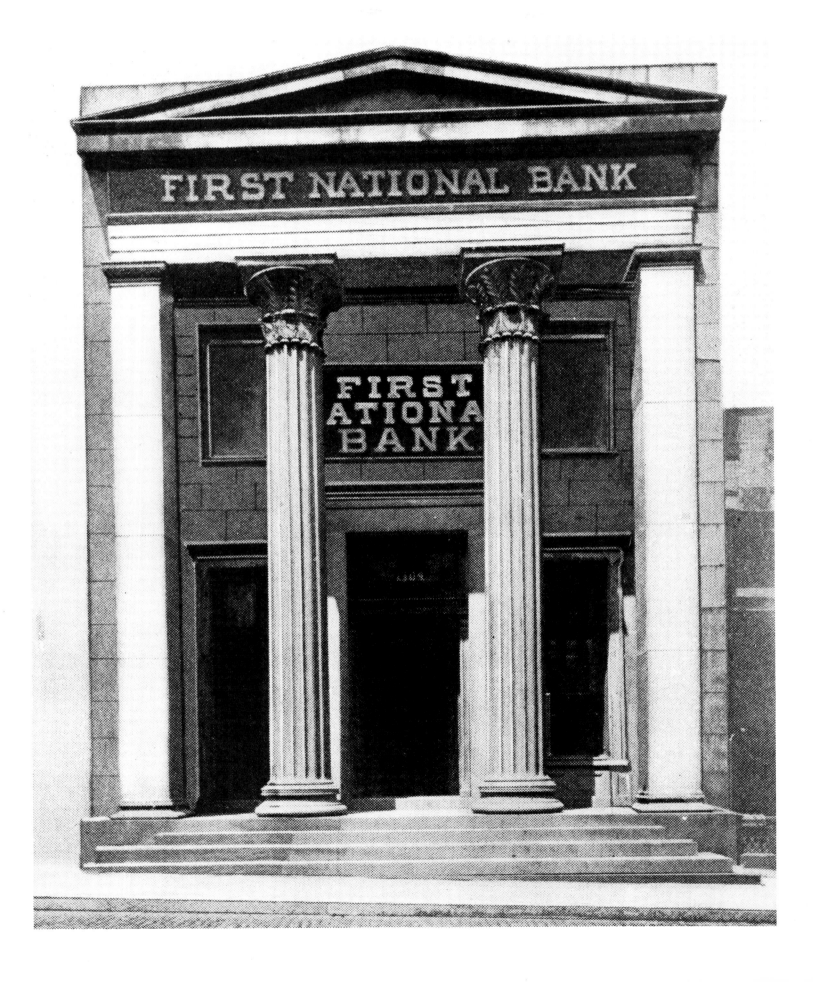

Right: These western Virginia farmers are shown cutting their wheat in the "old style," around 1900. Courtesy, Valentine Museum

Below: The livestock trade was one of the first industries to revive after the war. Because of the influx of people from the rural areas to the urban centers, the demand for beef increased. Courtesy, Valentine Museum

the Chesapeake area, spreading over 45,000 acres and producing annual crops valued at $6 to $7 million.

As the demand for Virginia produce grew in the North, the agricultural system recovered. Despite valiant strides, however, the state's agriculture never regained the prosperity of its antebellum glory.

As Virginia farmers struggled to find new markets, they also were faced with devising a whole new form of agricultural production. The plantation system had become a dinosaur.

Seeking economic freedom as well as legal emancipation, slaves deserted the plantations in droves. With no prospect of restoring the old gang-labor approach to working the soil, many planters broke up their farms and sold off large chunks or leased it to tenants.

Under the new system landowners rented tracts of land to sharecroppers, mostly freed slaves, in return for one-third to one-half of the profits. The landowner supplied tools, seed, land, and shelter; the sharecropper provided the labor. The system benefited both tenant and

Among the manufacturing concerns destroyed during the evacuation fire were the Haxall-Crenshaw flour mills located at Byrd and Twelfth streets. By 1870, however, the mills had been restored to full production and the company's famous F.F.V. (First Flours of Virginia) brand of flour was again available. Courtesy, National Archives

Right: Peaches, grown in Albemarle County, became a successful Virginia crop after the Civil War. Photo by Robert Llewellyn

Left: Because of the introduction of rapid transit and cooled railroad cars, farmers in the Shenandoah Valley were no longer limited to production for home consumption and nearby markets. They shipped their apple harvests to northern markets and coastal ports for export. The apple industry was generating revenues in excess of $1.4 million by 1899. Courtesy, Valentine Museum

owner. Croppers enjoyed their own incomes and a measure of independence; landowners found a way to generate revenue from their land. Planters preferred sharecropping to hiring wage labor because the croppers were less transient than hired hands and had an incentive to see crops through to harvest.

Some sharecropping contracts were written, but most were verbal. Some agreements included perquisites for the sharecropper, such as "a peck of cornmeal or the equivalent in wheat flour each week, a house, and garden" as well as "materials for making & manufacturing their winter coats & pants & leather for their shoes..."

Addenda might give the sharecropper permission to raise "a pig, keep 6 hens and 1 cock," or otherwise add to their personal food stock.

As sharecropping took hold and landowners broke up huge estates into small tenant holdings, the number of farms in Virginia tripled. Average farm size dipped from 336 acres in 1860 to 119 acres in 1900.

Although sharecropping accomplished the essential economic function of keeping farms in production and providing a livelihood for Virginia's 350,000 former slaves, it represented a regression to a semifeudal condition. Sharecropping mired much of the state's agricul-

While the tobacco crop suffered from competition with North Carolina following the Civil War, farmers in southside Virginia began to produce large quantities of peanuts. This circa 1890 photograph shows farmhands picking peanuts in Surry County, Virginia. Courtesy, Valentine Museum

After the slaves were freed, landowners devised a new system of agricultural production. They rented tracts of land to sharecroppers, mostly freed slaves, in return for a share in the profits. Pictured here are sharecroppers picking cotton in Surry County. Courtesy, Valentine Museum

tural economy in a state of seemingly permanent backwardness. While farmers in the great corn belt of America's Midwest boosted productivity with machinery such as combines and harvesters, Virginians had little incentive to innovate. Sharecroppers were too poor to buy the machinery, and their farms were too small to justify the use of such equipment. Landowners had no reason to invest in labor-saving equipment because sharecropping agreements entitled them to only a portion of the profits.

Sharecropping also perpetuated the master-servant relationship between blacks and whites. Although the legal status of blacks improved immensely, subject to the willingness of local authorities to enforce the law, economically they were powerless. Although most whites were left destitute by the war, at least many of them still had their land. Although their fortunes had been wiped out, they might have access to borrowed capital. The former slaves had nothing to offer but their labor. There was no more wilderness to conquer in Virginia, no more frontier land to be granted to those willing to settle it.

Many ex-slaves remained on their plantations because they had nowhere else to go. Others tried following the Union troops home. Thousands drifted into the cities, looking for work. Many former slaves cherished the groundless hope that the federal government would carve up confiscated plantations and award them free land. Preying upon this belief, carpetbaggers peddled them pegs to mark off their 40 acres.

Whether living in the city or on the land, uneducated former slaves made easy victims. One sharecropper complained that his landlord took all the profits from a year's crops. Drought had killed off half the yield and that half, the landlord said, was the sharecropper's. Carpetbaggers hustled ex-slaves at every turn, selling them Confederate money, worthless knickknacks, and lands to which they had no title.

In an attempt to protect former slaves from such exploitation, Congress established the Freedmen's Bureau to provide food, supplies, education, and shelter. In Virginia the bureau is-

The Freedmen's Bureau, a Federal agency established in the South to feed, protect, and educate former slaves, began operating in Richmond following the war. Schoolteachers came down from the North to instruct the blacks. The establishment of the Richmond Institute and the Richmond Normal and High School for the benefit of Negroes was a direct outgrowth of the bureau's activities. Courtesy, Harper's Weekly, *1865*

sued 178,000 rations before realizing that, at such a rate, funds would be exhausted before the ex-slaves had had a chance to adapt to their new way of life. It subsequently adopted a policy which denied aid to those who refused to work for fair wages.

During its five-year existence, the Freedmen's Bureau also attempted to protect blacks from other forms of exploitation. Any agent suspecting that a former slave had been denied fair treatment had the authority to fine or sentence the alleged offenders. In their zeal to reprimand the pettiest offenses, however, some agents ordered white farmers to ride great distances on short notice to answer such charges as "uttering offensive language." The agents also fed instances of racial abuse to the Northern radical press as evidence that Southern sentiment was both unrepentant and disloyal to the Union.

Although such tactics prolonged the disaffection of Southern whites, the bureau did fulfill many of its intentions. In addition to providing food and shelter for needy ex-slaves, it erected more than 200 schools and educated more than 50,000 blacks.

After rejoining the Union in 1870, the Commonwealth of Virginia plunged into a decades-long controversy over how to handle its prewar debt, a sum that totaled $45 million by 1870. The interest payments alone amounted to nearly $3 million, compared to the state's normal operating budget of about $1 million. If the state were to pay back its debt on schedule, however, it would be unable to meet obligations imposed by the new Underwood Constitution of 1869 to provide a free public education for its residents.

Although bondholders holding roughly a third of Virginia's debt lived outside the state—many of them in the North and in England—Virginia conservatives ardently supported total payback of the debt. Although some Southern states repudiated their antebellum debt, Virginians appealed to the ideals of honor and the state's unblemished fiscal record, arguing that failure to repay the debt in full would alienate potential Northern and foreign investors. Only by attracting outside interests, they reasoned,

could the economy resume its growth and the state generate tax revenues. Bankers, brokers, speculators, and railroad owners also supported the total payback, though their reasons were quite mercenary; the pledge would virtually force Virginia to sell its railroad stock. Eventually the debt issue became so entwined with railroad politics that the two became almost indistinguishable.

A key figure in both the debt and railroad controversies was Confederate war hero William Mahone. As president of three separate railroads in Virginia—the Norfolk & Petersburg, the Southside, and the Virginia & Tennessee—he wanted to secure legal permission to consolidate his roads. He received the support of representatives in Hampton Roads, Southside, and the Southwest, those regions that had the most to gain from unimpeded access to the coast and an increase in commerce through Virginia's own ports.

Mahone faced off against other railroad giants—most notably Baltimorean John W. Garrett of the Baltimore & Ohio. Garrett wanted to channel as much Southern trade as possible through the port of Baltimore. Controlling the Orange & Alexandria Railroad—Mahone's rival for Southwest trade—Garrett rallied allies around the state. Fearing that Mahone's railroad would reduce its canal-born trade with Lynchburg and build up the competing port of Norfolk, Richmond sided with Garrett. Lynchburg, which hoped to become profitable as a center for several railroads, wanted to be able to trade with Richmond, Norfolk, *and* Alexandria. The Valley, effectively serviced by the Orange & Alexandria, proffered like sentiment against Mahone's consolidation.

Mahone was just as motivated by self-interest as Garrett—he wanted to usurp some of the Ohio Valley trade from the Baltimore & Ohio. But he had the advantage of being able to tap the strong sense of Virginia patriotism by charging that "Baltimore gold" backed the opposition. The failure to consolidate lines running to Norfolk would allow other interests to consolidate rail lines running to out-of-state ports such as Baltimore and Philadelphia.

The industrialists courted lobbyists with greenbacks and booze. In the end Mahone prevailed. In 1870 the General Assembly granted him permission to merge his roads into the Atlantic, Mississippi & Ohio Railroad. It was a short-lived victory; within six years the railroad would be forced into bankruptcy.

Although Mahone won the consolidation controversy, he would not so brilliantly overcome the next issue. As bondholders clamored for redemption, the state government sought a means to pay them back. The state's heavy prewar investment in railroad securities offered one potential source of revenue. Northern industrialists, seeking access to the trade of the lower South, were eager to buy the Virginia roads. Sale of the state's railroad stock, it seemed, would be mutually beneficial.

Mahone would have been happy for the state to sell its interest in his three railroads—if he could afford to buy them. But he could not. Opening up the railroads to purchase by Northerners would allow interlopers onto his domain and would enable them to divert Southern trade to Northern ports. Mahone's bitter rivals, the Pennsylvania and the Baltimore & Ohio, supported the measure to allow sale of the state's stocks. A vicious legislative battle ensued. Both sides spent money liberally to buy votes, but

Mahone's dollars were wasted. Conservative members of the General Assembly supported the idea that anyone, regardless of origin, should have the right to buy or build a railroad as long as he did so without the state's money. On March 28, 1871, the state put its railroads on the auction block for anyone to buy.

The Pennsylvania Railroad secured interests in the Richmond & Danville and the Richmond & Petersburg railroads. The Baltimore & Ohio cemented its interests in the Orange & Alexandria, defeating Mahone in his quest to control access to western Virginia. Garrett's line then acquired the short Winchester & Potomac which, after 30 years' effort, had received permission to extend its lines to Baltimore, linking the Shenandoah Valley to that Maryland port as Mahone had predicted.

The Pennsylvania Railroad accessed Valley trade by building a line from Hagerstown, Maryland, through Front Royal and Waynesboro to the community of Big Lick near the Roanoke River. Later its residents would persuade the Pennsylvania road to join the Norfolk & Western—the result of the reorganization in 1881 of Mahone's Atlanta, Mississippi & Ohio—at their junction.

By early 1873, the Virginia Central ran all the way to the Ohio River. A few years later it became the Chesapeake & Ohio when California capitalist Collis P. Huntington assumed management. By the 1880s, another large trunk line had grown out of the Richmond & Danville. The parent company consolidated a number of short lines into a single, long system which provided a more direct route from Atlanta to commercial centers in the North. The company crashed in the 1893 depression but was reorganized by J. Pierpont Morgan as the Southern Railway Company.

Although Virginia would benefit greatly from the trade generated by railroads, it had surrendered its rail system to outside interests. By the 1880s, Northern corporations controlled rail transportation in the state.

The gentlemen planters of the antebellum era were mere specters in the General Assembly.

Confederate war hero William Mahone was successful in his bid to consolidate three railroad companies into the Atlantic, Mississippi & Ohio Railroad. Competition from other railroad lines vying for access to interstate and intrastate markets forced it into bankruptcy by 1876. Courtesy, Valentine Museum

In the Gilded Age, businessmen, industrialists, and financiers dominated the legislature. Issues of industry, finance, and the public purse supplanted those of agriculture.

The railroad sales failed to raise enough revenue to cover the state's debt. Because some companies paid for the railroad assets with unfunded bonds, Virginia gained little cash. Two days after approving the railroad sales, the General Assembly passed the Funding Act, also designed to facilitate payback of the debt.

According to the provisions of the Funding Act, the state issued $30 million of new bonds to retire the two-thirds portion of the debt that Virginia was prepared to assume. (The state abdicated responsibility for the other third, which legislators claimed was West Virginia's obligation; it wouldn't be until the twentieth century that West Virginia actually assumed the liability.) Payments on the new bonds, which yielded 6 percent interest, were stretched out over 30 years. The state guaranteed the interest with negotiable coupons which could be used to pay taxes, debts, or any other obligation to the state.

Although seemingly sound on paper, the Funding Act proved disastrous. As Virginians paid taxes with coupons, tax revenues dropped to less than half the amount needed to maintain public services and fulfill the debt obligation. As the state treasury fell into deficit, Virginians voted to replace 106 of the legislature's 132 members. The new Assembly voted to repeal both the Funding Act and the law providing for sale of the railroads. But the roads had been sold and Governor Gilbert C. Walker vetoed the measures. For years to come, conservative governors would stand firm against any legislation leaning toward repudiation of the debt.

Faced with the loss in tax revenue, the state government increased tax rates and cut expenses. Services, especially the school system, deteriorated sharply. In 1877, 127 schoolhouses closed down. In a desperate bid to restore the state's fiscal soundness, Culpeper delegate James Barbour crafted a bill modifying the terms of the debt settlement by restricting the amount of debt payment and funneling more money to the school system. Of every 50 cents collected on property taxes, 25 cents would go to state operating expenses, 10 cents to pay against the debt, and 10 cents would be earmarked for schools. But the legislation was blocked by yet another governor, Frederick W.M. Holliday. By 1878, almost half the schools ceased to operate.

By 1879, the state treasury was on the verge of bankruptcy, and opposition to the Funding Act was reaching a fever pitch. Recognizing that the power of the Republicans was too scattered and disorganized to overcome the

"Funders," Mahone forged a new party to stand against the debt payers once and for all. Joined by Barbour, John S. Wise, John Massey, William E. Cameron, and state senator Harrison Holt Riddleberger, Mahone spent the summer and fall stumping for a reduction of the state debt.

Riding the current of mass discontent, the so-called Readjusters swept through the state. They garnered support by proclaiming to be people of ordinary birth, interested in helping the masses instead of the privileged few. This populist party denounced foreign creditors as "vultures" and "shylocks" concerned only with accruing personal wealth. The new party contended that Virginia should not pay an interest rate that its people could not bear, that operating expenses should be met before money was sent to creditors in London or New York in payment of a debt of debatable legitimacy.

By election time, Mahone and his coalition of small-business owners, rural residents, and blacks who felt abandoned by the Republican party were ready to face the Funders, a party

The Underwood Convention, depicted in Frank Leslie's Illustrated Newspaper in February 1868, provided for a statewide system of public schools, establishment of a secret ballot, and changes in the tax structure. Blacks elected to the convention were (left to right) Hunnicutt, Snead of Accomac, Hodges of Princess Anne County, Lindsay of Richmond, and Morgan of Petersburg.

whose hallmark was privilege and old money. Mahone's organizational skills paid off at the polls: the Readjusters won the 1879 election by 82,000 to 61,000 votes. Replacing 56 of the 100 delegates in Virginia's House of Delegates and 24 of the 40 senators, they gained control of the legislature.

The Readjusters passed legislation scaling down the state's debt, repealing the poll tax, cutting the taxes on farmland and small business, raising taxes on corporations and corporate property, stabilizing mechanics' wages, and appropriating more money for public schools. Perhaps most important, the Readjusters changed the method of assessing corporate taxes. No longer were company officials permitted to appraise their own properties; state assessors determined the taxable value of holdings. The tax base soared: railroad and canal assessments rose from $9,876,306 in 1880 to $26,940,173

in 1881. By 1900, railroad and tax assessments reached a total value of $56,582,345.

In 1882 the Readjusters pushed through the Riddleberger Act to replace the 6 percent, 30-year bonds with 50-year bonds bearing 3 percent interest. The act also eliminated the practice of paying taxes with coupons. Readjuster policies relieved the burden of ordinary taxpayers and strengthened state finances. By the early 1880s, the Funders' deficit was replaced with a $1.5 million surplus. As Virginia trudged toward solvency, the question of who was to pay West Virginia's one-third of the debt remained unsettled. The debate between the two states continued until 1919 when the United States Supreme Court ruled that West Virginia was liable for $15 million in principal and accrued interest, payable over a 20-year period. The last payment was received July 1, 1939.

Right: A Norfolk & Western bunk car sits in the foreground of this view of Lynchburg, circa 1885. The city hoped to become a profitable railroad center by establishing connections with Richmond, Norfolk, and Alexandria. Courtesy, Valentine Museum

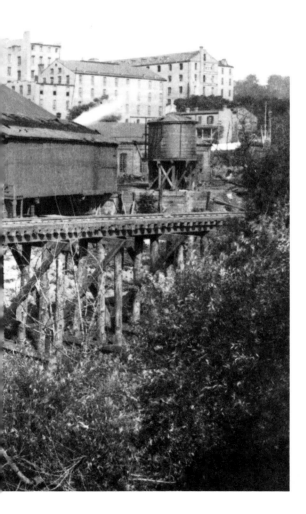

Above: Richmond was the only Southern city to have a major locomotive plant. The plant, started in 1865 as a farm machinery business, began locomotive production several years later. It continued its operations until 1927. This Chesapeake & Ohio Consolidation freight engine, the 350, was produced at the Richmond plant.

Left: James Barbour was a member of the Readjusters, the new political party formed in 1879 to work for the reduction of the state debt. From Cirker, Dictionary of American Portraits, *Dover, 1967*

*In 1887 the Richmond City Council
agreed to replace mule-drawn rail cars
with an electric trolley system. This group
of men posed with the last horse-drawn
car on the Richmond to Manchester line
in 1886. Courtesy, Valentine Museum*

THE RISE OF RICHMOND

The damage to Virginia's war-shattered industry went far deeper than torn-up railroad lines and burned-out factories. New track could be laid if the money was available, but the fortunes of most Virginians had been wiped out by emancipation, inflation, and unredeemable war debt. Factories could be rebuilt if the markets still existed, but a four-year blockade had taken Virginians out of the world economy. Worst of all, Virginia's entrepreneurial potential had been ravaged just as thoroughly as its farms and cities. Local businesses suffered a severe disadvantage competing against Northern industries bursting with profits and cash.

Immediately following the war, economic life was a struggle for economic survival. Jeremiah Morton, a prominent citizen of Orange County, wrote to a lady friend:

I was surrounded by every comfort which the world could afford—a delightful home and happy family of whites and blacks, an income of $30,000 annually, with a prospect of a yearly increase. The scourge of war has swept all from me, and at the age of 65, I stand a blasted stump in the wilderness of life.

Not only had the war shorn Virginia's business community of capital, it had also deprived them of the means to borrow. Collateral in the form of slaves, bank stocks, and savings was all gone. Money to finance new projects was unavailable except at extremely high interest rates. Wartime conditions had created a superficial demand geared to churning out war materiel as well as feeding and clothing thousands of soldiers. With peacetime those markets collapsed. In the brutal postwar economy, members of the old mercantile class resorted to manual labor just to survive.

Even so, there were opportunities. One Albemarle County farmer lost nearly $60,000 in property damages in the war. Selling his farm for $35,000, he paid his creditors in full, bought a stand for merchandising, and started a flourishing family business. An Orange County resident wrote to a friend that, although "under the new regime there cannot be the same pleasure" in farming, he planned to increase his operations and make more money.

As America's grain production shifted to the great wheat bowl of the Midwest and the Plains states, Virginia's flour milling industry never recovered. Yet some sectors of the economy performed handsomely. A decline in the cultivation of tobacco was counterbalanced by continued prominence in the processing of the weed; Virginians were instrumental in the development of the cigarette industry. Riding the great railroad boom of the late nineteenth century, iron and sawed lumber products as well surpassed prewar production levels.

Railroads were the driving force behind economic growth. In Virginia, railroad construc-

Virginia's railroads were nearly destroyed by the Civil War. In order for the economy to develop, Northern and Southern entrepreneurs invested money in reestablishing old rail lines as well as constructing new ones. Courtesy, Valentine Museum

tion kept dozens of local suppliers in business, reintegrated the state into a unified economy, and linked Virginia's industries to the larger world.

As it desperately funneled resources into the war effort, the Confederacy had cannibalized its rail system. Where poor maintenance failed to close the rail lines, Union raiders usually finished the job. In the spring of 1865, General George Stoneman's raiders ripped up railroad tracks and destroyed rolling stock all along the Virginia & Tennessee between Lynchburg and Petersburg. The Virginia Central had been almost completely knocked out; the Richmond & Danville, used by Jefferson Davis and his cabinet to escape advancing troops, had survived with only its rolling stock intact. Overuse and negligence had worn down the Southside Railroad as well. Rotting ties and general disrepair forced trains to travel slowly and caused occasional derailments.

When Richmond burned, the Richmond & Petersburg's bridge across the James River

went with it. The railroad's depot and workshops went up in flames; its books and records were reduced to ash. The same fate befell the records of the James River and Kanawha Canal Company when its general office and toll office ignited the same night. Scarcely a month before Appomattox, General Philip Sheridan's cavalry had trampled the canal's towpath and damaged locks from Scottsville to a point 30 miles west of Richmond. Locks were broken and canal boats burned, sunk, or taken over by former slaves for housing.

The canal system would never recover. Canal company officials tried to enlist outside capital to no avail. Northern industrialists wanted rail routes connecting their manufacturing centers to Southern markets and sources of raw materials; they had no use for a canal connecting Virginia communities to the sea. Besides, railroads had many advantages. Iron rails were less subject than canals to the whims of nature.

Virginia's canals, which revolutionized eighteenth century travel and commerce, could not compete with the railroad networks of the nineteenth century. Following the war, the Dismal Swamp Canal was in extremely poor condition and no money was available for repairs. The tugboat Emma K. is shown on the canal in 1913. Courtesy, Valentine Museum

Frequent floods damaged locks, dams, and tow-paths, periodically closing the canals. Freezes stopped traffic in the winter. Maintenance costs were frighteningly high.

Although the James River and Kanawha Canal Company reinstituted partial service by September 1866 and full service by mid-1869, the railroads usurped much of its business. Lynchburg was the only city of significance upriver from Richmond, and the promised connections between the James and the Kanawha—only 33 miles apart at their head-waters—were never made. The company cut its freight tolls steadily to attract more traffic, but the total take decreased yearly.

The Dismal Swamp Canal was in such poor condition that its company could not bor-row money. Revenues for the Rivanna Naviga-tion Company and the Roanoke Navigation Company steadily declined. On March 5, 1880, the James River canal company went out of busi-ness. The great canals that had revolutionized commerce and travel in the eighteenth century could not compete with the railroads of the nine-teenth century.

In contrast, railroad companies had no trouble finding financing. In the fall of 1865, President Andrew Jackson permitted railroad owners to reclaim their lines as long as they agreed not to press any damage claims against the federal government. The railroad managers could purchase equipment from the government, payable over two years at $7\frac{1}{2}$ percent interest on the unpaid balance. Under these liberal repay-ment terms Virginians reestablished several railroads. Meanwhile, the General Assembly's much-debated decision to sell its rail stock encouraged an influx of private capital. North-ern businesses seeking to tap the resources of the South funded the construction of many new rail lines and integrated the short, unconnected Vir-ginia lines into larger rail systems.

The Civil War had rendered most of Vir-ginia's 1,800 miles of track useless. Concentrat-ing on rebuilding old lines rather than creating new ones, Virginia's railroad companies had built only 107 miles of track by 1870. But

railroad expansion accelerated soon afterward: the next 15 years saw nearly 1,000 miles of track constructed. By 1885, 32 railroads sprawling across the state maintained a total of 2,430 miles of track.

Gripped by railroad fever, railroad com-panies extended lines down the Peninsula, through the Eastern Shore, into the Valley, and across the Piedmont. In 1870 the Virginia & Kentucky, which spanned the 100 miles between Abingdon and Cumberland Gap, was consoli-dated with Mahone's Atlantic, Mississippi & Ohio, creating a line all the way from Norfolk to Tennessee. (These lines would become the Nor-

Confederate veteran James H. Dooley, who invested in railroads, real estate, and steel, rose rapidly in Richmond's postwar business world. In 1890 he purchased 100 acres of land to the west of Rich-mond overlooking the James River. His estate, Maymont, included an enor-mously expensive Victorian mansion and fabulous trees, flowers, and shrubs from all over the world. Courtesy, Valentine Museum

folk & Western Railroad.) Virginia Midland Railway Company joined the Lynchburg & Danville Railroad with roads between Lynchburg and Alexandria, creating a line from north to south through the state. Stockholders of the Virginia Central line even agreed to consolidate with the yet-to-be-built Covington & Ohio to extend service to the Ohio Valley. The consolidation was completed on August 31, 1868. On that day the Chesapeake and Ohio Railroad Company was born.

These consolidations and others opened the channels of commerce around the state. By 1880, an extensive railroad system crisscrossed the state, paving the way for a more vigorous commercial and industrial development. The Virginia Central linked the state's eastern and western markets while the Richmond & Danville tapped the trade of the Carolinas and Georgia. The Richmond & Petersburg Railroad tied into the coastal plains of the Carolinas, while the Petersburg Railroad traveled southward through the Carolinas and Georgia. The Alexandria, Loudoun, & Hampshire channeled trade from the Valley to Alexandria in competition with the Baltimore & Ohio's road from Harper's Ferry to

The Virginia Midland Railway Company joined the Lynchburg and Danville Road with roads between Lynchburg and Alexandria, creating a solid north-south passage through the state. This 1907 view of the Virginia Railway shows the line passing through Charlotte County, Virginia. Courtesy, Valentine Museum

Winchester. The Seaboard & Roanoke, an 80-mile line, brought goods from Weldon, North Carolina, to the growing Hampton Roads port of Portsmouth.

Three lines—the Virginia & Tennessee, the Southside Railroad, and the Norfolk & Petersburg—traversed the Southside to Norfolk, bringing cotton, corn, flour, fruit, peanuts, potatoes, tobacco, wheat, and lumber from far inland. Before the war three lines hauled Valley trade to port. The Winchester & Potomac took produce to Baltimore, while the Manassas Gap Railroad tied the Valley to the port of Alexan-

dria. The Virginia Central ran from the Valley to Richmond. After the war damage was repaired, the only gap in the Valley was between Harrisonburg and Salem.

Towns and communities, new centers of trade, sprang up at railroad junctions. West Point, for instance, grew from a tiny town of 500 to a city of 5,000 after eight years of service by the Richmond & Danville Railway system. Briefly, before the trade shifted to Norfolk and Portsmouth with their superior ports, the town was the fifth greatest cotton-exporting port in the world.

Spurred by the railroads, Virginia entered a boom era. Developers carved fields adjacent to towns into lots. Weekly newspapers enlarged their presses to accommodate prospectuses inducing manufacturers to locate businesses in their circulation areas. Cities swelled in size as planters left their devalued lands in search of a better life. Former slaves flooded the cities, providing a ready supply of factory workers. An estimated 15,000 blacks came to Richmond after the war, doubling its black population. Although agricultural workers still outnumbered factory laborers, factory work commanded higher wages, affording an average annual income of $198 compared to $60 to $120 earned in the fields. Blacks working in skilled positions in the iron, tobacco, or flour milling industries were generally paid the same as whites. But because unskilled blacks worked for lower pay than whites, many earned less in a week than they had as factory slaves working overtime.

America had entered one of the most dynamic periods of economic expansion the world has ever seen. Virginia shared in that remarkable growth and prosperity. As early as its 1865-1866 session, the General Assembly approved charters for 44 new manufacturing and mining companies. The following year the legislature provided for the creation of another 39 firms. But the war-torn Old Dominion lagged behind many of its neighbors.

Before the war Virginia held a commanding lead as the South's most industrialized state, producing goods valued at $42 million. Tennessee was a poor second with $18 million. In 1870 Virginia was producing only $38 million, still falling short of its prewar output. In contrast, Tennessee's manufacturing had almost doubled to $34 million, and Georgia was not far behind with $31 million.

The ruin of Richmond, the leading antebellum manufacturing center of the old South,

A triple-decker railroad crossing was built at Seventeenth and Dock streets for the Chesapeake & Ohio, Seaboard, and Southern railroad lines in 1900. Eleven years later, these three steam locomotives were photographed at the crossing. Courtesy, Valentine Museum

accounted for much of Virginia's overall industrial decline. Before the war Virginia's capital was the thirteenth most important manufacturing center in the country; more than 300 manufacturing companies turned out an aggregate value of $12 million. But on the morning of April 3, 1865, the smokestacks lay in toppled heaps. Where factory exhaust had billowed, only wisps of smoke arose from the ruins.

Nine-tenths of Richmond's business district, 900 buildings, had been razed; 230 of the best business houses and their contents had been reduced to cinders. The fire had incinerated rolling mills, flour mills, and tobacco warehouses. Nine brokerage houses, more than 20 law firms, and every bank and saloon had been consumed by the inferno. More than two dozen groceries—and four-fifths of the food supply—were wiped out. When the Union army occupied the city, a third of the population was forced to rely on federal rations of codfish and cornmeal for sustenance. The lone silhouettes of the "Burnt District" were the granite customhouse, former headquarters for the Confederate government, and the Tredegar Iron Works, saved by Anderson's Tredegar battalion. Damage estimates ranged from $2 million to $30 million.

Citizens and occupying troops worked together to restore order. As the economy revived, Richmond became a city of contradictions, where hope glowed amid the ashes of desolation. As new buildings rose, garbage rotted in the streets. While some residents scraped together their resources to start anew, others robbed and burglarized. The Burnt District was said to be crawling with garroters, thieves, and pickpockets.

Because native Virginians had no capital, much of the new construction was fueled by Northern interests. One of the earliest infusions of greenbacks came from sutlers, army provisioners who followed Union troops into Richmond. Some opened stores on Broad Street, the temporary center of retail trade, while others leased lots in the Burnt District from local businesses which lacked the money to rebuild. In the early days of recovery, sutlers were practically the only

source of goods, although most moved on shortly for want of business.

The currency shortage eased with the opening of new banks, most of them established by Northern investors. Within two weeks of the fire, Hamilton G. Fant, a partner in a Washington business firm, and a group of his associates banded together to create the First National Bank of Richmond. As the largest stockholder, Fant became president of Richmond's first postwar bank. On May 10, only a month after Appomattox, First National commenced operations in the former customhouse.

Five days later the National Bank of Virginia, also backed by Northern investors, began operations in the same building. The next month the National Exchange Bank under the leadership of a German-born Washington resident opened its doors. The infusion of money accelerated the pace of rebuilding. The resulting building boom restored the capital to its former preeminence as a great commercial center.

Buildings were erected with great haste, so that many were shoddy structures. Ever mindful

After the war an estimated 15,000 blacks moved from rural areas to Richmond in search of work. These former slaves, posed beside the James River and Kanawha Canal circa 1865, were facing an uncertain future. The ruins of Richmond's business district in the background emphasize Virginia's war-shattered economy. Courtesy, Valentine Museum

Dunlop Mills, located on the south side of the James River in Manchester, survived the evacuation fire of 1865 but suffered financially in the early days of Reconstruction. The wheat crops of 1865 and 1866 failed miserably, and competition from the Midwest and Plains states hindered the recovery of Virginia's flourmilling industry. In 1902 the mill was purchased by Warner Moore and Company, and it continued to provide for domestic consumption until 1935, when it closed. Courtesy, Valentine Museum

Hamilton G. Fant and others banded together to create the First National Bank just two weeks after the evacuation fire, with Fant becoming its president. Completed in 1913, the bank's building at Ninth and Main streets is shown decorated in 1922 for a Confederate States Army reunion. Courtesy, Valentine Museum

Following the evacuation fire, buildings in Richmond's business district were erected with great haste. The city council outlawed wooden buildings in the area surrounding the state capitol, so iron fronts became a popular addition to the commercial district. Courtesy, Valentine Museum

Following the evacuation fire and subsequent rebuilding of Richmond's business district, scrap iron became a valuable resource. Bits and pieces, collected from vacant lots and battlefields, were resold to foundries, blacksmiths, and metal workers. This circa 1890 photograph was taken near Virginia and Dock streets and shows the one-story Southern Freight Depot and the Watkins-Cottrell building on 14th Street. Courtesy, Valentine Museum

of the recent fire, the city council outlawed wooden buildings in areas near the State Capitol. Likewise, the city banned lumberyards from the Burnt District, and merchants discouraged use of wood in new constructions anywhere in the commercial center. Brick was the material of choice. Iron fronts, used frequently in the North before the war, became a popular addition. Easily maintained with paint, the ironwork added ornamentation and strength, and allowed the installation of large windows for natural lighting and displays.

By October 1865, Richmond's *Whig* noted that at least 100 new buildings were being built in the business district alone. The boom furnished Richmonders with construction-related jobs and created a market for lumberyards, iron foundries, and metalworking shops. Scrap metal became a valuable resource, and junkyards profited from buying bits and pieces culled from vacant lots and battlefields around the city, then reselling them to foundries, blacksmiths, and metalworkers. Scrap metal became so profitable, in fact, that hawkers were known to rip out iron fences and pilfer iron stopcocks from gas streetlamps. One even stole the lead pipes from the kitchen of Richmond's Roman Catholic Bishop John McGill.

Richmond grew rapidly during its postwar renaissance. By 1867, the city's population had reached 38,710, and its corporate limits had doubled from 2.4 to 4.9 square miles. In the next four years the number of homes increased by 62 percent to 8,033 dwellings.

Ten years after the Civil War, Richmond's economy was again prospering. Large sailing ships could be found at the city docks and railroad lines traversed the James River. The business district featured the smokestacks of Tredegar Iron Works and Gallego Mills (left center). Five bridges spanned the James River, including the Mayo Bridge (directly below the Capitol). Courtesy, Valentine Museum

Commercial activity was facilitated by the rapid rebuilding of four of Richmond's five antebellum railroad lines: the Richmond, Fredericksburg & Potomac; the Virginia Central; the Richmond & Danville; and the Richmond & Petersburg. These roads, along with the York River line, which was restored later, reestablished Richmond as a leading transportation center. In both 1868 and 1869, more freight tonnage entered Richmond than Baltimore, Philadelphia, and Norfolk combined. Richmond ranked second only to New York in incoming freight tonnage.

As before the war, tobacco, milling, and ironworking dominated the city's industry,

comprising 85 percent of the city's total manufactured product. These major manufacturers took longer than the small, retail-oriented businesses to reestablish their operations. It was two years before the Tobacco Exchange was reorganized and the Corn and Flour Exchange reopened. But by then Richmond was a town on the move.

Most heavy industry was situated in Shockoe Valley or along the river or the canal. Factories were rebuilt east of Shockoe Creek for accessibility to docks and railroad depots. Flour mills, dependent upon a source of running water, clustered along the river and on the canal basin. Large ironworks and rolling mills lined the riverfront at the western edge of the city.

Blacksmiths, tailors, milliners, carpenters, and other small manufacturers dotted the downtown landscape.

Workers usually walked a mile or two to their jobs. While the omnibus provided crosstown transportation in horsedrawn cars, the fare was high. Within 18 months, however, horse-drawn railway cars were back in service along a short in-town route. The 10-cent fare was high but not prohibitive, and residents jammed into the stuffy railcars for the short ride around town. Three years later the street railway would carry travelers from various rail and steamship depots into the urban center. A westward extension of the line enabled city residents to travel to the country for a quiet weekend or a day trip at a reasonable price.

The number of manufacturers in Richmond doubled from 262 in 1860 to 531 by the end of the decade, though the total value of their manufactured product declined 15 percent. Factories and shops were smaller than before the war, employing only one-half the average number of workers per establishment. Population, on the other hand, had escalated 35 percent in the same decade, moving Richmond up a notch from 25th largest American city to 24th.

Of its 51,038 residents, 18,545, or 36 percent, worked in the labor force. Despite the revival of industry, the number of workers

Following the war, small retail businesses were quick to reestablish their operations. From 1874 to 1901, Davenport and Morris, wholesale grocers and commission merchants, operated in this impressive building at the intersection of Seventeenth and Dock streets in Richmond. Courtesy, Valentine Museum

Richmond's iron industry recovered quickly after the Civil War. Although a number of foundries forged rails, steam engines, and machinery, Tredegar retained its leading position. Courtesy, Valentine Museum

employed in manufacturing was 10 percent lower than the average for cities comparable in size. The number of employers involved in professional and personal services, however, was well above the national average. Only 311 Richmonders, or less than 2 percent of the population, worked on farms.

When the Panic of 1873 struck, the nation's economy dipped radically. The panic broke out with the failure of the New York financial house of Jay Cooke & Company in September and spread to Virginia not long after. Runs on Richmond banks occurred, and two small

banking establishments quickly went out of business. The ensuing depression cut short Virginia's commercial recovery. Richmond's resurgence in particular was slowed significantly as several railroads, banks, and factories were forced into bankruptcy or receivership. Several factories and small businesses closed.

In the fall of 1875 the Chesapeake & Ohio Railroad passed into the hands of receivers. Even the Tredegar Iron Works declared insolvency due to the bankruptcy of several of its Northern railroad clients. By the late 1870s, the effects of the panic were still visible in Rich-

mond. Many businesses had yet to recover and people were still jobless. As the depression began to wane, there were still approximately 175 applicants for every position on the local police force.

Recovery came with the new decade. The prosperity of the 1880s was reflected in real estate figures: in 1886, 400 houses were built; the following year saw 500 homes go up. In 1889 the figure increased to 600 new dwellings. Only one building and loan association had been established before 1880; seven were organized after 1886. But the boom was surprisingly frag-

ile. The city had lost its position as the South's leading industrial center to New Orleans, and its major industries were facing tremendous challenges.

While Richmond's three greatest industries—iron, tobacco, and flour milling—continued to dominate the city's economy, their progress after the Civil War was uneven. Iron was the only industry to increase its product value in the first five years after the war, but it encountered tremendous competition from the booming steel towns along the Ohio River Valley and the Great Lakes. The shift of tobacco production to

Kentucky and other states impeded the recovery of the tobacco processing industry. Similarly, the development of large, efficiently farmed wheat fields in the Midwest and the Great Plains also enabled Midwestern cities to supersede Richmond as a major flour milling center.

Yet none of these long-term trends were apparent in 1865. Immediately after the war the shared primary goal was to rebuild. Richmond's ironmaking industry, stoked by the demands of the railroad boom, recovered quickly. Within two years of Appomattox, more than a dozen foundries were forging rails, locomotives, steam engines, and machinery for a variety of purposes. By 1870, various iron foundries were producing goods worth approximately $3 million a year.

Tredegar Iron Works retained its leading position. That same year the 800 workers there accounted for a third of the city's ironworks production. The company had the advantage of possessing one of the few industrial plants to have survived the great fire. It also had the capital to quickly resume production. President Joseph Anderson had wisely forestalled payment on quantities of cotton shipped during the war. When the hostilities ended, Anderson and his associates were remunerated with $190,000 in greenbacks.

Tredegar was largely responsible for Richmond's rise to the status of regional center of the iron industry. Even after the depression of the 1870s, Tredegar expanded its operations to become the leading firm of its kind in the South. A visitor in 1870 wrote:

The Tredegar Ironworks, reconstituted since the war, if not the largest of its kind in the United States, execute an almost unequalled variety of work, not only making iron, but every kind of iron castings—from railway spikes to field artillery—with equal resource and success, and are carried on with vigour and activity, employing a thousand hands.

Ironmaking flourished throughout the 1870s, generating revenues of $5.5 million in 1872, surviving a depression drop to $1 million, and climbing again to $5.25 million in 1881. From there, however, Richmond's iron industry

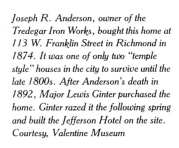

Joseph R. Anderson, owner of the Tredegar Iron Works, bought this home at 113 W. Franklin Street in Richmond in 1874. It was one of only two "temple style" houses in the city to survive until the late 1800s. After Anderson's death in 1892, Major Lewis Ginter purchased the home. Ginter razed it the following spring and built the Jefferson Hotel on the site. Courtesy, Valentine Museum

Lewis Ginter, tobacco magnate and philanthropist, came to Richmond from New York in 1842 and opened a home furnishings store which grossed $40,000 in 1860. After serving as quartermaster under General Joseph R. Anderson during the Civil War, he associated himself with a New York stock brokerage which failed. Ginter then returned to Richmond and entered into a partnership with John R. Allen. He is shown seated at the desk of Thomas Jeffress, a business associate, about 1890. Courtesy, Valentine Museum

began a slow decline. Although iron ore had been mined in Virginia since the eighteenth century, the state simply did not possess high quality reserves in quantities sufficient to sustain production levels demanded by the nation's roaring industrial economy. Richmond's coal reserves, too, proved to be inadequate. The nearby Midlothian mines were quickly depleted, driving up the cost of production. Meanwhile, cheaper coal was being mined at far less expense in the distant Appalachian coalfields. By the 1880s, shortages of locally produced coal and iron ore forced Richmond's foundries to seek sources

from other states; the cost of transporting the raw materials put Richmond at an enormous disadvantage compared to cities along the Ohio River basin. By 1890, Richmond's production had dropped to $4.25 million. By the turn of the century, Richmond's once-powerful iron industry was on a steady decline.

The war had thrown Virginia's tobacco industry into total turmoil. The manufacturers of tobacco products faced many of the same problems as their rural brethren, the tobacco planters. The Northern blockade had kept Virginia's darkleaf tobacco from reaching its profitable

markets in America and overseas; like her planters, Virginia's manufacturers had been supplanted by those of Kentucky, Ohio, and Missouri. Furthermore, the emancipation of slaves had created an inconsistent and unreliable work force in Richmond factories. The adjustment to paid labor would take time.

Before the war Richmond had been located at the center of the nation's tobacco belt. As cultivation spread, however, it became impractical for farmers to carry their product to the Richmond market. By necessity other centers of trade and manufacture in the leaf sprang up.

As farmers in the Piedmont, the Southside, and in North Carolina grew more of the popular new "bright" leaf, Richmond lost ground to Danville, then to Raleigh and Durham in North Carolina. Although more than three-fifths of the state's entire crop was brought to Richmond for inspection and sale at the Tobacco Exchange, the number of local tobacco factories dropped from 50 in 1860 to 38 a decade later; product value slipped from $5 million to approximately $4 million.

Still, tobacco remained Richmond's single most important industry after the war, employing nearly 4,000 hands in 1870. One of the most important postwar firms was Allen and Ginter, headed by Major Lewis Ginter, a New York native who had fought on the side of the Confederacy. Ginter sparked the Richmond industry in the mid-1870s when, observing the growing popularity of cigarettes, he employed 20 women to roll the new product. The Richmond-made cigarettes won wide acclaim at the Centen-

nial Exposition held in Philadelphia in 1876. By 1881, cigarette manufacture in Richmond had risen from 3 million to 65 million a year. Ten years later Richmond firms were turning out 100 million a year. Cigarettes had become the most important element in the tobacco industry.

But Ginter missed a phenomenal opportunity to regain Richmond's former dominance.

The rolling cigarette machine, invented by James A. Bonsack in 1883, is pictured in the Allen and Ginter Tobacco factory about 1890. Bonsack had offered his invention to Ginter, who refused it. Bonsack then took the machine to James Buchanan Duke of Durham, North Carolina, who moved to the forefront of the cigarette industry by 1887. Courtesy, Valentine Museum

James A. Bonsack, a Lynchburg resident, invented a cigarette rolling machine and offered it to Allen and Ginter. The Richmond manufacturer tried the machine in 1883, but discarded it. Bonsack took his innovation to James Buchanan Duke of Durham, North Carolina. With the new contraption Duke promptly began outproducing and outselling his rivals, and soon

moved to the head of the industry. By the time Allen and Ginter adopted rolling machines in 1887, Duke dominated the industry. The Richmond firm subsequently merged with Duke's firm and others in 1890 to form a tobacco trust which would control 95 percent of the nation's cigarette market.

Although North Carolina came to dominate the tobacco industry, Richmond remained a major player. In 1885, 74 million pounds of leaf came through the city's exchange; half was shipped off and half was locally turned into marketable products. By the early twentieth century, more than one-third of the total industrial capital invested in Richmond had been earmarked for tobacco manufacturing.

While the flour milling industry ranked second to tobacco in product value before the Civil War, it was the slowest to recover. With a scanty wheat crop and most of its mills inoperable, Virginia milled little flour in 1865. The Gallego and the Haxall mills, which had burned in the great fire, had to be rebuilt. The Dunlop operation survived physical devastation but was hurt by the wheat crop failure.

Eventually the wheat crop recovered and some mills resumed operation, but the trade in Richmond was slow to develop; the lack of stor-

As the popularity of cigarettes grew, Lewis Ginter employed women to roll the new product, as seen in this circa 1910 photograph. Courtesy, Valentine Museum

age facilities after the fire increased spoilage. Richmond merchants lost the business of many farmers in western Virginia who took advantage of the new railroad combinations, particularly the Baltimore & Ohio and its subsidiaries, to ship their wheat to Baltimore. Richmonders also found themselves unable to compete in their old export markets. Before the war they had run wheat to South America in fast brigs and along the coast on some 23 schooners. After the war Richmond businessmen had to hire foreign- or Northern-owned vessels, which ran up their transportation costs. Three years after the war's close, production levels of Richmond's flour mills were considerably lower than the half-million barrels a year produced before the war. In 1870 city mills turned out less than 200,000 barrels, of which only one-third was exported.

Despite the economic obstacles, a rash of fires, and unreliable waterpower, the flour milling industry managed to increase its postwar revenues to $3 million a year between 1881 and 1883. But competition from other wheat-producing regions proved insurmountable. Meanwhile, flour milling concerns in the Midwest used technological developments to gain a competitive edge over Richmond mills. California was another formidable rival, often shipping flour to the East Coast for sale at lower prices than those of Richmond's mills. After peaking in the early 1880s, Richmond's milling industry entered an irreversible decline. By 1887, flour production fell to $1.5 million, rose again to $2.5 million in 1892, then dove to less than $1 million in 1897.

By the turn of the century, only one of Richmond's three major mills survived. The Haxall-Crenshaw mill failed in 1891—after 100 years of operation—when its South American market disappeared. The Gallego operation passed into the hands of receivers. Only the Dunlop Mill, which served domestic markets in the South and the Southwest, continued operations.

As the mainstays of Richmond's traditional economy declined, the city developed other businesses. Following Reconstruction, iron,

As Richmond's industries stabilized the economy, improvements were made to the city. City Hall, located on the block bounded by Capital, Tenth, Eleventh, and Broad streets, was completed in 1894 at a cost of $1,440,000—almost five times the original estimate. Courtesy, Valentine Museum

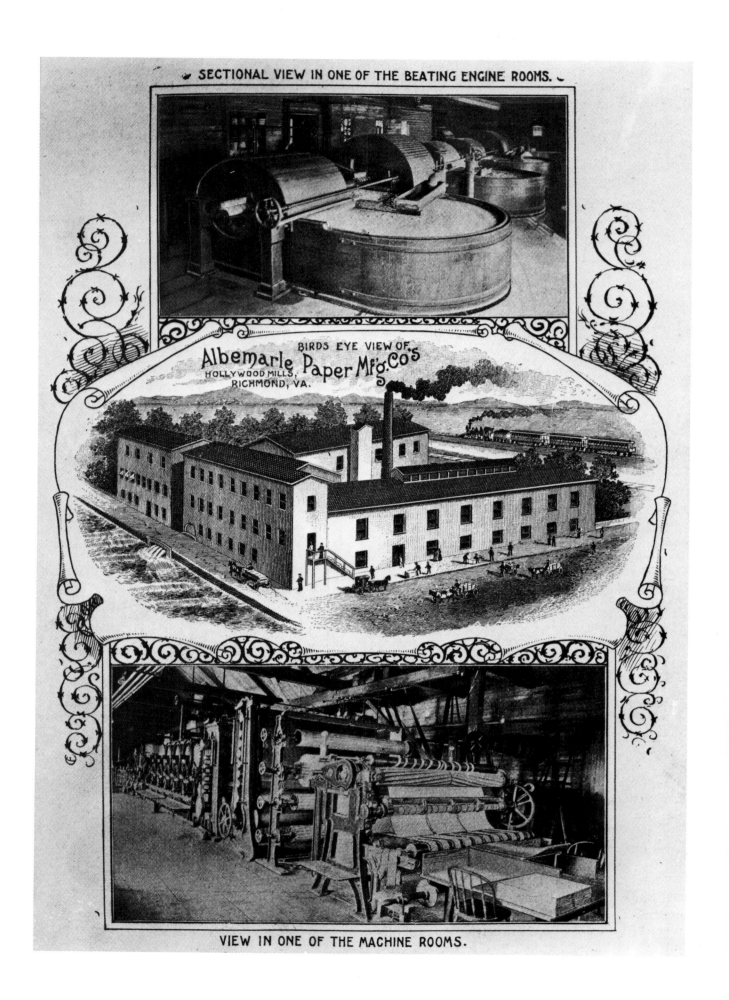

SECTIONAL VIEW IN ONE OF THE BEATING ENGINE ROOMS.

BIRDS EYE VIEW OF. Albemarle Paper Mfg.Co's HOLLYWOOD MILLS, RICHMOND, VA.

VIEW IN ONE OF THE MACHINE ROOMS.

flour, and tobacco accounted for 89 percent of the city's total manufactured products. The contribution of the big three dropped to 63 percent by 1880, and to 43 percent a decade later.

The building boom created a heavy demand for construction materials. Brickmaking was one of the earliest secondary trades to become a major industry. The city produced more than 13 million bricks a year in the 1870s. Other factories turned out stoves, wagons and carriages, boxes, soap, plywood, farming tools, and barrels.

Fed by six railroad lines, Richmond attracted a number of other industries: lumber, chemical fertilizer, paper products, and flavoring extracts. Thirteen confectioners and 20 bakers kept Richmonders supplied with sweets. The Southern Fertilizing Company and Richmond Chemical Works turned out significant volumes of acids and fertilizers. The Richmond Cedar Works was the world's largest woodworking plant. Albemarle Paper Company produced newsprint in the same decade, then switched later to blotting paper, matrix, and filter papers. Of the numerous coffee and spice manufacturers, the C.F. Sauer Company would come to be renowned for its Old Dominion Baking Powder as well as for its ground spices and extracts.

One important Richmond business, founded by Mann S. Valentine II, was based on a formula for beef extract. Produced initially on a small scale for the local market, the formula ultimately enjoyed renown on five continents. The Empress of Russia praised Valentine's Meat Juice after its use in the Russo-Turkish War. After President James Garfield was shot and wounded in 1881, he breakfasted on toast soaked with the juice. Explorers to the North and South poles considered the award-winning juice standard equipment.

Blacksmiths, wheelwrights, carpenters, shoemakers, tailors, milliners, and dressmakers occupied city storefronts, while "objectionable" industries—breweries, a tannery, a soap and candle factory, and the city's gasworks—stood on the outskirts of the city where their noxious odors and wastes were less of a nuisance.

Richmond was not hospitable to all industry. While dry goods merchandising expanded, cotton manufacturing was altogether abandoned. The two postwar mills, the Marshall Manufacturing Company and the Manchester Cotton and Wool Company, closed down by 1900. The Richmond-Virginia Woolen Mills, a small operation started in the 1880s, died after a few years. Shipbuilding and car manufacturing came and went quickly. Chartered in 1888, Trigg Shipbuilding Company constructed the South's first torpedo boat before being forced into receivership after 14 years. Kline Motor Car Corporation, producer of Stanley and White steamers, moved its operation to Richmond from York, Pennsylvania, in 1911, only to go out of business 12 years later.

Electricity came to Richmond in 1881 with the organization of the Virginia Electric Lighting Company. On the theory that competition would keep rates low and service high, the city council approved charters for two more companies. In 1884 the city became involved in the power business as well, replacing the city's gas lamps with electric streetlights and constructing a power plant the following year. Wires soon crisscrossed Richmond as the city provided electricity for streets and parks while private companies supplied power to private customers. But the arrangement failed to live up to the council's expectations. Believing that electricity was a natural monopoly, the council in 1890 chartered the Richmond Railway and Electric Company which bought out four other power and streetcar firms.

As Richmond's population topped 63,000 in 1885, the need for a more expedient means of travel became apparent. In 1887 the council agreed to replace the mule-drawn rail cars, which ran top speeds of three miles per hour, with an electric trolley system. Richmond became the first city in the nation to employ overhead trolleys powered from a central system. By 1890, eight streetcar companies traveled over more than 32 miles of track. As Richmond continued to grow, pedestrian viaducts were built, bridges were improved, and streets and sewers were extended.

Albemarle Paper Manufacturing Company's Hollywood Mills produced newsprint during the 1890s. Later the mills switched to blotting paper, matrix, and filter papers. In 1969, James River Corporation purchased Albemarle Paper Company and expanded it to produce not only specialty papers but also paper towels, paperboard packaging, custom-coated films, and imaging products and pulp. From Richmond: City on the James, *1893*

Mann S. Valentine II founded the Valentine Meat Juice Company in 1871, and the business grew rapidly for several years. The meat juice can still be found in some U.S. pharmacies, but it is more readily available on foreign markets. Valentine (in the rear, center) is shown with some of his employees. Courtesy, Valentine Museum

But the city would not continue its reign as Virginia's undisputed leader in commerce and manufacture.

In the early 1870s Richmond was still the state's busiest port and rail center. But the city's upriver location, which had served it so well a century earlier, was now a disadvantage. Oceangoing trade was being conducted on much larger vessels than in 1800, and the trip up the undredged, silted-over channel of the James River made slow, tedious sailing. It was far easier for the big, iron-hulled vessels that predominated in the late nineteenth century to dock at Baltimore or Hampton Roads, both of which were well served by railroads.

As Richmond entered the twentieth century, its commerce had leveled off to a steady, unremarkable tempo. Tobacco processing remained a mainstay, while the paper and chemical industries contributed an element of stability.

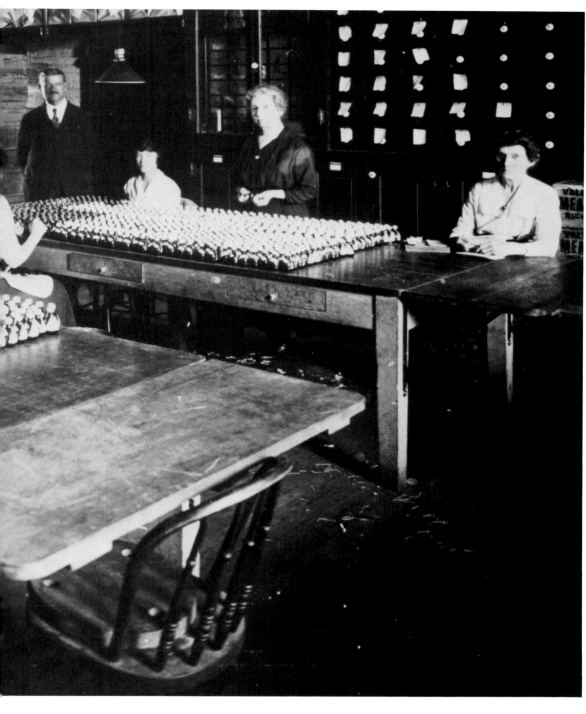

Its position as a major rail center increased with the coming of major railroads like the Atlantic Coast Line and the Southern Railway Railroad Company, and the city was recognized as a notable regional financial center when it was chosen as the headquarters for the Fifth Federal Reserve District in 1914. Yet the ironmaking and flour industries had all but disappeared, and competition with Norfolk had reduced Richmond forever to the status of a second-class port.

As worldwide economic forces turned against the port of Richmond, they worked to the advantage of the port cities of Hampton Roads. William Mahone's newly consolidated Atlantic, Mississippi & Ohio Railroad, which connected with Norfolk, funneled considerable Southside trade from Richmond to Norfolk. Later as the large, consolidated lines—the Norfolk & Western and the Chesapeake & Ohio—carried coal, cotton, and produce to port, they

In the 1930s dry goods merchandising expanded along Broad Street in Richmond. Thalhimers Brothers and Miller & Rhoads added onto their department store complexes to meet the demands of a growing population. This 1932 view of Broad Street, looking west from Eighth Street, shows the city's preparations for a Confederate States Army reunion. Courtesy, Valentine Museum

sought deep-water ports from which to export their cargoes. At Norfolk ships could transfer their cargo directly from dock to train and vice versa. Large freighters, too large to navigate Richmond's inferior channel, poured into Norfolk's harbors.

In 1881 Norfolk's exports totaled nearly $18 million, more than nine times Richmond's exports in the same year. As Norfolk's shipments rose, Richmond's plunged. The value of Richmond's imports between 1875 and 1880 declined from $575,000 to $40,000.

Produce and manufactured goods traveled the rails to Norfolk from all over Virginia and other Southern states. By 1874, the port ranked third in volume along the country's cotton exporting ports. Ten years later nearly a half-million bales a year would pass through the city, half of it bound for Europe.

In the late 1800s the Norfolk & Western began shipping millions of tons of the "black diamond" through Norfolk from the newly opened Pocahontas coalfields in Virginia and West Virginia. Between Norfolk and nearby Newport

News, the cities of Hampton Roads would become the largest coal-exporting ports in the world.

The port activity created a wealth of jobs. Between 1880 and 1910, Norfolk's population tripled. When the Chesapeake & Ohio extended a rail line down the Peninsula, Newport News grew from a small fishing village to a vibrant town. Newport News Shipbuilding and Dry Dock Company, founded by Chesapeake & Ohio tycoon Collis P. Huntington, became the state's largest employer with 5,000 workers. In the 1890s the company began building ships for the United States Navy. Soon it was one of the country's major builders of warships and steamships.

Railroads created other commercial centers around the state to compete with Richmond. The linkup of the north-south Shenandoah Valley line and the east-west Norfolk & Western line created western Virginia's first full-fledged metropolis. The population of the village of Big Lick increased from 669 to 24,495 within 20 years. Roanoke, as the community was

Right: In 1899 William R. Trigg, a prominent industrialist, opened a shipyard in Richmond on the James River. Although it was at first successful, obtaining contracts for two U.S. Navy torpedo boats, the company began to struggle when Trigg's health declined. He died and the company went into receivership in 1902, never to return to full operation. Courtesy, Valentine Museum

Above: The paper and chemical industries contributed to the stability of Richmond's economy at the beginning of the twentieth century. The Standard Paper Company's mill, located at Hull Street and Canal in Manchester, is shown here. From Richmond: City on the James, *1902-1903*

Workers plowed the cobblestone streets so that Richmond's electric streetcar tracks could be laid. The new transportation system helped to create the city's suburbs by allowing workers to move beyond the traditional neighborhoods. By 1890 Richmond had eight streetcar lines. This photograph shows track construction near First and Broad streets. Courtesy, Valentine Museum

The Norfolk harbor was bustling with activity in 1912 when this photo was taken. In the 1870s Norfolk replaced Richmond as the state's commercial center. Railroad lines located there could transfer their cargo from train to ship with great ease. Cotton and coal became the two largest exports from the Norfolk area. Courtesy, Valentine Museum

renamed, also became a major center of heavy manufacturing, boasting the South's largest locomotive factory and a number of iron foundries.

No longer were communities slaves to the geography of coastlines and navigable rivers. As railroads probed into every corner of the state, they gave rise to numerous smaller centers of commerce and industry. The railroads opened up the coalfields of the farthest western reaches of Virginia: Pocahontas and Big Stone Gap became prosperous mountain towns.

The restoration of the Richmond & Danville Railway brought life to the textile industry that would make Danville one of the country's chief textile centers. Drawing upon the cotton and wool resources of the Southeast, Riverside

Cotton Mills arose along the banks of the Dan River in 1882. As the tobacco industry spread, Danville also became the world's largest market for loose-leaf bright tobacco.

Farmville, Bedford, Chatham, Lynchburg, Martinsville, and South Boston also became centers for handling tobacco. Like Danville, Petersburg's rail accessibility boosted its tobacco and textile industries. As early as 1885, five cotton manufacturers with an aggregate number of 26,554 spindles were operating there.

In the Piedmont, Lynchburg quickly renewed its antebellum reputation as a commercial center. The world's largest loose-tobacco market before the war, the city of seven hills rebuilt its tobacco industry within a few years. Shortly after the end of Reconstruction, a visitor to Lynchburg reported that the city's 35 tobacco factories employed "great numbers of negroes, men, women and children ... [who] earn good wages, work faithfully, and turn out vast quantities of the black ugly compound known as 'plug.'" Shoe and candy businesses grew into important enterprises in the new century. Ranking first in the Union in per capita income in 1850, Lynchburg was still one of Virginia's wealthiest cities for its size a half century later.

The small Piedmont town of Charlottesville, home of Thomas Jefferson's University of Virginia, had one substantial industry that predated the war: a woolen mill. Burned by Sheridan's army, the mill was rebuilt by businessman Henry Clay Marchand. Resuming operation in 1868, the Charlottesville Woolen Mills became one of the nation's leading woolen manufacturers and continued business until 1964.

The railroad boom extended to Northern Virginia as well. Alexandria, a busy port city on the Potomac, benefited from the extension of rail lines into the nation's capital. By the early 1870s, three rail lines traversed Fairfax County: the Washington & Ohio; the Orange, Alexandria & Manassas (later the Midland Railroad); and the Alexandria & Fredericksburg. While some industries such as brickmaking and lumbering took root, Northern Virginia remained largely rural, a magnet for well-heeled Washingtonians in search of respite. The resort at Wiehle—on the present site of the planned residential community of Reston—boasted a lavish hotel with bowling alley, tennis courts, and lakes. The surrounding woods were popular for horseback riding and hunting.

By the 1880s, Fairfax was becoming known as a bedroom community for Washington. Northern Virginia residents from Falls Church to Herndon commuted daily to jobs in the District of Columbia. The Loring Company made the first effort to promote Northern Virginia as a suburb rather than as an agricultural supplier to Washington. "Its nearness to the town of Washington ... renders it most desirable to persons employed in that city and wishing for a healthful country home," explained a company pamphlet touting the new community of Dunn Loring.

With its superior ports and its elaborate rail networks, Virginia had a well-developed industrial-agricultural economy by the turn of the century. In 1920 the value of Virginia's manufacturing had risen to $650 million. Although the state was still overwhelmingly rural, Virginia was no longer a plantation society; industrialists and financiers had totally replaced the planter-merchants as the leading entrepreneurs. Towns and cities with more than 2,500 residents, accounting for 18.3 percent of the state's population in 1900, had become hotbeds of entrepreneurial energy.

Nevertheless, Virginia was far from regaining its preeminence as one of the leading states of the Union. As was the case with the other states of the old Confederacy, the average income of Virginia's citizens trailed far behind the rest of the nation. None of Virginia's cities could compare to such bastions of capitalism as New York, Philadelphia, Pittsburgh, or Chicago. And to a degree never seen before the war or since, Virginia's economic destiny was controlled by outsiders. But by the turn of the century, the state had completed the vital task of repairing the war damage. Virginians were in a position to unleash their native entrepreneurial genius.

Coal mining and iron ore production brought thousands of families into the southwest region of Virginia. Mining opened up the land between Pocahontas and Clinch Valley for settlement. This coal mining plant in Pocahontas is pictured in 1974. Courtesy, Roanoke Valley Chamber of Commerce

*This 1946 photograph shows Water
Street in the Tazewell County coal mining
town of Pocahontas. The painted green
and white "company houses" were rented
to miners for $2.75 per month per room.
Courtesy, Richmond Newspapers, Inc.*

VIRGINIA'S "WILD WEST" BOOM TOWNS

◆

America's westward expansion with its gold rushes, mining towns, gunplay, and intercontinental railroads has always captured the popular imagination. During the same period, from 1880 to 1900, Virginia's own west was booming as railroads drove deep into the mountains to exploit a vast wealth of timber and coal. To the newcomers Appalachia seemed an untamed land, and its ruggedly independent mountain folk were as alien to the brash nineteenth-century capitalists as were the Plains Indians. But unlike many western communities, which turned into ghost towns as the gold and silver ran out, Southwest Virginia's towns survived.

The sale and consolidation of Virginia's railroads gave rebuilding and expansion new impetus. As various roads extended into the hinterlands of the Old Dominion to tap vast resources of mineral wealth, the Southwest entered a period of boom growth. New towns sprang up at railroad junctions and at mining camps that were their destinations. Quaint crossroads sparked to life as prospectors and speculators came to chip their fortunes out of the land. Mountain towns like Clifton Forge, Pocahontas, Pulaski, and Covington blossomed along the rail lines probing into the heart of the Appalachians.

Roanoke showed the most remarkable growth during the period, exploding from the tiny hamlet of Big Lick with such speed as to earn the sobriquet, "The Magic City." In the early 1800s, Big Lick was nothing more than a settlement beside a spring, a stagecoach stop for Tennessee-bound travelers. By the 1870s, it had become a small center for trade, with a number of mills, stores, saloons, factories, and warehouses crammed into its one square mile; yet its population had yet to top 700. Despite the Virginia & Tennessee Railroad depot there, Big Lick was still mainly a way station for cargo and travelers bound for the California gold rush. Land sold for $30 an acre then, a fraction of what it would go for a decade later when one citizen claimed to have asked and got $50,000 per acre.

Roanoke might still be a mountain hamlet today had not a throng of farsighted citizens pooled their resources to solicit the attention of Norfolk & Western officials in June 1881. Seeking a site to link the Norfolk & Western with the Shenandoah Valley line, railroad representatives were combing the area between Lynchburg and Salem for such a location. When some of Big Lick's civic-minded citizens called a town meeting to discuss the future of their community, one resident suggested that the Norfolk & Western might take a harder look if a subscription of several thousand dollars were raised.

Clifton Forge was one of several mountain towns that sprang up along the rail lines in the late nineteenth century. Later, large plants for manufacturing iron and other products were located there. Courtesy, Virginia State Library

In a few hours the money had been raised. Reports vary as to the exact sum, but it is known to have been between $7,000 and $10,000. Railroad officials were in Lexington that evening, considering that town as a point of connection. The townspeople of Big Lick hastily dispatched a special courier to convey the bonus.

The courier rode into the night to Arch Mills where he handed off the papers to another rider who took the package to Lexington. The committee was in session when the bearer burst through the door. Impressed by the zeal of Big Lick's townspeople, Colonel U.L. Boyce, one of the chief movers in the railroad project, declared, "Gentlemen, this brings the road to Big Lick." The following February the Virginia General Assembly issued the city its charter, and Big Lick formally became Roanoke.

The town erupted with activity as people prepared for the coming of the trains. The Roa-

The western Virginia town of Big Lick exploded with the consolidation of the state's railroads. In 1881 citizens of the town solicited the attention of the Norfolk & Western Railroad, which was looking for a site where it could link up with the Shenandoah Valley line. This aerial view of Roanoke, looking southeast, shows Mill Mountain in the background at right and the American Viscose Corporation in the background at center. Courtesy, Roanoke Valley Chamber of Commerce

noke Land & Improvement Company, formed in August 1881, oversaw the purchasing and laying off of lots which sold at prices ranging from $100 to $500. Real estate soared as speculators snapped up properties. The town grew so quickly that real estate agents stopped relying on the survey-and-stake method of dividing lots and took to pacing them off, using boot heels as markers. Building materials were in such great demand that even the supplies of nearby towns were exhausted. As lumber piled up at intersections of newly graded streets, Roanoke was said to be "the most excavated place in the United States."

The speculators were not to be disappointed. Railroad employees would double Big Lick's population. The Norfolk & Western planned to move its general offices from Lynchburg, and the Shenandoah Valley Railway had similar plans for its Hagerstown, Maryland,

headquarters. A building craze ignited as hundreds of employees sought accommodations. In the town's first year, the Norfolk & Western and its subsidiaries erected more than 130 dwellings. A mill, 2 office buildings, 15 stores, and 7 homes went up on lots bought from the railroad. When Norfolk & Western official Frederick Kimball sought a new bank to process the railroad's financial transactions, Roanoke got its second bank. Kimball guaranteed subscription if city financial leaders could raise $25,000 locally. The money was raised and the First National Bank was chartered. When the first train rolled in on June 18, Roanoke was ready.

Industry blossomed with the coming of the railroads. The Roanoke Machine Works were operating by May 10, 1882, producing and repairing railroad equipment with capitalization of $5,000 and 1,000 employees. And the big Crozier Furnace was lit. A crowd gathered for that event. The first iron was drawn and declared to be of the finest quality. By 1883, Roanoke Gas Company was organized to provide for the burgeoning population. As brilliant gaslights replaced feeble oil burning lamps, Roanoke began to take on the appearance of a real city.

Workmen found ready jobs in a plethora of trades. As the labor force swelled, the building boom accelerated. Brick houses erected by the Roanoke Land & Improvement Company were the envy of the shop mechanics, while railroad officials and clerks purchased more lavish cottages near the Hotel Roanoke. Clever contractors built long blocks of brick structures and divided them into apartments.

Rapid growth had its problems. Roanoke residents, many of them fresh off the tenant farms of Virginia and North Carolina, clung to provincial habits such as tossing "the accumulations of both chamber and kitchen into their yards." Such methods of disposal combined with crowded living conditions to render Roanoke vulnerable to disease. Meanwhile, so busy were Roanokers with building, buying, and selling buildings that street construction took a backseat. After even the slightest rain, roads became veritable quagmires, clogging up traffic and making a general mess of things.

With the frenzy of construction came hearty laborers who played as hard as they worked. Saloon owners, enjoying a boisterous business, stayed open all hours. As they sought to quench their thirst at the local saloons, day laborers often became overzealous in their pursuit of leisure. With great regularity, the town sergeant was forced to incarcerate rabble-rousers in the famed "calaboose."

Although prostitution houses would later become a problem, such transactions in the early days were confined to assignations at one of the city's several hotels. "Wenching, drinking and gambling" were considered normal pastimes. Men toted guns, even to work. A *Baltimore Sun* reporter noted, "At night, with the red light beacons of the bar-rooms all ablaze over the plank sidewalks, and the music of the violins and banjos coming through the open windows, the town suggests a mining camp or a mushroom city in Colorado."

By the end of its first year, Roanoke had grown to a bustling city with 63 merchants, 44 tobacco and cigar dealers, 17 liquor dealers, 12 factories—most of which were for tobacco—and enough real estate and insurance agents to defy enumeration.

The boom continued into the mid-1880s. Ravines were filled and hills leveled. Grazing land was graded for streets. According to the second report to the shareholders of the Roanoke Land & Improvement Company, the number of buildings rose from 119 in 1881 to 747 in 1883, including 2 office buildings, 54 dwellings and 6 stores. The number of saloons quintupled in the same period. Assessed value of real estate and personal property more than tripled to $1,079,012 between 1882 and 1883.

Some people came to town to stay, others just to visit. Roanoke quickly acquired the reputation of a convention town with 50 to 60 hotels and boardinghouses. The grandest dame of them all was the Hotel Roanoke. It exceeded all others in elegance with its barber shop and attached bathroom fully equipped with hot and cold

water, an elevator, a grandiose dining room seating 200, and gaslit chandeliers.

By 1883, Roanoke had evolved into a stable if somewhat raucous community, with a militia and enough schools, including two private schools, to educate its young. Several businesses were established which would last into the twentieth century, including a branch of the J.P. Bell Printery of Lynchburg, later nationally known as Stone Printing and Manufacturing Company. Rorer Iron Company was transporting 200 to 250 pounds of washed ore daily to the Norfolk & Western yards for shipment to Iron Town, Ohio. Electricity, telephones, and streetcars all came to Roanoke in the 1880s.

The new payroll became the lifeblood of Roanoke's economy. Tapping the resources of the Southwest, the railroad brought steady business to the town. In 1883, 65,675 bales of cotton passed through the city on their way to Northern mills, while 1,604 carloads of cattle,

sheep, hogs, horses, and mules came through on their way to various destinations. On June 21 of that year, 16 carloads of coal, the first of thousands, traveled through en route to Norfolk. After iron mining began just south of Roanoke, freight trains carried 200 to 250 tons of the brown hematite ore in a normal day's load. As tonnages mounted, the Roanoke Machine Works—having been purchased by the Norfolk & Western—prospered.

As the 1880s wore on, a recession settled on the country, and Roanoke's boom pace slowed. Unemployment became a serious problem and businesses suffered. Speculators who had bought unimproved real estate were forced to sell at sacrifice prices. A number of merchants closed their shops and moved on, leaving vacant stores and houses with "for rent" signs swinging on their doors. The machine shops were nearly dormant, except for repair work. Unable to find steady employment, mechanics left town to seek

Roanoke's industrial growth paralleled that of the Norfolk & Western Railroad Company. In 1941 the company had 7,000 employees in the Roanoke area with an annual payroll of $14,500,000. This photograph, taken from the cement stack at the powerhouse, looks west from the upper end of the railroad yards. Courtesy, Roanoke Valley Chamber of Commerce

work elsewhere. Widespread rumors that Roanoke was a pest hole for noxious fevers exacerbated the depression. Rail passengers could be seen closing windows as they passed through town to guard against contamination. Even the most successful, prominent Roanokers were caught by the disaster. Ferdinand Rorer, whose family predated the city, sold his Rorer Park Hotel for $30,000 and left town, "cleaned out." Former Mayor Marshall Waid lost his beautiful brick house and headed home to Waidsboro, never to return.

But Roanoke's energy quickly buoyed. In 1885 Mayor J. H. Dunston reported to city council:

With the New Year, the clouds have begun to break and roll away and flashes of sunshine to brighten the firmament of our city. Prices of produce have arisen to gladden the hearts of our farmers; orders are coming into our factories, which brightens the faces and keeps busy the hands of our mechanics; and relieves the pressure of shelves loaded with merchandise and gives pleasure and profit to our merchants. The increased demand for goods will soon act on our ener-

getic, enterprising young and indominable people; and the factories and enterprises which a short time ago nearly culminated, will be taken up again and carried to a successful conclusion, and our people who have so steadfastly stood by...will soon earn the reward of their ... perseverance.

The recession had lifted. Spurred by a nationwide shift to standard gauge rails that enabled railroad cars to move between rail systems without cumbersome hoists, Roanoke's machine shops gained new business. Real estate and personal property values climbed to $3.2 million—

nine times the 1882 figures. City finances recovered as the tax base swelled. By 1886, Roanoke was back in the black: total receipts were almost $30,000, surpassing expenditures of $26,000.

Nineteen new land companies were chartered. The Hotel Roanoke added 52 rooms. Saloons, bawdy houses, and gambling houses proliferated. On November 22, 1889, the editor of the *Roanoke Times* wrote:

More internal improvements are needed but so many buildings are in the course of construction and so

The Hotel Roanoke was the finest establishment of its kind when it was built in the booming city of Roanoke. This was the hotel's lobby. Courtesy, Virginia State Library

Roanoke's remarkable growth and activity attracted investors from other parts of the country, who came to Roanoke to survey the situation. Airmail began in the city in 1934. This group ushered in the new service at Woodrum Airfield. The rate was six cents per ounce. Courtesy, Roanoke Valley Chamber of Commerce

many houses going up in the suburbs, the streets are littered with bricks, mortar, lathes, and building debris that cannot be helped, nor can sidewalks be constructed fast enough to keep up at once with the grading of the new streets.

Articles in Northern journals about Roanoke's remarkable growth and activity spurred investors from other parts of the country to come to Roanoke to survey the situation. By 1890, the city was enjoying a new wave of prosperity. Prospective buyers and potential investors from all over the country arrived in trains and in caravans of carriages. As full-page newspaper ads touted spectacular land buys, an average of five families moved to Roanoke daily. "The rush of vehicles to various parts of the city

is continuous and every agent seems to have all of the business he can attend to," noted the *Roanoke Times*. On a single day in February, real estate agencies reported sales of $150,000, while private sales exceeded $200,000. Prices soared. Property once assessed at $70 an acre brought $50 to $200 per front foot. Meanwhile, construction continued at a furious pace to meet the demand for homes and business houses. A million dollars worth of buildings were erected between 1890 and 1891.

As real estate mania took hold, investors snatched up bond issues for streets and bridges over the railroad but ignored the need for a new hospital. Local capitalists poured money into the construction of a railroad, the Roanoke &

Southern, to tie the city to Winston-Salem, North Carolina.

Between 1890 and 1891, 1,025 business licenses were issued to merchants, lawyers, doctors, house builders, real estate agents, and owners of various establishments. Census takers estimated the city's population as between 16,000 and 17,000.

In the Gay Nineties, a veneer of civility settled over the rough-and-tumble frontier town. The city managed to pave some of its roads with vitrified brick. Men still packed guns and patronized houses of ill repute, and professional gamesters still catered to the gambling crowd. But across town, gloved ladies held "tiddly wink parties" and "violet teas." The wealthiest citizens

sank small fortunes into lavishly furnished private railroad cars, the ultimate status symbol.

The fever was spreading across the Roanoke Valley. With the completion of a dummy line to Vinton, lots there inflated in value. Speculators descended upon the village, making first payments with the intention of quickly unloading their purchases at a profit. Land companies like the Vinton Land, Loan and Building Company bought up hundreds of acres of grainfields and grazing lands for development. Skilled workers quit their trades and took up speculation. Vinton quickly outgrew its original boundaries. Across the valley, Salem burst into activity with the organization of a dozen or more land companies. Banks opened; ironworks, machine works, brick works, and mills were established. In Norwich rows of cottages were built to accommodate the laborers who flooded the area.

The Norfolk & Western consolidated its dominance in the local economy by purchasing the bankrupt Shenandoah Valley Railroad and absorbing the Roanoke & Southern line. By doubling the capacity of its freight station, the Norfolk & Western continued to feed the commerce of Roanoke and its adjoining settlements.

Roanoke's boom was one of the greatest explosions of vitality in Virginia's 375-year history, and the indisputable success story of the late nineteenth century—an era when eastern Virginia was still dogged by the legacy of the Civil War destruction, sharecropping, and the decline of iron, textiles, and grain milling. But there were limits to the city's growth. Iron reserves were meager, not sufficient to sustain a steel industry in the face of competition from the emerging Birminghams and Pittsburghs. Lacking access to rivers and ports, Roanoke remained on the periphery of world trade. Hemmed in by mountains, Roanoke could never realistically aspire to being more than a regional center of commerce. Inevitably, the boom lost its fizzle.

Some believed that a paralyzing snowfall, which suspended business, precipitated Roanoke's downward spiral. Others attested that the weakening of English investment and unwise currency legislation triggered the collapse. Whatever the reason, Roanoke was swept up in the Panic of 1893, an economic catastrophe that washed over the entire United States.

With money tight, several prominent citizens admitted an inability to pay debts. Some were forced to auction their holdings in order to pay taxes. In May 1893 the Roanoke Times carried full pages of advertisements offering properties for sale under deeds of trust. To ease climbing unemployment, the city council hired laborers to work on streets alongside chain gangs. Families petitioned the council for relief.

Despite the hardship, the Magic City fared better than other nascent metropolises across the country. Property values fell, and the days of easy money were gone forever. Fair-

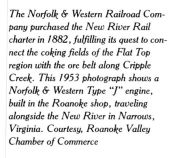

The Norfolk & Western Railroad Company purchased the New River Rail charter in 1882, fulfilling its quest to connect the coking fields of the Flat Top region with the ore belt along Cripple Creek. This 1953 photograph shows a Norfolk & Western Type "J" engine, built in the Roanoke shop, traveling alongside the New River in Narrows, Virginia. Courtesy, Roanoke Valley Chamber of Commerce

weather businesses packed up and left town, leaving a nucleus population of stalwart citizens to carry on the task of building a stable economy.

By 1895, depression had bottomed out, and citizens found cause for sober optimism. Real estate was cheap, and families were again moving to Roanoke. Houses could be bought with a $10-cash down payment. New houses were built and more were under construction. Some clever investors bought empty cottages in Norwich and moved them to more desirable sections of Roanoke for sale at a profit.

Merchants returned to steady businesses. Furnaces and factories resumed full-scale operations. The Norfolk & Western, which had passed into receivership, announced reorganization plans. The machine shops surged back into action with new orders. By February 1896, payroll at the shops had increased to $70,000. By the end of the year, every empty house was reoccupied and nearly every vacant store reopened.

A *Roanoke Times* editorial on New

Year's Day, 1899, greeted residents with a message of hope: "the New Year finds the city entering upon an era safely said to be better than anything in its history." Roanoke was back on its feet, striding confidently into the new century.

"It takes a railroad to bring progress and culture," wrote John Fox, Jr., author of *The Trail of the Lonesome Pine*, a turn-of-the-century novel set in Appalachia against a backdrop of clashing cultures: capitalism triumphant versus the primitive economy of the mountaineers. Before the coming of the trains, Southwest Virginia was a land of dispersed settlement and subsistence farming. Industry was of the most rustic sort, geared to local consumption rather than faraway markets. Although Northern states had been producing coal and coke for several years, the counties of Southwest Virginia remained a primeval forest. As the industrial revolution stoked the fires of growth all around, the richest coalfields on the face of the earth remained inaccessible, guarded by walls of mountains.

The existence of coal was no secret. In

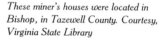

These miner's houses were located in Bishop, in Tazewell County. Courtesy, Virginia State Library

increased the demand for coal—the boiler fuel of railroad locomotives, steamships, electric generators, and industrial plants; as well as raw material in the steel-making process—Northern capitalists turned their attentions to Virginia's Southwest. They had long been aware of the abundant resources in Virginia's wilds. When the county of Wise was created in 1856, the edition of the Philadelphia *Pennsylvanian* which carried the news sold out. A second edition was printed so that no interested party would miss the story of a new county in "the land of vast natural resources." A *Richmond Dispatch* writer noted the keen interest of outside capitalists: "The great resources of Virginia seem to be everywhere more highly appreciated than by herself." Indeed, as the 1880s progressed, a significant amount of capital invested in the Southwest would come from Pennsylvania and England.

As the railroads penetrated deeper into Virginia, investors plumbed the far reaches of the state for coal reserves and iron. In the early 1880s railroads running through Bristol in the Southwest transported primarily cotton and agricultural products. Ten years later coal had become the major commodity.

Mining camps and small towns like Coeburn—named for the Norfolk & Western's chief engineer—sprang up along the rail lines, providing humble if not sophisticated settlements for miners and their families. People flocked to the mining communities. Big Stone Gap, Norton, and Wise rapidly doubled in population, overwhelming the resources of local authorities to maintain order. Rowdies routinely shot the glass out of streetlights. Women were imported from Philadelphia to remedy the lack of eligible females. Promiscuous spending and reckless gambling were the hallmarks of the boom years across the Southwest.

As settlements grew, land prices inflated. Dazzled by unprecedented prices, longtime locals sold land and mineral rights for what seemed a fortune. In fact, they virtually gave their wealth away. Outsiders assembled huge tracts of coal reserves that would still be generating millions of dollars in annual royalties a full century later.

Far left: Frederick Kimball, chief operating officer of the Norfolk & Western, pioneered the railroad's move into the Pocahontas coal fields. Courtesy, Virginia State Library

1750 both Christopher Gist exploring for the Ohio Company and the Loyal Company's Dr. Thomas Walker discovered the black rock in their travels through the Southwest. Walker even dubbed the area "the coal land." But, with seemingly limitless timber, local inhabitants saw no need to chip into the ground for fuel.

As early as 1852 Dr. George W. Bickley wrote of Tazewell County, "Coal exists everywhere, though wood is so plenty that it has not been used as fuel to any extent ...Coal has been found below, and in every direction around, and no doubt, exists generally through the county. When shall we have an outlet for this coal?" Twenty years later geologist J.P. Leslie reported to the American Philosophical Society on the nature of coal deposits in the Southwest: "It is good blacksmith coal and no doubt will make good coke." By the mid-1870s, a mining engineer reporting for the Virginia Board of Immigration declared the Southwest to be rich in valuable deposits of iron and coal.

But roads were poor, and the horse-drawn wagons were crude, laboriously slow, and uneconomical. As the industrial revolution

Following the Civil War, General J.D. Imboden spearheaded the development of the coal reserves in southwest Virginia. A native of Washington County, he convinced several capitalists to invest in his Tansalia Coal and Iron Company, which later became Virginia Coal and Iron Company. Courtesy, Valentine Museum

A handful of coal men from Pittsburgh, the coal and steel capital of America's industrial revolution, spearheaded the development of Virginia's coal reserves in the winter of 1879-1880. At a dinner gathering, General J.D. Imboden, a former resident of Washington County, told his colleagues of the potential he saw for development of Virginia's mountainous southwest, which was about to be tied by rail to Bristol. Two guests offered Imboden $500 and expenses to examine the potential of the region for iron manufacturing. The expedition was a success.

Imboden returned bearing samples enough to convince the capitalists to invest in the Tinsalia Coal and Iron Company (later to become the Virginia Coal and Iron Company).

Tinsalia purchased mineral lands, including land at Big Stone Gap and in the Wild Cat Valley, and acquired a controlling interest in the Bristol Coal and Iron Company Narrow Gauge Railway. The first plans for the railway, which would become the South Atlantic & Ohio Railway, included an extension to Big Stone Gap.

Tracks were speedily thrown down, extending deeper and deeper into the mountain wilderness. In 1887, under a joint agreement, the Louisville & Nashville and the Norfolk & Western had begun laying tracks toward a connecting point in Wise County. Meanwhile,

the South Atlantic & Ohio brought its first passengers to Big Stone Gap in May 1890. A year later, the Louisville & Nashville railroad also reached Big Stone Gap, while the Norfolk & Western brought life to the nearby town of Norton.

The 1890s found all three railroads converging on a point just north of Big Stone Gap for access to the rich mineral fields that lay beyond. "Gappers" had anticipated the boom. Even before the first train pulled into town, a development company advertised a great land sale, and competing purchasers deposited checks totaling three times the sum asked by the com-

The Norfolk & Western Rail Company was responsible for the operation of 144 mines in southwestern Virginia. The company located its shops in the city of Roanoke; in this 1936 photograph a locomotive is getting a major overhaul. Courtesy, Roanoke Valley Chamber of Commerce

pany. Land was auctioned at such a price that one old farmer who had sold his land for $100 an acre bought some of it back for $1,000 a lot. Taking advantage of the impending building craze, one Northern businessman recruited a corps of gunslingers from the Tennessee mountains to work in his brick plant at the Gap. These folks did not always mix well with the locals, and Virginia's Wild West often erupted in violence.

Analysts' reports commenting on the superiority of the coal deposits of the Southwest generated excitement in iron and coal circles around the country. Lots advertised in prospectuses and in metropolitan newspapers piqued interest. For

the August 1891 land auction, some 30 Pullman cars brought potential buyers from distant cities. The town's hotel overrun, speculators used the sleeper cars as living quarters. Small-time fortune hunters slept in tents. "Big Stone Gap, seat of empire," wrote the editor of the *Stone Post*. "Such will be unless an earthquake swallows it."

The only earthquake was one of cataclysmic change. Twelve different railroad lines were surveyed into the Gap in 1891. Laborers, engineers, surveyors, and coal operators found ready work. Shrewd investors and slaphappy speculators flocked in on stagecoaches, wagons, horses, mules, and even on foot. Real estate transactions

were conducted at the Grand Central Hotel, where newcomers slept eight to a room, paid a dollar a gallon for oil, and feasted on potatoes that cost 10 cents apiece. "Poker ceased," noted one magazine writer. "It was too tame in competition with this new game of trading in town lots."

An old iron furnace in St. Louis was dismantled and reconstructed at Big Stone Gap, initiating the production of iron. Coal companies bought more land and opened more mines. In the fall of 1892 the first shipment of Wise County coal was shipped out over the South Atlantic & Ohio Railroad. Three years later the Louisville & Nashville carried out Wise's first load of coke.

Before the coal boom Tazewell County had been nothing more than an agricultural community of 1,922 farmers, 10 doctors, 8 lawyers, 36 teachers, 22 merchants, "and a total of 91 persons engaged in non-productive callings," according to the 1850 census. In Tazewell the seed of the coal boom sprouted early. In 1872, believing that existing charcoal furnaces would eventually shut down for lack of blast, 26 investors, including William Mahone and Montgomery County delegate Gabriel C. Wharton, established the New River Railroad, Mining and Manufacturing Company for the purpose of developing the coal beds of the Flat Top Mountain region for production of coke.

The development of the Pocahontas coal beds brought thousands of miners and consumers to Tazewell County. Pocahontas coal, known for its superior quality, was specifically requested by the U.S. Navy as well as by premier transportation companies. This 1983 photograph shows a Norfolk & Western train carrying the high quality coal out of the Virginia hills. Courtesy, Roanoke Valley Chamber of Commerce

But local businessmen had little capital. Wharton and his associates looked north for cash support. Hearing of the great mineral riches of the Flat Top region, some Philadelphia financiers and promoters invested in the company. Their cunning reorganization schemes resulted in the formation of the New River Railroad. The Norfolk & Western absorbed the road in 1882 in its quest to connect the coking fields of the Flat Top region and the ore belt along Cripple Creek.

Norfolk & Western's chief operating officer, Frederick Kimball, pioneered the railroad's move into the Pocahontas fields, a basin containing the highest quality metallurgical coal in the world. Prompted by Professor J.P. Leslie's 1881 report of various coal showings in Southwest Virginia, Frederick Kimball set out to locate and examine the outcroppings. Using Leslie's maps, Kimball and his party moved throughout Tazewell's most isolated, inaccessible countryside, through Abb's Valley to Hutton— the future site of the town of Pocahontas. Before they dismounted their horses, Kimball and his accomplices could see a 12-foot-thick vein of coal. Kimball chipped out a few chunks with his knife and lit it. As the combustible rock burned, Kimball noted, "This may be a very important day in our lives." Thrilled with his find, Kimball rerouted the New River line through the Flat Top region to Pocahontas.

By the twentieth century coal mining dominated the economy of Virginia's far western edge. One hundred and forty-four mines were operating along the Norfolk & Western lines by 1905. This 1983 photograph shows one of the modern coal preparation plants served by the N&W system. Courtesy, Roanoke Valley Chamber of Commerce

After the Norfolk & Western purchased the New River Rail charter, it financed development of the area by organizing the Southwest Virginia Improvement Company. Capitalized at $1 million, the company held mineral rights to approximately 100,000 acres of land. Houses and other buildings were hastily constructed by the Crozier Land interests to accommodate the Norfolk & Western's growing labor force. It would be two years before the railroad extended its line west from Radford to Pocahontas; but by 1883, coal producers could ship directly to Norfolk.

Even before rail lines were complete, the Pocahontas fields produced 40,000 tons of coal. Within a year of its beginnings, the village of Pocahontas possessed a hotel, seven stores, and related facilities to serve 1,000 inhabitants. The town became the socializing center for miners from neighboring camps. "Almost every other building was a saloon," recorded one coal operator. "I concluded that Pocahontas was the toughest little town I had yet seen in my travels from Maine to Texas." Weekends were stained by shootings and "sudden deaths," as Pocahontas was the chief liquor supplier for neighboring camps.

The development of the Pocahontas and Flat Top coal beds had brought thousands of miners and consumers to Tazewell County, establishing good markets for farm products that had previously been marketed only locally.

By 1890, the boom in the Southwest was climbing to a crescendo. Virginia miners produced 784,000 tons of coal that year, and total coal tonnage handled by the Norfolk & Western alone had long since topped one million tons. Virginia had risen from seventeenth to sixth place among U.S. iron producers since the beginning of the boom 10 years before. New furnaces were expected to increase Virginia's yearly output by more than 300,000 tons. But with the Panic of 1893, the surging economy began sputtering.

As the national economy slipped into depression, demand for coal and iron slumped. Coal mining was almost discontinued in the prosperous Pocahontas fields and in Wise County. Norton and Graham, at opposite ends of the Clinch Valley Railroad, became veritable ghost towns. The coke ovens at Pocahontas were

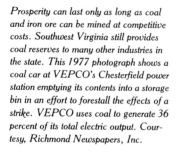

Prosperity can last only as long as coal and iron ore can be mined at competitive costs. Southwest Virginia still provides coal reserves to many other industries in the state. This 1977 photograph shows a coal car at VEPCO's Chesterfield power station emptying its contents into a storage bin in an effort to forestall the effects of a strike. VEPCO uses coal to generate 36 percent of its total electric output. Courtesy, Richmond Newspapers, Inc.

Coal and iron mining provide a livelihood for many in Virginia's southwestern region. Elsewhere, the iron and coal reserves have been mined out. This view of the Roanoke Valley from Mill Mountain shows the industrial area along Interstate 81. Courtesy, Roanoke Valley Chamber of Commerce

abandoned, save for hogs who had made their beds there. Promoters lopped off lots into small farms for sale. Many lots reverted to their original owners on deferred payments, and some landowners were forced to give up their lands for auction due to delinquent taxes.

By 1897, the depression was over and growth in Virginia's coal industry resumed. By the turn of the century, 39 mining operations were back in business, 25 of which were on Pocahontas land, and new ventures were started. The demand for high quality coal was so high that the Norfolk & Western got a premium $25 per acre on its leases. Pocahontas was buzzing again as 23 trains stopped each day to unload coal miners from neighboring coal camps. In the twentieth century, Pocahontas coal would maintain its superior standing, specifically requested by the U.S. Navy as well as by premier transportation companies like the Cunard Steamship line. By 1905, 144 mines were operating along Norfolk & Western lines, from Pocahontas to Clinch Valley, including the Tug River, Thacker, and Kenova districts in West Virginia.

By 1920, coal mining had consumed the entire economy of Virginia's far western tip. Mines were opened in Lee, Dickenson, Buchanan, and Russell counties. Farming was all but abandoned as the local populations with single-minded intensity devoted themselves to the extraction of the "black diamond." With the smaller volumes mined in Montgomery, Pulaski, Augusta, Botetourt, Bland, and Wythe counties contributing to Virginia's output of more than 12 million tons, Virginia ranked as one of the leading coal-producing states in the country.

Iron ore production also grew into the new century. In 1920 production totaled 320,109 long tons with a value of $1,227,601, while pig iron valuation equaled $16,086,946. Clifton Forge, Covington, and Pulaski had large plants for manufacturing iron and other products; similar plants were established throughout the Southwest. The total value of all mineral products mined and quarried in Virginia that year totaled $82,662,945, representing a 40-percent increase over the preceding year.

Prosperity built upon the extraction of minerals can last only as long as the mineral—be it coal or iron ore—can be mined at competitive costs. In Virginia, such prosperity has been fleeting. Only in the far Southwest, blessed by abundant reserves, does mining provide a livelihood today. Elsewhere the iron and coal eventually was mined out, and the local mineral-based industries shriveled. But the railroads, paid for by hauling coal, remained in place to ease the transition to a more stable economy.

Lacking land, capital, and an education, many Virginia blacks were forced to sharecrop. This circa 1890 photograph shows a mother and her son standing outside their cabin in Chesterfield County, Virginia. Courtesy, Valentine Museum

THE DUAL ECONOMY

◆

Emancipation abolished slavery, but it did not end the economic and legal oppression of blacks. Lacking land, capital, and education, Virginia's blacks slipped into a subtler form of servitude: sharecropping. And outnumbered by whites who shamelessly wielded their political dominance to disenfranchise the former slaves, blacks were powerless to seek political redress. After Reconstruction and Jim Crow blacks could legitimately ask if emancipation were anything more than a polite fiction. For the thousands of blacks who swarmed the cities, unprecedented freedoms awaited. Yet freedom and opportunity were not to be confused.

Where slavery had forced blacks into servitude, post-emancipation discrimination almost as strongly enforced their subordination. While life's basic necessities had been provided under a system that simultaneously permitted harsh treatment, suppression, and hard work for little or no compensation, emancipation invited blacks to provide for themselves under an unwritten code that placed them at the lowest social and economical rungs of a society which defined racial equality in its own terms.

Faced with the challenge of surmounting or enduring the limitations placed on them through written as well as attitudinal codes of suppression, black Virginians forged their own economic structure. "Jim Crow" laws were intended to create separate societies, but they also created separate economies and insulated markets for black businesses. Banned from the political arena, blacks channeled their energies into the development of black enterprise.

Secret societies, initiated in the days of slavery, gave birth to mutual aid organizations which became the benefactors of black enterprises and the forerunners of black-owned banks and insurance companies. When blacks were restricted residentially, small vibrant communities sprang up with their own stores, banks, restaurants, and barber and beauty shops, catering to and patronized by black clientele. Ironically, "Jim Crow" laws created the conditions for the greatest surge of entrepreneurial energy in black Virginians' history.

Discrimination against blacks was not unique to the South. While Northerners verbally promoted black freedom and cursed the South for its oppression of blacks, they failed to enforce equality on their own turf. One black leader in Boston observed in 1860 that "it is ten times as difficult for a colored mechanic to get work here as in Charleston."

Given the prevailing attitude, emancipation proved to be no panacea. Blacks were no longer the property of another man, but their freedom was hemmed in by numerous legal restraints. Under the gun of Northern occupation troops, Southerners were somewhat tolerant of black political activity.

Little had changed for blacks by 1900. An unwritten code placed them on the lowest social and economic rung of society. Courtesy, Valentine Museum

The polls as well as seats on juries and even in state government were opened to blacks for the first time. Blacks voted and held office while whites who had served as officers in the Confederacy could not. In the 1870s and 1880s, blacks and whites mixed in the marketplace and traveled on trains with no segregation.

But white legislatures began undermining black freedoms as soon as they had the power to do so. Separation was enforced at theaters and on public conveyances. Mixed marriages were punishable with a $100 fine and a year in jail.

When federal troops withdrew in 1877, a new wave of "Jim Crow" laws was inaugurated. Hotels and restaurants usually enforced separate seating. Those hospitals, private establishments, and public buildings that permitted blacks enforced segregation. While blacks continued to vote and hold elective and appointive offices, many public facilities excluded them or limited them to certain hours.

By the turn of the century, racial sentiment was so strong that laws were adopted to enforce the discrimination already in practice. Every

to impose this "color line." For the next 60 years discriminatory laws tightened the noose of racism. Where state laws left leeway, local regulations took up the slack. Blacks were relegated to seats in the rear of streetcars and later buses, and to separate seating at theaters, restaurants, and parks. Signs specifying "White Only" and "Colored" appeared in profusion over drinking fountains and entrances to bathrooms, theaters, boardinghouses, and other public buildings.

The most damaging law restricted blacks' right to vote. By requiring voters to read and explain any section of the state constitution as well as to pay a poll tax, Virginia's white politicians virtually wiped out black voting power. When the registration books closed in 1902, only 21,000 of the state's 147,000 blacks of voting age were registered. When the poll tax took effect in 1905, less than half of those could afford to pay it. With the diminished strength of the black electorate, blacks had little hope of enacting legislation to ease their worsening economic plight.

The effects were far reaching. The General Assembly allocated disproportionate shares of funds to the education of whites. In the Southside counties, where school-age blacks were concentrated in 1915, only $1 per child was spent to educate blacks as opposed to the $12 per child spent on education of whites. Cities instituted their own plans for residential segregation. Richmond and Ashland, for instance, designated blocks as white or black according to the majority of residents. Citizens were forbidden to reside in any block "where the majority of residents on such streets as occupied by those with whom said person is forbidden to marry." Similar plans were mapped out in other cities.

Most effective in maintaining the suppression of blacks, however, was the unwritten code that limited their employment. In 1902 Richmond's city council threatened to block a white contractor from a job because he employed black mechanics. Virginia's larger cities excluded blacks from a majority of municipal occupations. Those who were able to secure

Southern state except Virginia had adopted a law applying to segregation on trains. After Governor J. Hoge Tyler awakened in his train berth to find black passengers above, opposite, and in front of him, Virginia likewise enacted a law forcing blacks to ride in separate rail cars.

Giving voice to the growing feelings of racism, the *Richmond Times* in 1900 called for segregation "in every relation of Southern life" on the basis that "God Almighty drew the color line and it cannot be obliterated." The Virginia Constitutional Convention of 1901-1902 attempted

Facing page: Stores, banks, restaurants, and movie theaters owned by blacks were easily accessible from this black residence, located at 612 North Third Street in Jackson Ward. In spite of residential segregation and employment discrimination, the black economy developed and thrived in Virginia's inner cities. Courtesy, Valentine Museum

Right: Sedley D. Jones displays samples of his goods outside his store at 726-728 North Second Street in Jackson Ward in this photo, circa 1905. Because of the restrictions on blacks, they opened their own stores, banks, and restaurants, catering to and patronized by black clientele. Courtesy, Valentine Museum

employment in skilled jobs often received less pay than their white counterparts.

The black freedman often fared worse as a free laborer than he had as a slave before the war. In 1860 hired-out slaves earned $105 a year plus rations and clothing; in 1867 freedmen working as laborers earned a flat $102 a year. In many cases skilled black laborers were denied union membership. Unions that did admit blacks sometimes negotiated separate contracts for

whites. Other unions forbade promotion of blacks. The International Brotherhood of Blacksmiths, Drop Forgers and Helpers (AFL) would not allow black members to be promoted to positions as blacksmiths or as helper-apprentices.

However oppressive, residential segregation and employment discrimination were two of the primary factors in the development of a separate black economy. The desire to improve their

plight and upgrade their employment prompted blacks to start their own businesses and to hire other blacks.

Black residential communities provided the setting. Stores and businesses had a captive clientele in residents who were pleased to work, shop, and pursue entertainment in their own neighborhoods. Usually the business activity centered around one main street within the neighborhood. Second Street in Richmond's Jackson Ward had a number of hotels, restaurants, and movie houses, a law office, a tailor shop, and a bicycle and repair shop. Roanoke had its Henry Street; Norfolk, its Church Street; Portsmouth and Danville, their High Streets. These communities were microcosms of the white urban economy.

If residential communities were the seedbed for black economic development, churches were

the fertilizer. For blacks the church was far more than a religious organization; it was the chief organ of social, religious, and economic exchange. At camp meetings, all-night shouts, and Sunday services, black ministers admonished their flocks to "save money," "get an education," "live within your means," and "buy homes." Worshipers were advised to pay poll taxes and to vote. It was at church that the former slaves and their progeny found the moral support and encouragement to help them make their own way.

After the Civil War, blacks left the white-run churches in droves to form numerous independent denominations. Some were direct counterparts of the orthodox religions their former masters had shared with them; others were off-shoots or independent churches. Pastors were elected from field hands, coal miners, and former slave preachers. The separation was momentous.

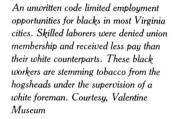

An unwritten code limited employment opportunities for blacks in most Virginia cities. Skilled laborers were denied union membership and received less pay than their white counterparts. These black workers are stemming tobacco from the hogsheads under the supervision of a white foreman. Courtesy, Valentine Museum

While whites excluded blacks from every other aspect of day-to-day life, blacks voluntarily withdrew from the white-dominated churches.

Church leaders were often great fund-raisers, leading drives and campaigns to raise money for their churches. The building and furnishing of a church was a sacred duty in which no expense was to be spared. Some preachers showed extraordinary entrepreneurial talents. One very popular minister was Bishop Daddy Grace. While other pastors solicited contributions for God's work, Bishop Daddy published a magazine and peddled a variety of products under his own label. "Freely you receive," he said, "freely you give." With the proceeds Bishop Daddy built a two-story, stone and steel church in Newport News for his following of 5,000.

Too poor to build new churches, many black congregations purchased churches vacated by whites. By 1900, expanding black urban communities encroached on white neighborhoods, stimulating white flight and driving down property values. "Segregation has been a boon to Negro congregations," observed one writer. "As Negro districts expand, white residents move away, and expensive church buildings go on sale at a fraction of their cost."

By 1930, 48 percent of Virginia's black urban residents as well as 62 percent of its rural blacks were regular churchgoers. Churches would continue to play a powerful role in the economic development of the black community, providing the foundation and the voice of civic reform.

Thomas Jefferson's wish to educate "every description of our citizens from the richest to the poorest" had yet to be fulfilled by the end of Reconstruction. Although education was theoretically available to every Virginian, higher education for blacks in the public system was virtually unknown.

Even before emancipation, schools for blacks existed in Virginia. And the Freedmen's Bureau had provided education for approximately 50,000 black Virginians. By 1880 Virginia had 1,256 black schools, staffed mostly by

In March 1878 the Reverend John Jasper, minister of Sixth Mount Zion Baptist Church in Richmond, Virginia, preached his "Sun Do Move" sermon which challenged Galileo's observations on planetary motion. So great was his oration that audiences almost unanimously agreed with him. Jasper preached this sermon to white and black audiences in Philadelphia, Baltimore, Washington, D.C., and throughout Virginia. Courtesy, Valentine Museum

white teachers. Yet it would be 45 years before Virginia would have its first accredited black public high school. In a state whose constitution provided for education for all, black Virginians found that their opportunities for advanced education were severely limited. White politicians denied that blacks needed education beyond the primary level. Eager to move ahead, blacks sought ways to provide further education for their own.

Missionary societies and other church organizations created schools to supplement public facilities which would provide higher learning for blacks. For instance, Norfolk Mission College, founded with the support of the United Presbyterian Church of North America, provided four years of Latin study, Bible courses, English, science, mathematics, history, home economics, and industrial arts. Tuition was 50 cents a month, charged only to those who could afford it. By the 1880s, Virginia had three institutions of higher learning for blacks.

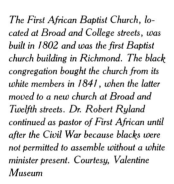

The First African Baptist Church, located at Broad and College streets, was built in 1802 and was the first Baptist church building in Richmond. The black congregation bought the church from its white members in 1841, when the latter moved to a new church at Broad and Twelfth streets. Dr. Robert Ryland continued as pastor of First African until after the Civil War because blacks were not permitted to assemble without a white minister present. Courtesy, Valentine Museum

In some cases the students themselves pitched in to raise funds for their schools. Students at Hampton Institute, chartered in 1869 to provide higher education for "young people without distinction of color," raised substantial amounts of money. When a $20,000 donation from the Freedmen's Bureau in the early 1870s didn't cover the cost of a building, the Hampton Institute Singers brought in another $20,000 through a performance tour of 500 concerts in seven states and Canada.

Schools were often built on land bought by community groups or donated by landowners. Churches, unions, lodges and other organizations generated funds for these black schools which were referred to interchangeably as "institutes," "colleges," and "universities."

A number of funds established by individuals in the North benefited Virginia's black students. The Slater Fund, the Jeanes Negro Rural School Fund, and the Phelps-Stokes Fellowship were just a few of the foundations dedicated to the education of blacks. Yet black schools would continue to suffer from underfinancing well into the twentieth century. As late as 1939, 62 percent of black public schools in Virginia had only one room and one teacher.

Even before the Civil War, blacks were active in a variety of businesses. Entrepreneurs were divided into two groups: free blacks who had accumulated through labor the capital to establish their own businesses, and slaves who parlayed their plantation skills into marketable services. In some cases the proceeds of these efforts were used to purchase freedom. Larger cities with concentrations of blacks supported black-owned labor and service enterprises such as barbershops, restaurants, caterers, and undertakers. While undertakers stayed within color lines, black caterers were especially popular among the white well-to-do. Many survived the Civil War and its aftermath.

Reconstruction saw the expansion of black business into other areas. Butchers, clothiers, boot makers, mechanics, and draymen ran flourishing businesses. By the 1880s, the black entre-

preneur was no longer a rarity, and the barbershop and the pool room were no longer the only black businesses. Blacks competed in numerous areas of commercial enterprise, including building and loan and land improvement businesses.

Racial discrimination drove blacks together. Black neighborhoods became microcosms of the cities in which they existed, providing necessities as well as niceties to a clientele which would otherwise be forced to travel to distant business districts for goods and services. Blacks entered the commercial sector in increasing numbers. As early as 1890 black merchants

Blacks fill every available seat and crowd into the aisles to hear the sermon in this Harper's Weekly *engraving of the interior of the First African Baptist Church in Richmond. Courtesy, Virginia State Library*

numbered 1,068 in Virginia. By 1899, Richmond was one of only 20 cities in the country with 20 or more black businesses of considerable size. Three years later blacks in Hampton owned 20 mercantile establishments as well as 40 to 50 small shops.

By the second decade of the new century, black economic consciousness solidified. In 1913 the National Negro Business League, conceived by Virginia native Booker T. Washington, opened a chapter in Virginia. The league's stated objective was to encourage blacks to develop "their own resources, to establish more business enterprises among themselves, to patronize them for their own racial benefit . . ." Mottoes like "Share your trade with Negroes" and "Don't trade where you can't work" cemented segregation in business while bolstering trade among blacks. Businesses were encouraged to offer services and prices comparable to their white counterparts in an effort to draw trade.

Through the league, business leaders began to exchange ideas and to share knowledge of merchandising, office management, corporation financing, salesmanship, and advertising. "With the growth of the league," observed one black magazine writer, "ignorance and narrow-mindedness are disappearing." By 1919, black Virginians had three insurance companies, nine banks, and five building and loan associations capitalized at a total of $710,000 and gross resources of $407,487.

Black enterprise received extensive support from a black banking system which developed out of the secret societies of slave days. These mutual aid societies also formed the foundation for the life insurance business which would become the largest, longest sustained business conducted by blacks in the United States.

Dating back to the eighteenth century, benevolent societies provided for members in illness and in death from a treasury supported by an initiation fee and small periodic payments from each member. Like the tribal systems of Africa, these societies served as centers for social activities and religious worship. In the event of illness members were provided stipends; in death

After the Civil War, the Freedmen's Bureau opened schools for black children in Virginia. These schools met in black churches and homes, despite difficulties in obtaining adequate teachers and books. Courtesy, Valentine Museum

Virginia Union University developed from the Richmond Theological Seminary School for Freedmen, founded in 1865. Incorporated as the Richmond Institute in 1876, the school was moved from Lumpkin's slave jail to the Union Hotel, a former military hospital, in 1870. Soon after its merger with the Wayland Academy of Washington, D.C., construction was begun on Kingsley Hall, shown here. The building is still used by the university as a dormitory. Courtesy, Library of Congress

they were afforded decent, and sometimes lavish, burials. By the time of emancipation, more than 30 such orders existed in Richmond alone.

In the late 1800s, when a number of publications proclaiming blacks to be poor insurance risks caused several white insurance companies to cancel policies held by blacks, these mutual aid societies expanded their insurance offerings. Through this business many organizations amassed large sums of money which they reinvested in land and buildings. As the orders grew, they developed various commercial enterprises and subsidiaries. The Grand Fountain of the United Order of True Reformers that was organized in Richmond in 1883 eventually counted a bank, a weekly newspaper, a retirement home, a building and loan association, and a real estate agency among its subsidiaries.

Of the commercial enterprises in which these secret orders engaged, banking was the most significant. Early in the nineteenth century, society leaders loaned not only their own money, but also the savings entrusted to them by others. Military savings banks established during the Civil War offered blacks their first experience as a group with formal banking practices. After the war the Freedmen's Bank provided banking services to the black community, but its collapse in 1873 left blacks distrustful of banks.

As the black economy expanded in the 1880s, blacks realized the need for credit. Unable to secure loans from most white banks, they sought backing from their mutual aid organizations. Banks became a logical outgrowth for societies seeking investment opportunities. One of the first black banks was the Savings Bank of

Above: The Lancasterian School, based on the educational concepts of English Quaker Joseph Lancaster, opened in Richmond in April 1816. The school operated with only one teacher; older pupils assisted the younger ones. Underwritten by both public and private endowments, the school opened at its permanent site, Marshall Street near Fifteenth, in 1817. In 1871, after public education was established in Richmond, the building became the Valley School for Negroes. Courtesy, Valentine Museum

Facing page: Chartered as a normal and agricultural school, the Hampton Institute, in Hampton, Virginia, was among the first colleges for blacks. Courtesy, Virginia State Library

According to the 1900 Richmond city directory, there were two black-owned drugstores in the city that year. They were the Duval Street Pharmacy and the Thompson and Benson Pharmacy. In 1901 the directory listed George A. Thompson and John M. Benson as the proprietors of both stores. It is not known which of the two stores is depicted here, but it is probably the latter. Courtesy, Library of Congress

the Grand Fountain United Order of True Reformers, established in Richmond in 1887.

Once black banks opened their doors, aspiring entrepreneurs spurned by white banks had a new source of credit. Black banks would be the wellspring for economic development within the community. While one function of white banks was to boost circulation of money, black banks were inaugurated mainly to provide financial services to the black community and to serve as a depository for its money. By encouraging and assisting black entrepreneurs, banks inspired new confidence and spawned a variety of enterprises. By the early 1900s, Richmond, with its four black banks, was a major center of finance for black Virginians. The St. Luke Penny Savings Bank, chartered in 1901 under the leadership of Maggie L. Walker, still exists as the Consolidated Bank and Trust Company, the oldest black-owned and -operated bank in the country today.

By the 1920s, hotels, restaurants, bakeries, barbershops, and undertaking firms were common in the black marketplace. And black

commercial enterprise had expanded into entertainment, newspapers, real estate, savings and loans, clothing, and confectionery establishments. These began to comprise significant segments of black commercial activity. In 1927 more than 70,000 black businesses across the country did a volume business of half a million dollars. Richmond was the self-proclaimed "Negro Business Capital of America"—although Atlanta and Durham, North Carolina, made the identical claim—leading the country in the number of black cooperative enterprises.

Blacks enjoyed the pleasures of success. Still excluded from white hotels and resorts, they patronized establishments run for and by blacks. The Rappahannock Hotel and the McGuire Hotel in Fredericksburg were at one time the largest black hotels in the state. And the Bay Shore Hotel near Fort Monroe, with its piazzas, pavilion, and pier, gained national acclaim, drawing patrons from as far away as Indiana, Alabama, and Georgia.

As the century wore on, the legal plight of blacks gradually eased. Although racism persisted, discrimination with legal sanction was on its way out. In 1929, two years after the U.S. Supreme Court ruled that residential segregation ordinances were unconstitutional, Richmond's city council voted to enforce segregation. Yet the U.S. District Court and the U.S. Circuit Court of Appeals each ruled against the measure. Twice the city sought a reversal by the U.S. Supreme Court; twice it was denied.

The black vote strengthened in 1931 when the Virginia Supreme Court of Appeals clamped down on the practice of purposely confounding prospective registrants, requiring electoral officials to be more conscientious in their choices of questions regarding the state constitution. By 1936, the greatest number of blacks since Reconstruction voted in state elections.

Although most white-owned businesses still hired primarily whites, blacks were no longer excluded from municipal jobs. In 1937 the city of Richmond listed 281 black employees on its payroll. In 1941 a federal requirement directed that "all contractors getting defense contracts" could not discriminate against anyone on the basis of race, creed, color, or nationality.

In 1940 Virginia ranked eighth in the United States in black population and third in the number of black businesses. While most black-owned retail businesses were confined to a half-dozen major categories—predominantly restaurants and general merchandise stores—there were nearly 1,000 black-owned stores in Virginia by 1930. By 1938, net sales of black retail businesses amounted to more than $5 million.

Black-operated beauty parlors were the state's fastest-growing business, numbering 300 in 1940. Restaurants were still a major factor in black economy across the state; nearly every town had at least one. Meanwhile, black areas in cities often had two or three for every other kind of business.

More than three dozen black newspapers had been established. The white journalistic community acknowledged the competition by initiating "special colored editions" distributed in black areas.

By the time Chief Justice Earl Warren delivered the Supreme Court's unanimous opinion in 1954 that segregation in public schools was unconstitutional, the era of "Jim Crow" was drawing to a close. Segregation in housing was no longer legal. In the 1960s, laws would be passed to phase out legal discrimination on every level. Ironically, integration would weaken the black business structure that had evolved out of necessity during the years of segregation. As blacks moved into the mainstream, racial loyalty to enterprises owned and operated by blacks diminished. The lines dividing black and white commerce gradually blurred, and Virginia's dual economy was obliterated.

Virginia native Booker T. Washington (1856-1915) conceived the National Negro Business League. A chapter opened in Virginia in 1913. From Cirker, Dictionary of American Portraits, *Dover, 1967*

Consolidated Bank and Trust Company, formerly the St. Luke Penny Savings Bank, was founded by Maggie L. Walker in November 1903. It is the nation's oldest black-owned bank. Located at 329 North First Street, the bank building was demolished in 1974 and replaced by a more modern structure. Courtesy, Valentine Museum

Maggie Lena Walker

... in twenty-five years, a small spiritless company of men and women is converted into a compact army; a dilapidated dwelling house is replaced by a magnificent office building filled with earnest and zealous workers ... Where once stood a residence, now stands a bank, and the once empty treasury, like the widow's oil, is being constantly increased. The once unknown school teacher becomes a national figure, and your Organization is favorably spoken of from East to West ...

—Reverend T.J. King, then pastor of Fifth Street Baptist Church in Richmond, at a Testimonial of Love in honor of Maggie L. Walker, November 30, 1924

Maggie L. Walker distinguished herself not only in Richmond's black community as a leader of remarkable business acumen, but also in the national business arena as the country's first black bank president and the first woman to hold such a position. As leader of the Independent Order of St. Luke, the founding organization of the first black bank in the nation, Walker transformed the order from an indebted fraternal society careening toward financial disaster into a thriving organization with numerous black-run subsidiaries. By the time of her death in 1935, Walker had emerged as one of this century's great black leaders.

Reputedly the illegitimate issue of a white abolitionist writer and a cook in the household of Union spy Elizabeth Van Lew, Maggie Lena Mitchell was pressed into work at an early age, helping her mother take in laundry to support the family after her stepfather was found murdered. Although her natural father wanted to send her to boarding school in Baltimore, Maggie stayed at home and attended Richmond Colored High and Normal School.

At the age of 14, Maggie joined the Independent Order of St. Luke. She rose quickly through the society's ranks, holding a variety of positions throughout her teen years. After graduating from high school in 1883, she worked as an insurance agent for the Women's Union and attended night classes to learn bookkeeping before returning to her alma mater as a teacher. Three years later she married Armistead Walker, Jr., the son of a locally respected building contractor, and left teaching to raise her family.

Maintaining her commitment to the Independent Order of St. Luke, Walker occupied every office in the organization. As national deputy, she formed councils throughout Virginia and West Virginia; she called for the formation of a juvenile branch of the Independent Order of St. Luke, a division which would grow to a membership of 20,000 during her lifetime; and she oversaw the growth of the society into a vibrant organ which provided revenues, cared for the sick, and buried the dead.

But as the order expanded, its assets diminished and membership flagged. When the society's secretary-treasurer resigned in 1899, the 1,080-member order had only $31.60 in the treasury and $400 in unpaid bills. Walker stepped into the position and assumed the burden of reversing the downward spiral. In March 1902, under her leadership, the *St. Luke Herald* began a publishing career that 25 years later would be acclaimed as one of the best association newspapers in the country. In November 1903 she created the St. Luke's Penny Savings Bank, which would eventually grow into Consolidated Bank and Trust Company, the nation's oldest black-owned bank. As president of the bank Walker customarily stood near the front doors,

welcoming customers. By 1927, membership in the order had grown to 100,000 and assets reached nearly $400,000.

Walker worked her financial miracle despite a series of personal tragedies. The second of her three sons died in infancy. A crippling fall in her late 30s eventually forced her into a wheelchair. One of her sons mortally wounded her husband, mistaking him for a prowler; eight years later that son died. Yet Walker steadfastly continued her life's work.

In addition to her service through the order, Walker made numerous contributions to the development of the black community. She raised money for humanitarian endeavors such as the creation of a school for delinquent girls near Richmond, a nursing home, and a community center. She also served as president of the Virginia NAACP.

In 1912 Walker formed the Council of Colored Women to raise money for various black-promoted organizations. She was instrumental in establishing a tuberculosis sanitarium for blacks at Burkeville and in providing support for the Colored Industrial School at Peaks. By 1927, the club had grown to nearly 1,000 members and had contributed more than $36,000 to black causes.

Until her death in 1935, Walker worked diligently. She had dedicated her life to furthering the progress of the black community. In recognition of her efforts, a Richmond high school was named for her and her home has become a National Historic Landmark.

...she, by whose energy and tireless efforts most of this has been accomplished, may smilingly exclaim, "These are my jewels," and rejoice that she heard and answered the call.

—Reverend T. J. King.

Maggie Lena Walker. Courtesy, Valentine Museum

Even the Great Depression did not halt the growth of the tobacco industry in Richmond. Pictured here is "Tobacco Row" on Cary Street near Twentieth. Courtesy, Dementi-Foster Studios

ROARING TWENTIES, WHISPERING THIRTIES

◆

On the heels of World War I, America entered an age of peace and prosperity. It was the decade of good times, when "flappers," hounded by "parlor snakes," went to "speakeasies." It was a decade of conspicuous consumption, when grocers stocked caviar and pate de foie gras, when millions of Americans bought their first autos, stoves, refrigerators, and radios. Buoyed by unprecedented optimism, the economy rode a seemingly endless wave of euphoria. Stock market speculation became a national obsession; the average prices of common stock doubled. Hints of imminent economic disaster were drowned in the boisterous tide of the decade.

Along with the nation, Virginia roared with the twenties. Bridge parties, suspended during the war, were all the rage. Even the slightest occasion was an excuse for a party for which revelers donned togas, medieval garb, or other thematic costumes. Country clubs were on the rise, and in the horse country of Albemarle County hunt clubs were the choice of the gentry.

Shocked by corsetless females, racy theatrical performances, and moonshine liquor, ministers railed from pulpits about loose practices of the day. Meanwhile, many of the clergy joined their flocks in clubs like the Rotary and Kiwanis,

discarding their conservative attire for stylish business suits.

While the popular passions pandered to indulgence, Virginia's strict regimen of fiscal conservatism and efficient management of public funds stood the state in good stead. With his "pay-as-you-go" system of highway building and a reorganized tax system, Governor Harry Flood Byrd was building a surplus in the state coffers. Virginia's per capita wealth was the greatest of the Southern states. Her percentage of bank suspensions was among the lowest in the nation, while her automobile population and wholesale and retail trade volumes placed her in the top half of the 48 states. While 47 percent of Americans owned their homes, 51 percent of Virginia residents owned theirs. Between 1925 and 1929 Virginians enjoyed sizable increases in wages and salaries as industrial output rose approximately 50 percent.

Where the Civil War had devastated Virginia's economy, World War I had stimulated it. When the United States entered the war, the Hampton Roads area blossomed into one of the country's largest centers for shipping and shipbuilding. It was the site of the headquarters for the Atlantic Fleet as well as of the largest

Black soldiers form up ranks at Camp Lee during World War I. Courtesy, Virginia State Library

army supply base in the country. With a superior railroad system linking it to the rest of America, Hampton Roads served as a conduit for war materials, food, and soldiers to Europe.

The war-induced prosperity spread throughout the state. Virginians shipped thousands of tons of produce, tobacco, petroleum products, and seafood to other American ports. Mines spewed out coal as Pocahontas coal became the preferred fuel for steam-powered engines. Railroads upgraded their track to handle the inflated exports of the Hampton Roads ports. Munitions plants at Hopewell and at Penniman on the York River offered employment to thousands of Virginians, as did Newport News Shipbuilding and Dry Dock Company, which produced merchant and naval ships to transport American soldiers and supplies overseas. Camp Lee, with its facilities for 45,000 men, greatly bolstered commerce in Petersburg and Richmond.

Virginia's transition from an agricultural to an industrial economy was not painless, however. Glutted overseas markets pushed down prices, and lower prices shoved thousands of laborers off the farm. Meanwhile, wrenching changes in the tobacco and timber industries knocked out the props of two mainstays of rural and small-town Virginia. Nature also tormented the Virginia farmer in the twenties. A drought in 1922 was so

severe that car traffic ground dirt roads into powdery dust six inches deep. Three successive bad seasons virtually destroyed the apple and peach harvests of the rich Crozet orchard area. Insects, worms, tornadoes, and hail sabotaged Virginia's agricultural recovery. In 1929 gross farm income was 33 percent lower than it had been a decade before. Rural population and the number of farm acres in use declined as farmers looked to the cities for employment.

Meanwhile, as tobacco cooperatives bought out and consolidated smaller factories, the role of the small manufacturer diminished. Even before the war, Southside manufacturers were being eclipsed by the American Tobacco Company and Reynolds Tobacco Company across the border in North Carolina.

For more than 200 years, Virginians had eschewed the state's vast timber resources to make tobacco the lynch pin of its economy. Yet the lumber industry enjoyed success on a smaller scale. It is believed that a sawmill was in operation in the Old Dominion as early as 1608, cutting wood for the building of homes. Later, timber from the thick, green forests of the Piedmont would be used in shipbuilding and in the production of naval stores. Not until the late nineteenth century, when Northern forests had been depleted, were Virginia's forests industrially harvested.

In 1909, with a significant number of logging operations and large sawmills, Virginia's total production peaked with 2.1 billion board feet. By 1917, the lushest forests of the Coastal Plain and the Piedmont had been plundered, forcing loggers into the mountain ridges to meet the growing demand. The lumber industry thrived, especially as the number of furniture manufacturers increased. By 1930, Virginia's forests were severely depleted.

Large-scale lumbering operations were no longer possible except in virtually inaccessible areas like the Dismal Swamp. Large mills were replaced with small, mobile circular saws which were looked upon as the scavengers of the industry.

The overcutting that had occurred prior to World War I had a long-lasting effect. Ironically, the Great Depression with its low demand for timber helped save the industry by giving Virginia's forests time to rest and replenish. As demand resumed in the late thirties, Virginia's

forests were green again and mills were back in operation. By 1942, 2,618 sawmills were turning out 1.2 billion board feet of lumber.

The abundance of Virginia's forestry resources was instrumental in creating what would become another major industry. As the tobacco industry faded, a handful of tobacco growers turned to the furniture industry. In 1902 John D. Bassett gave up tobacco speculating and put his full attention toward making the family sawmill into the Bassett Furniture Company. Four years later Tazewell County native Ancil Davidson Witten and North Carolinian Charles Blackwell Keesee founded the American Furniture Company. By the twenties, these two businesses had spawned six furniture companies, a cotton mill, and two textile and three lumber plants, as well as other smaller industries in the Henry County area.

The Martinsville-Henry County area enjoyed a burst of homegrown entrepreneurial energy the like of which was seen nowhere else in

Munitions plants such as the DuPont Powder Company in Hopewell offered employment to thousands of Virginians during the war. Courtesy, Appomattox Regional Library

At the turn of the century tobacco was still the leading industry in Virginia. As a result of anti-trust litigation, the American Tobacco Company divided into four firms—Liggett & Myers, R.J. Reynolds, P. Lorillard, and American Tobacco—all of which had plants in Richmond. During the Depression, tobacco cooperatives such as R.J. Reynolds and the American Tobacco Company, headquartered in North Carolina, bought out and consolidated smaller factories while maintaining their operations in Richmond. Courtesy, Valentine Museum

the state in the years between the two world wars. Local merchants, hungry for the employment and payrolls that such industry could provide, pledged backing for new companies, such as Hooker-Bassett and Stanley Furniture Company. By the early twenties, approximately 40 percent of Henry County's population was employed in the manufacture of furniture.

It was not long, however, before textiles came to rival furniture for preeminence in manu-

facture. Since the development of the rail system, millions of pounds of cotton rolled through Virginia, bound for the textile mills of the North. But by the early twenties, Virginia was making use of its cotton connection. In 1919 Chadwick-Hoskins Company of Charlotte, North Carolina, purchased the Martinsville Cotton Mills and boosted local employment. In 1925 William L. Pannill founded Pannill Knitting Company to manufacture underwear. By the end of its first

Virginia's lumber production peaked with 2.1 billion board feet in 1909. Twenty years later, the state's forests were severely depleted. Courtesy, Virginia State Library

The abundance of forestry resources in Virginia allowed for the development of furniture production as a leading industry in the state. Virginia's southern Piedmont area is second only to North Carolina in furniture production. Courtesy, Richmond Newspapers, Inc.

fiscal year, Pannill Knitting Company boasted sales of $207,000. All stock was locally held. In time, Pannill gave rise to Sale Knitting Company and Bassett-Walker Knitting Company. In later years the three knit mills would so dominate the production of fleeced knitwear that Martinsville would boast of being the "Sweatshirt Capital of the World." Martinsville was almost unique among Southern mill towns in hosting so many strong, locally owned firms.

Entire communities grew out of some mill operations. Marshall Field & Company purchased 25 separate tracts of land in Henry County to create its Fieldcrest Towel Mill. Fieldale, with its own grocery stores, post office, furniture store, theater, bank, and school, provided Fieldcrest's 300-plus employees with more than the basic necessities. Fieldale had no

charter and no statutes, no taxes except county property taxes, and no governing body; but when amenities like street repair or lighting were necessary Fieldcrest provided them. Like the 100-house village of Stanleytown, created by Stanley Furniture Company, Fieldale provided a convenient, self-contained residential community for its employees.

Thirty-five miles to the east, Danville, a textile center since the 1880s, had built a city around its Dan River Mills. At the turn of the century, 20 or more tobacco factories provided employment to its citizens. Dan River Flour Mills ground 500 barrels a day by 1913. In the twenties Danville buzzed with the construction of a municipal building, a Masonic Temple, a hotel, and a theater. In Roanoke to the north, textiles were affording similar security; the Viscose

Right: Between the two world wars, the Martinsville-Henry County area enjoyed homegrown entrepreneurial energy in the furniture industry. Local merchants pledged backing for new companies. The Lester Brothers plant, located in Martinsville, began its operations at this time. Courtesy, Richmond Newspapers, Inc.

Below: In 1906 Ancil D. Witten and Charles B. Keesee founded the American Furniture Company in the Henry County area. The American Furniture Company and other furniture plants in and around Martinsville made the city one of the largest furniture-producing centers in the world. By the early 1920s nearly 40 percent of the Martinsville-Henry County population was employed in this industry. Courtesy, Richmond Newspapers, Inc.

Danville, Virginia, a textile center since the 1880s, built a city around its Dan River Mills. This aerial view shows some of the mill buildings in the center and background. In 1963 the Danville plant employed about 9,800 workers, including 1,100 blacks. Courtesy, Richmond Newspapers, Inc.

Corporation, established in 1917, employed 70 more people at its "silk mill."

The revision of the Virginia tax structure under Byrd attracted new industries to the state. In fiscal year 1927, Virginia surpassed all other states in industrial development with an infusion into the state's capital of $265 million. Textile and chemical producers came in droves, attracted by the abundant water supply, labor supply, and good transportation system. Tubize-Chatillon Corporation opened a rayon plant at Hopewell, and Industrial Rayon Corporation opened at Covington. After the arrival of the E. I. du Pont de Nemours Company in 1929, with its rayon plant in the suburbs of Richmond and another in Waynesboro, Virginia became the leading state in the nation in the manufacture of artificial silk yarn. By 1930, Virginia was responsible for one-third of the country's—or, one-ninth of the world's—rayon production.

When the Depression hit, every industry would feel its effects—all except for one: bootlegging. Virginia's outspoken Anti-Saloon League began campaigning against the demon rum as early as 1901. When the league joined forces with the Women's Christian Temperance

Union in their fight to control the sale and consumption of liquor, it convinced the General Assembly to tighten alcohol restrictions. As a result more than 500 saloons across the state closed.

By 1916, Virginia's "drys" had gained enough sway to institute statewide prohibition—three years before the Eighteenth Amendment prohibited the manufacture, sale, or transportation of liquor throughout the country. When nationwide prohibition nullified Virginia's One Quart Law (allowing residents to buy from out-of-state one quart of liquor, a gallon of wine, or three gallons of beer), bootlegging became big business.

Bootlegging was a "social crime" and a profitable one at that. Aspiring purveyors could buy a half-gallon of moonshine for three dollars or less and sell it for 20 cents per two-ounce shot, making more than 100 percent profit on the deal. Not everyone made or sold liquor, but nearly everyone bought it. Country club conversations often centered around how to contact one's bootlegger. Poor brewing or distilling techniques caused explosions, and loud booms commonly could be traced to closets or basements in the most respectable homes. Despite strong "dry" sentiment across the Old Dominion, many leading citizens had few inhibitions about violating the prohibition law.

Bootlegging knew no class distinctions. From the poorest to the wealthiest, Virginians illegally bought liquor. During the twenties, the "blind tiger"—where liquor could be purchased without seeing the seller—came into being. Speakeasies, which filled the function of saloons as well as many restaurants, were popular meeting places. Locked doors with peepholes replaced the swinging doors of saloons.

Business was conducted in backrooms, basements, or first-floor flats. In Richmond the heart of the bootlegging district was conveniently located several blocks west of its business district. Folks in Alexandria reportedly floated kegs of liquor in the river and tethered them to the shore. The Wickersham Commission reported that 99 percent of Franklin County was connected, directly or indirectly, with the illegal manufacture or distribution of "white mule." Jewelers and department stores all over the state featured stylish hip-flasks for personal consumption.

By the mid-1920s, raids on suppliers were routine. These were not all good-natured affairs. In many cases, especially in moonshine country, gunplay and bloodshed often accompanied the seizure of mountain stills. Headlines in the Charlottesville *Progress* told of "Another Killing in the Foothills of the Blue Ridge." Others were more sporting: "Over 29 Gallons of Christmas Cheer Poured Into Sewer At Police Station." In less volatile areas of the state, police bartered confiscated liquor on the sly.

With the Layman Act of 1924, which allowed the most strident measures, including entrapment, in the pursuit of a bootlegging arrest, liquor dealers invented numerous ploys to avoid being caught. One Roanoke purveyor used a trap whereby a mason jar was tilted for

Right: Tobacco is big business in Danville, Virginia. This redrying plant next to the Dan River was just one of 20 plants providing employment in the 1950s. Courtesy, Richmond Newspapers, Inc.

Left: Bootlegging was all the rage in Virginia and elsewhere during Prohibition. Stills such as the one shown here began operating even in the most respectable places. Courtesy, Virginia State Library

emptying, then flushed with a stream of water. Some bootleggers outfitted their cars' exhaust pipes with contraptions that emitted thick smoke to blind pursuing officers.

Throughout Prohibition the courts were clogged with dry law violations. Penalties for bootlegging involved a jail sentence and a fine. Those found guilty were barely locked up before a spouse or a cohort was on hand to post bond.

After 17 years of Prohibition, Virginians joined the national tide for repeal. In a dual referendum in 1933, almost twice as many voted for repeal of both federal and state prohibition laws as those who cast their votes in favor of retaining them. Although illicit liquor trafficking did not cease completely, related killings and arrests dropped off significantly.

When the stock market crashed in 1929, Virginians thought it was a temporary setback. As the resulting depression seared America's economic landscape, Virginia staved off its harshest effects for two years. Buffeted by the financial stability of the Byrd Administration as well as by recent industrial development, Virginia rested on sturdy ground when the economy plunged.

The stock market crash failed to dampen Virginia optimism. With their own peculiar brand of hubris, Virginians considered themselves exempt from doom. Before leaving office Governor Byrd commented, "The close of the year 1929 sees Virginia facing a bright future. Never, probably in the long history of the Old Dominion has she faced a destiny more filled with promise." In an article entitled "A Billion Dollar Manufacturing State by 1930," economist James E. Ward wrote that: "this State is even now entering into an expansion of industrial activities on a scale never before equalled in its history."

As year-end statistics rolled in it looked as if the optimists might be right: Norfolk & Western announced 1929 to be its best year since 1926, with a net income of $11,059,571 over 1928. Roanoke's cost of living was the lowest in two years. Norfolk retail merchants noted that Christmas sales were up from the preceding year,

and a group of Richmond industrialists announced construction plans to the tune of $15 million for the coming year. But the national picture was ominous. Steel operations were running at 50 percent capacity; automobiles were being stockpiled; freight tonnages were sliding; and commercial failures were rampant.

The nation's somber mood was reflected in everything from farm prices to fashions. Ballroom dancing replaced the wilder dances of the Roaring Twenties. Stutz Bearcats and cries of "whoopee" died out. Gloom soon gave way to desperation. Banks closed. Bread lines grew longer, and able-bodied men sold apples on the street. It was an oft-repeated joke that when someone registered at a hotel, the clerk wryly asked, "Do you want the room for sleeping or for jumping?"

With low-bonded indebtedness and low taxes, Virginia was better equipped to face the Depression than other states. State finances were not overextended and the industrial expansion of the twenties provided a cushion. With major industries of high demand and necessity—tobacco and textiles—Virginia was less vulnerable to depression. An income well-balanced between agriculture, manufacturing, and trade was as hearty a defense as state officials could hope for.

Although it became apparent that the Depression was no passing phase in the economic cycle, Virginia weathered its earliest days admirably. Her industries were indispensable to the consumer: food, clothing, and cigarettes. (People didn't stop smoking; they simply bought cheaper brands.) Richmond's well-balanced economy and its stable tobacco industry buoyed that city. Lynchburg's sound banks and construction start-ups fueled her economy. In Norfolk, where the navy spent $20 million a year, conditions were also relatively stable. While banks around the country closed their doors, not one Norfolk bank closed.

A severe nationwide drought in the summer of 1930 seemed to be a harbinger of doom. Virginia's rainfall for the year registered at 60 percent of normal. In the Shenandoah Valley a 42-day dry spell ruined crops. Virginius

Dabney, then correspondent for the *New York Times*, noted: "The usually fertile Shenandoah Valley ... almost looked ... as if Sheridan had just finished his devastating ride through it." Dried-out grazing land in Northern and Southwest Virginia affected the livestock trade. And truck crops in the Tidewater were choked as well. The tobacco crop was the meagerest since 1876. Farmers feared the lowest crop production since the earliest figures recorded in 1860.

Yet Virginia's agriculture, like her industry, was better prepared to meet the Depression than other states. Crop diversity allowed for a balanced farm income. Proximity to eastern markets gave some stability to prices. With a high percentage of subsistence farmers requiring little or no income to maintain their exiguous existence, a great number of Virginia farmers would be little affected by the consequences of the crash. While farm tenancy posed problems in the tobacco-growing regions of the state, Virginia

had the third-lowest ratio of tenants to farmers in the U.S. Furthermore, the state ranked sixth lowest in farms under mortgage. In fact, as economic conditions worsened, Virginians returned to the soil in great numbers to feed their families. Between 1930 and 1935 the number of farmers rose 16 percent.

As the stock market continued to plunge throughout 1930, manufacturing production nationwide dipped below 1928 levels. Although the lumber and flour milling industries suffered, Virginia remained seemingly aloof from the thunderous disaster. Industrial output dipped from $897 million to $814 million, a modest decline. And while the production value of tobacco declined slightly, the shipbuilding, fertilizer, and chemical industries increased the value of their output in 1930. Although unemployment in the Old Dominion rose to 50,000 that year, the percentage of those out of work was far lower than the national average.

The Norfolk & Western Railroad had a very good year in 1929, despite the national economic picture. Shown here is a passenger train on the main line circa 1930. Courtesy, Virginia State Library

Following the 1920-1921 organization of Virginia farmers into the Virginia Crop Improvement Association, the marketing of certified seed became a problem for the association's 500 members. As a result, the Southern States Cooperative was formed in 1923 to serve the farmers' seed requirements. The cooperative has since grown into one of the largest farm-related operations in the United States. Shown here are the feed mill and grain receiving station at First and Hull streets in Richmond. Photo by John Salmon

By 1931, Virginia began to feel the crushing weight of the Depression. Industrial output plunged 17 percent to $679 million, pushing up unemployment across the state. Even Norfolk, where shipping maintained a steady pace, declared that its rolls had doubled. During the first seven months of the year, unemployment in cities and towns rose 15 percent. The most extreme situations were in industrial centers or in the Southside tobacco region. The cities of Roa-

noke, Richmond, and Petersburg and the counties of Alleghany, Wise, Halifax, and Pulaski took the hardest blows. Half of Halifax's work force was unemployed, and coal production in Wise had dropped to three percent of normal levels, leaving hundreds of coal miners hungry.

Norfolk laid off firefighters, police officers, and garbage collectors. Several teachers were fired; others took salary cuts. A cutback at the Viscose plant in Roanoke affected 4,500 workers. In some areas college graduates were reduced to begging on the streets. Yet Virginia's 19 percent rate paled next to the nation's 30-plus percent.

By the next year, farm prices had dropped to one-half the 1929 figures, and farm cash income was the lowest in 26 years. Wheat sold for 50 cents a bushel, the lowest price in 132 years. Tobacco prices were hacked to $6.63 per 100 pounds, the lowest price since 1920. Prices were so low that farmers could not even meet production costs much less make a profit. Rather than market their crops at such a loss, farmers let them rot.

The state surplus, earmarked for new public buildings, went to meet immediate expenses. In Richmond the Social Service Bureau provided relief to 926 families. Three thousand Hopewell residents ate from a public dispensary. School children in the mountain

Left: President Franklin Delano Roosevelt revived the troubled American economy during the Great Depression by rushing through Congress a number of fiscal and social reform measures and setting up agencies to tackle the reorganization of industry and agriculture. From Cirker, Dictionary of American Portraits, Dover, 1967

Below: The West Virginia Pulp and Paper Company, located in Covington, is shown here. Courtesy, Virginia State Library

regions were fed at soup kitchens, and striking mill employees in Danville were near starvation.

Responding to cries of desperation, Governor John Garland Pollard cut state expenditures, which included a 10 percent reduction in his salary. The General Assembly approved a diversion of highway funds to schools and transferred the burden of road repairs to county governments. As a result of the latter, many unemployed Virginians were soon back at work repairing secondary roads. As the relief rolls grew fatter and tax collections shrank, Virginia looked to the federal government for help.

With Franklin Delano Roosevelt's inauguration the country had a New Deal. FDR's Alphabet Soup—which included the AAA, the FCA, the REA, the CCC, the PWA, the WPA, the FERA, and the NRA—fed the nation's hungry, including a quarter million Virginians.

Virginia farmers benefited greatly from the programs. Under the Agricultural Adjustment Administration (AAA), farmers were given acreage allotments and benefit payments in exchange for reduced crop production. By the end of its first year, the AAA had proven its success. With production down 13 million pounds, tobacco had doubled in price. Across the board, crop values, prices, and farm cash income had registered remarkable gains. Also of benefit to the farmer were the Farm Credit Administration (FCA), which coordinated all farm credit activities, and the Rural Electrification Administration (REA). The FCA reduced the number of foreclosures and helped stabilize farm income, while the REA provided electric power to small towns and family farms.

The Civilian Conservation Corps (CCC) and the Works Progress Administration (WPA) provided thousands of Virginians with employment. The Public Works Administration (PWA) was a major supplier of funds for relief in Virginia, providing millions of dollars for various projects, including construction of navy vessels, harbor improvements in Newport News, a hydroelectric plant for Danville, a sewer complex in Arlington, a public housing project in Rich-

mond, and waterworks for Lynchburg. In its first year of operation, the PWA approved $90 million worth of projects in Virginia.

The National Recovery Administration (NRA) aided industrial recovery by allowing businesses to administer their affairs with limited governmental supervision. Wage and hour standards were instituted and, in exchange for their acceptance, antitrust laws were suspended. Thousands of Virginia workers received wage raises, and State Drive Chairman Mason Manghum estimated that the NRA was responsible for the rehiring of 10,000 Virginians in its first three months.

By 1934, however, the NRA had outlived its usefulness. Consumers, industry, and labor decried the resulting high prices and the reluctance of business to recognize labor. Wage and hour violations were numerous; many employers had subscribed to the NRA's policies on paper but not in spirit. The NRA's code deficiencies as well as its lack of enforcement power laid the groundwork for its demise. In 1935 the United States Supreme Court declared the NRA and its wage fixing unconstitutional.

In Virginia the Federal Emergency Relief Administration (FERA) carried the brunt of relief appropriations, doling out more than $26 million around the state, primarily for school improvements, malaria control, airport projects, parks, and streets. While FDR's New Deal provided greatly needed relief, Virginia's relief rolls were smaller than those of almost any other state.

In 1933 the number of Virginians on relief declined noticeably: on a national unemployment census, Virginia showed the second lowest percentage in the country of people on relief. Employment across the state was up 20 to 25 percent. The value of manufacturing output climbed to $616 million, increasing the Old Dominion's percentage of U.S. manufacturing

With the opening of the E.I. du Pont de Nemours Company in Ampthill in 1929, Virginia became the leading state in the manufacture of artificial silk yarn. A year later, Virginia was responsible for one-third of the nation's rayon production. This aerial view shows the plant at Bellwood just south of Richmond. Courtesy, Richmond Newspapers, Inc.

production from 1.06 percent in 1929 to 1.62 percent. By 1935, Virginians had put their starving years behind them.

Virginia's economy was in many ways better than it had been before the Depression. In 1937 all manufacturing indices of 1929 had been surpassed. Virginia led the nation in increased value of industrial products. The value of manufactured goods in Virginia had increased 31 percent, while their value nationwide had decreased 11 percent over the same period. The state's per capita wealth increased 4 percent during that time, while the country's declined 20 percent. Wages and salaries were higher and more people were employed.

In 1939 the Census of Manufactures showed that Virginia was responsible for one-quarter of the nation's production of rayon yarn, nylon, and cellophane. Coal production reached a decade high with 13.2 million short tons. Tobacco, paper, and pulp products, furniture and metal machinery manufacturing, and automobile and railroad repair work were making similarly significant strides.

Virginia had weathered the painful years and emerged with a sizable surplus in its general fund and the lowest state and local debt per capita of any state in the country. A stable economy, plentiful work force, and good transportation system made the state attractive to new industry. Its favorable tax system, relatively low wage rates, plentiful raw materials, and good climate enticed businesses to settle in the state. Virginia was on the verge of its second industrial boom.

Between 1935 and 1940, 510 new manufacturing plants began operations in the state. A $500,000 silk printing and dyeing plant went up in Richmond; a $1 million insulation-board plant appeared in Jarratt; Franklin became home to a $2.5 million pulp and paper plant; and Pearisburg in Giles County was selected as the site for the $10 million American Cellulose and Chemical Company plant.

With industrial output up 44 percent over 1929 levels, Richmond was now the fastest growing industrial center in the country. Unlike most other industrial centers, Richmond had weathered the Depression well. The expansion of the tobacco industry buffeted the city from the harshest effects, as did the arrival of new businesses in the twenties.

The twenties had brought a flurry of business to Richmond. Southern States Cooperative, currently one of the largest owners and operators of farm-related industries, located its headquarters in Richmond. Harry Marks Clothing Company, later Friedman-Marks Clothing Company, began manufacturing its garments in the city in 1925. Two years later Southern Biscuit Company came to town. By the onset of the Depression, the E.I. du Pont de Nemours Company had opened a huge rayon yarn plant on the city's outskirts and Reynolds Metals Company acquired the Lehmaier, Schwartz & Company foil works.

Richmond became an important retail center. Ranking seventh in the South in retail sales in 1939, the city was responsible for 20 percent of Virginia's retail sales. The financial district grew as well. The 1929 Economic Census notes that 24 financial institutions and 21 insurance companies had made the city their headquarters.

Tobacco manufacturing boomed. The American Tobacco Company manufactured 100 million cigarettes a day at its two plants. Leggett and Myers and Larus and Brother expanded their operations. Philip Morris & Company, a firm of British origin, began manufacturing cigarettes in Richmond in 1929. By 1940, a third of all U.S.-made cigarettes were produced in the city.

Served by six railroads, two steamship lines, three inner-city transport lines and, after 1927, a major airport, Richmond was more than hospitable to business. In a decade the volume of Richmond's industrial output had increased 59 percent. The city had reestablished its position at the forefront of the nation's commercial development, ranking second among the country's 19 major industrial centers.

Except in isolated pockets, such as the homegrown furniture and textiles firms in Martinsville, Virginia did not owe its progress to entrepreneurial genius. The strength of the state's economy rested in its conservative governmental policies, low-cost labor, weak labor unions, low taxes—in sum, its favorable business climate. Virginians could take much comfort from their superior economic performance. But there were hidden weaknesses in the state's economic growth.

To an unusual degree Virginia's was a branch-plant economy; the important decisions concerning hirings, firings, expansions, and shutdowns were made in the centers of Northern capitalism. Virginia's economic growth also was tied to the unprecedented growth in the federal government. Northern Virginia became the bedroom community for federal employees in Washington; Hampton Roads owed its growth far more to military mobilization than to its natural advantages as a commercial center. Even so, while the rest of the nation was clawing its way out of the Depression, it was hard to argue with prosperity.

Inside the Philip Morris plant on "Tobacco Row," men operated the machines that loaded cigarettes into packs, which women then sorted into cartons. With machines to speed the work, some plants could turn out millions of cigarettes a day. Courtesy, Dementi-Foster Studios

Newport News grew from a small fishing
village to an industrial center with the
founding of Newport News Shipbuilding
and Dry Dock Company by Collis P.
Huntington. The company employed
nearly 5,000 workers. By the 1890s it
began building ships for the United States
Navy. This 1925 photograph shows the
USS Virginia under construction. Courtesy, Valentine Museum

MILITARY BUILDUP AT HAMPTON ROADS

◆

Since the settlers arrived in Jamestown in 1607, war has been the single most influential factor in the development of Hampton Roads. With each successive altercation, population and commerce jumped, pumped up by seamen, soldiers, dock laborers, and shipbuilders. Today Hampton Roads is Virginia's second largest population center, home to one of the nation's finest ports, a vigorous shipbuilding industry, and a vast military establishment.

The stretch of water at the confluence of the James River and the Chesapeake Bay is one of the finest natural harbors in the world. Not only does it offer superb protection from storms, it also permits access by ships with 45-foot drafts—all but the largest cargo carriers and oil tankers. By the mid-eighteenth century, ports had been established in Hampton on the peninsula and Norfolk on the south channel. Hampton Roads was thick with commerce during the Revolutionary War when Virginia's little navy patrolled its waters.

The ports of Hampton Roads survived the Revolution, only to fall subject to future battles. The War of 1812 had a shattering effect as the British blockade and the U.S. embargo in 1813 brought trade to a standstill. Counteracting the negative effects of the war, the federal government strengthened fortifications and expanded the Gosport Navy Yard in Norfolk for the construction of heavy war vessels.

By the mid-nineteenth century, Hampton Roads had gained prominence as a major East Coast port. With the development of Virginia's rail network, produce from all over the state, as well as from North Carolina, came to Hampton Roads for export. Local boat builders averaged 1,000 tons of shipping a year. And the U.S. Navy continued to pump money into the area, spending an estimated $1 million a year on the navy yard alone.

The Civil War interrupted the region's growth. Federal troops burned the Gosport Navy Yard—by then the largest in the nation—before surrendering it to the Confederate states in 1861. The next year, evacuating Confederate soldiers burned it again. The ironclads *Virginia* and *Monitor* battled for control of Hampton Roads. Although the duel was a tactical draw, the *Virginia* withdrew, leaving the Northern fleet in control. Shut off from trade by the Northern blockade, commerce withered. By the war's end, Norfolk's docks, once the center of commercial activity, were frighteningly quiet.

RULES

For the Regulation of the Navy-Yard at Gosport.

IT being essential to the Public Interest, that the Officers, Workmen, and others employed in the Service of the United States, at the NAVY-YARD at GOSPORT, should conduct themselves with Order and Regularity in the execution of their several Duties, whereby the same may be carried on with Economy and Dispatch.—I DO HEREBY ORDER AND DIRECT, That all Officers, Workmen, and others of every denomination whatsoever, employed therein, do conform themselves to the following REGULATIONS as a GENERAL RULE for their conduct.

OFFICERS.

Each Officer will receive from the Constructor, such Orders and Instructions, from time to time, as may be judged best for the Public Service, to which he must undeviatingly adhere: He will have such persons placed under his directions as may be deemed necessary; he will direct them in the performance of such parts of the works as he may entrusted with, which it will be his duty to forward by all the means in his power, and see that the same be properly and efficiently executed, at the smallest expence possible.

He will discourage those placed under his direction, from quarrelling, committing excesses of any kind, or absenting themselves from work. He will use his utmost endeavors to protect all public property placed under his charge, or otherwise disposed. It is expected, that he shall attend to the business of the Navy Yard in preference to any other whatever, and shall on no account absent himself therefrom, without leave, except in case of sickness, or other unavoidable cause. He will be careful to check each person under his direction, for the time he may be absent from his work; and observe those who shew an idle disposition; and in all cases to report transgressors.

ARTIFICERS, LABOURERS, &c. &c.

All persons on being entered in the Navy-Yard, will report their real Names to the Constructor and Clerk, that they may be inserted in the roll.

Such Wages will be allowed to each Workman or other person, as the Constructor may judge his qualifications entitle him to receive, which shall be paid on the Saturday of each week, (or as soon after as can be done) to himself, or the person who may be qualified to receive the same, as circumstances may be.

To each Workman who may be sent on board any ship or vessel to work, the same lying below Fort Norfolk, one quarter of a dollar per day, will be allowed him in addition to his Wages at the Yard; to those who may work on board any ship or vessel above that place, the same wages will be paid him, as if he had actually worked in the yard, and no more.

As soon as possible after his name has been entered on the roll, he will be placed under the direction of a Quarterman, or other Officer, as occasion may require, to whom he will apply for instructions respecting his work, &c. and from whose orders he shall in no wise deviate, (unless directed to to do by a Superior Officer) but in all respects he is to execute the same with diligence, care, fidelity, œconomy and dispatch.

The time of Daily Labour will be from Sun-rise until Sun-set: The commencement and termination of which will be noticed by Ringing of the Yard-Bell, as well as at Breakfast and Dinner; for the former three quarters of an Hour in Winter, and one Hour in Summer will be allowed; for the latter, one Hour in Winter and two in Summer: The Winter to be considered from the first of September to the first of May; and the Summer from the first of May to the first of September following. N. B. From Sun-rise to Noon is to be understood as comprising one half a Day's Work; and from Noon to Sun-set the remaining half —and he shall not at any time quit his Work, before the Bell rings for that purpose, without leave, of his Officer, unless compelled thereto by rain or other unavoidable cause.

To perform his work in the best and most expeditious manner, he shall provide himself with such Tools as the officer placed over him may deem requisite for his occupation ;—He shall not make use of Tools belonging to another person, without his leave, neither shall he conceal, injure, nor destroy them.

He shall not loiter at his work, nor set an example of idleness to others by unnecessary conversations or otherways—He shall neither Game, Quarrel, give abusive Language, get Intoxicated, or insult any Person whatsoever within the Yard, nor when absent on Public Duty.

He is not to perform work for individuals during the hours of Work, without leave being first obtained; and it will be expected that he shall not leave his Work to perform Military Duty without leave (except in case of emergency) unless the Fine for absence shall exceed the amount of a Day's Work.

He shall not wilfully Waste, Destroy, nor Embezzle any part of the Public Property, nor suffer others to do it; and it is strictly forbidden to cut up any serviceable Timber, Boards, &c. for Chips—He is not to break the Fence of the Yard, or Enclosures, nor take off any Boards, &c. from the same, nor suffer others to do it, without leave being first obtained from the principal Officer at that time in the Yard.

In case of Fire happening in the Yard, or to any Ship of War, or other Public Vessel lying in the vicinity thereof, it will be required of him to use every endeavour in his power to extinguish the same, and preserve and protect all Public property that may in any wise be endangered thereby—And it is strictly ordered that no Fires shall be kindled in the Yard, but at such places as may be appointed for that purpose.

He will be accountable for such Tools, Implements, &c. belonging to the United States, as he may occasionally be furnished with, and in case they are lost, or wilfully destroyed, the amount of their value will be deducted from his wages.

If any Person finds himself insulted, or personally aggrieved, he is required to make his case known to the Constructor, or in his absence to the Superior Officer, who will take the same into consideration, and afford him such redress as circumstances may dictate.

As it may happen that Workmen and others, whose residence is distant from the Yard, may have occasion to quit their Work on Saturday Afternoons at an early hour, those will have the time noticed, and when the same shall amount to a Days Work, it will be deducted from their wages.

A PRINTED COPY of the preceding "Rules for the Regulation of the NAVY YARD," shall be hung up in the CLERK'S OFFICE, or some other conspicuous place, for the perusal of all Persons concerned; and no plea will be admitted of ignorance of any part thereof.

Given under my hand at the NAVY YARD, Gosport, this   day of   18

JOSIAH FOX, Navy Constructor and Superintendant.

NORFOLK: PRINTED BY WILLETT and O'CONNOR.

Right: These are the earliest extant regulations for the Gosport Navy Yard, circa 1800. Courtesy, Virginia State Library

Below: The Gosport Navy Yard, shown here in a bird's-eye view, was burned twice during the Civil War—once by federal troops and once by evacuating Confederate troops. From Frank Leslie's Pictorial History of the War of 1861-62. Courtesy, Virginia State Library

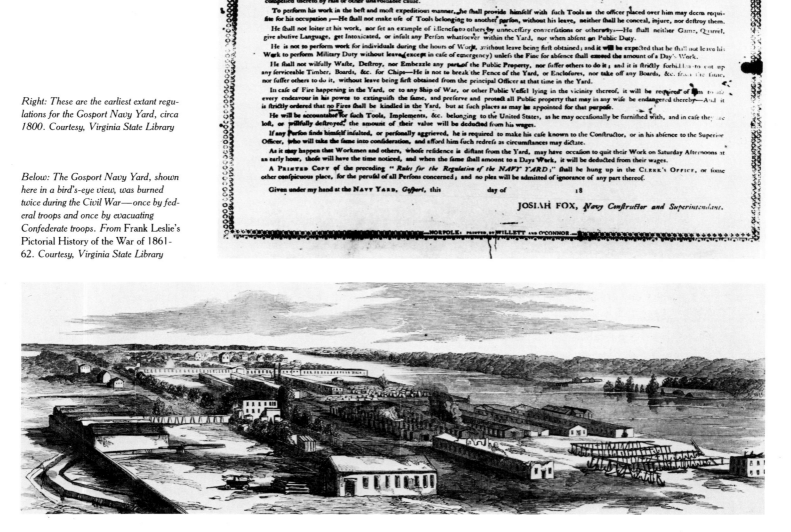

Norfolk was a big cotton port by the mid-1870s. Courtesy, Norfolk Redevelopment and Housing Authority

Despite wartime starvation and suffering, the cities of Hampton Roads revived with a vigor not seen since the days before Jefferson's Embargo of 1807. By the close of Reconstruction, port activity had attracted thousands of tradespeople, shipbuilders, laborers, and others seeking work in port-related jobs. The populations of Norfolk and Portsmouth swelled to two and three times their numbers of a half century earlier.

Shipbuilding became the driving force behind the region's economy, employing some 7,000 workers by the turn of the century. The industry's first boom came with the Spanish-American War as the Gosport Navy Yard and the Newport News Shipbuilding and Dry Dock Company, a private company founded in 1866 by railroad magnate Collis P. Huntington, sped to build the U.S. fleet "Manifest Destiny."

Throughout history, wars shaped the economy of Hampton Roads. Its shipyards would bustle again with the outbreak of hostilities in Korea in 1950. Its naval and military installations would become a gateway to America's involvement in Vietnam. But none of America's military conflicts had quite the effect of the world wars.

With a vast harbor and railroad ties to the interior, Hampton Roads became the focal point of the United States' participation in World War I. The advantages of both ocean and rail traffic made the region the ideal site for the country's largest army supply base and the headquarters of the navy's Atlantic Fleet.

With every available local worker employed in the construction of military installations, agents scoured the nation for laborers. Lured by tales of sky-high wages, employment seekers came from all over the country to cash in on the building craze. "If you see any unbelievably wide-brimmed hat," noted the *Virginian Pilot*, "there is either a Texan or a Kentuckian under it."

Overseas and coastal trade burgeoned. Guns, food, and war materials from around the country funneled through Hampton Roads for export to Europe. To better handle the inflated wartime exports, railroads and port facilities were upgraded and expanded. In 1917, as the United States entered the war, exports from Norfolk and Portsmouth alone totaled nearly 11 million tons.

America looked to the shipyards of Hampton Roads to create the world's best navy. Shipbuilding sparked the local economy, employing thousands in the construction and overhaul of the nation's warships. Between 1917 and 1919, the payroll at Newport News Shipbuilding and

Dry Dock Company rose from 7,600 to 12,500, while employment at the Portsmouth Navy Yard reached 11,000. By 1918, employment at Norfolk Shipbuilding and Dry Dock Company had reached 20 times the level of two years before.

As war vessels, both foreign and domestic, sought its ports for repairs and rest, Hampton Roads thundered with activity. Hundreds of thousands of soldiers and sailors came to the Hampton Roads region during the war. For some it was a way station en route to a European platform. Others brought their families to put down roots. Still others came for a short leave, overtaxing filled-to-capacity housing. As the population ballooned, a housing shortage ensued. Servicemen were hard put to find living space for their families. Workers crowded into vacant rooms. Charges of profiteering were rampant. Finally the government responded with the emergency construction of a handful of residential developments.

To serve the booming war economy, private industry built new plants and expanded old ones. The American Chain Company, the British-American Tobacco Company, and Linde

Air Products began operations in Hampton Roads, as did E.I. du Pont de Nemours and Company, Virginia Coal and Navigation Company, and Standard Oil Company. The Chesapeake and Potomac Telephone Company doubled its exchange, adding 10,000 new phones to accommodate the skyrocketing population.

Just as war had quickened the pulse of the Hampton Roads economy, peace signaled a downturn. Although the volume of exports diminished rapidly, it was still 10 times larger than in 1914. Coal shipments fell, yet millions of tons of the fuel were dumped as waste each month over Hampton Roads' piers. Grain exports flourished and Hampton Roads was on its way to becoming the world's greatest tobacco port. Cotton, flour, starch, lumber, and livestock left the docks, bound for Germany, Italy, Great Britain, and Japan. While exports fell off, imports rose, constituting 15 percent of the port's foreign trade in 1928, compared to 4 percent a decade earlier.

Shipbuilding sustained the sharpest blow. Operating at top speed with 23,000 workers at the war's end, the industry suffered a direct hit. Three years later the Conference for the Limita-

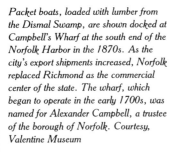

Packet boats, loaded with lumber from the Dismal Swamp, are shown docked at Campbell's Wharf at the south end of the Norfolk Harbor in the 1870s. As the city's export shipments increased, Norfolk replaced Richmond as the commercial center of the state. The wharf, which began to operate in the early 1700s, was named for Alexander Campbell, a trustee of the borough of Norfolk. Courtesy, Valentine Museum

tion of Armaments cut even deeper into the industry, promptly halting tens of millions of dollars worth of work in progress. Employment at the shipyards plunged.

The mere threat of war, however, was enough to reenergize Hampton Roads. In the 1930s President Roosevelt launched a major naval shipbuilding and improvement plan. The Hampton Roads shipyards began to hum again, preparing to rebuild the Pacific Fleet. Under the naval improvement plan, new construction employed 15,000 workers at Norfolk's naval base alone.

By 1940, unemployment in Hampton Roads was only 8.6 percent, significantly lower than Virginia's 9.5 percent rate and way below the country's 14.4 percent rate. The government was the largest employer, followed by retail and wholesale trade and services. Even before the war, with its 400,000 inhabitants accounting for only 15 percent of the state's population, Hampton Roads comprised 22 percent of Virginia's wholesale trade, 21 percent of its retail trade, and 25 percent of its total service receipts for 1940.

As the nation braced for war, the military presence expanded rapidly. The navy outgrew the Norfolk base and spilled east into Princess Anne County and west nearly to Williamsburg. By the war's end, the area's 10 prewar military establishments would number 26, and their personnel would increase seventeenfold.

The government spent more than $267 million constructing nonmanufacturing army and navy establishments and another $107 million on manufacturing plants. As with World War I the building boom of World War II drew thousands of workers from all over the country. This time growth did not stop until the entire Hampton Roads area was converted into a huge construction camp. The Camp Peary project alone brought 10,000 workers to a community whose inhabitants had numbered less than 3,000 before the war.

As war workers and military personnel poured in, the population soared. During the first two years of the war, some 28,000 families

moved to the region; by 1943, the civilian population alone had risen about 40 percent. During the war years the region's share of Virginia's inhabitants increased to 20.6 percent.

The construction boom failed to keep pace with the burgeoning population. People were pushed out into the streets. Rooms were rented in shifts. Landlords split their houses into several units and then divided them again, sometimes forcing several families to share a single bath. With a hospitable spirit some hotels agreed to reserve rooms until evening while servicemen and war workers looked for more permanent dwellings. A war housing program of more than 14,000 new dwellings was little help: 90 percent of the units were snapped up even before completion.

Transportation was so miserably overtaxed that some construction companies built on-site dormitories for their workers. Sailors commonly were seen piling atop streetcars or hanging onto the rear platforms. A local joke referred to a motorman who always succeeded in crowding yet one more on, not realizing that for every new passenger, one was shoved off at the rear.

By 1874 Norfolk ranked third in volume among U.S. cotton exporting ports. Ten years later nearly half a million bales a year passed through the city. This 1923 photograph shows a cotton field at the Robinson Farm in New Kent County, Virginia. Courtesy, Valentine Museum

Facing page: Pictured here is a giant crane in use at the Newport News Shipbuilding and Dry Dock Company. Courtesy, Virginia State Library

Left: Because native Virginians lacked capital following the Civil War, much of the new construction was funded by Northern interests. This engraving, sketched by T.R. Davis, depicts the rebuilding of the Burnt District of Richmond—the city's financial and commercial center. Courtesy, Valentine Museum

Below: Philip Rahm's Eagle Foundry, located on Cary Street between 14th and 15th streets, was one of 13 iron foundries operating in Richmond in 1860. Lithographed by W.H. Rease and published by T.W. Bovell, this advertisement shows the various commercial and domestic ironworks manufactured in the city. Courtesy, Valentine Museum

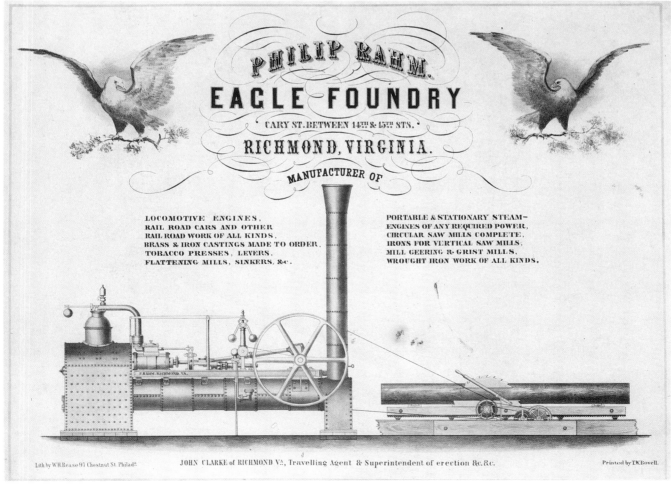

PHILIP RAHM.

EAGLE FOUNDRY

CARY ST. BETWEEN 14TH & 15TH STS.

RICHMOND, VIRGINIA.

MANUFACTURER OF

LOCOMOTIVE ENGINES,
RAIL ROAD CARS AND OTHER
RAIL ROAD WORK OF ALL KINDS,
BRASS & IRON CASTINGS MADE TO ORDER,
TOBACCO PRESSES, LEVERS,
FLATTENING MILLS, SINKERS, &c.

PORTABLE & STATIONARY STEAM-
ENGINES OF ANY REQUIRED POWER,
CIRCULAR SAW MILLS COMPLETE,
IRONS FOR VERTICAL SAW MILLS,
MILL GEERING & GRIST MILLS,
WROUGHT IRON WORK OF ALL KINDS,

Lith by W.H.Rease 97 Chestnut St Philadᵃ. JOHN CLARKE of RICHMOND Vᵃ., Travelling Agent & Superintendent of erection &c. &c. Printed by T.W.Bovell.

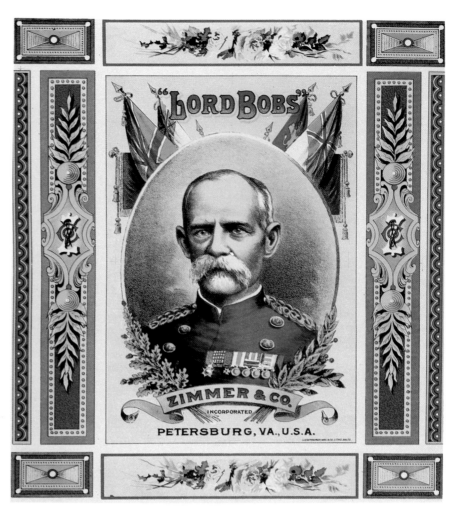

Virginia tobacco companies used a wide variety of colorful images to market their product. Shown here are advertisements and labels from several different companies. Courtesy, Virginia State Library

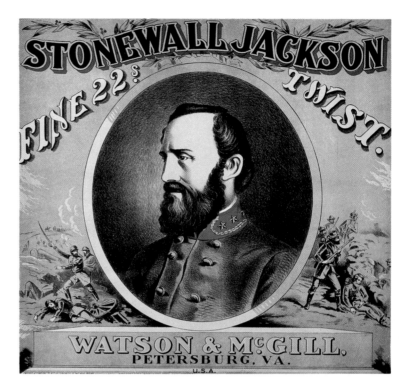

Facing page: A picturesque fall day in Nelson County. Courtesy, Virginia Tourism Corporation

Right: Isolated mountain farmers looked to Ed Mabry and his mill to grind meal long before transportation brought commerce to the Blue Ridge region. Photo by Carol Cotter

Below: The Jefferson Hotel, financed by tobacco magnate Lewis Ginter, opened in 1895 in Richmond. The design of the elaborate structure was based on the Villa Medici in Rome. Although the hotel burned in 1901, the Franklin Street façade was saved. The remainder of the building was reconstructed and the hotel reopened in 1907. Courtesy, Virginia State Library

WINTER SEASON
AMERICAN & EUROPEAN PLANS.

THE JEFFERSON
RICHMOND, VIRGINIA.

SUMMER SEASON
EUROPEAN PLAN EXCLUSIVELY.

ROOMS $1.50 PER DAY AND UPWARDS.

LITH. BY A. HOEN & CO. RICHMOND, VA.

Right: George Washington's Birthday Parade in Alexandria attracts tourists and locals alike. Photo by Alexandria Convention and Visitor's Bureau. Courtesy, Virginia Tourism Corporation

Below: Colonial Williamsburg is one of the largest and most comprehensive restored villages in the world. Here, some visitors enjoy a carriage ride. Photo by Mark Gibson

Above: Yorktown Battlefield is the site of the final, major battle of the American Revolutionary War and the symbolic end of Colonial English America. Courtesy, Virginia Tourism Corporation

Left: Winchester's Handley Library. Courtesy, City of Winchester

Above: Taliaferro Cole Garden in Colonial Williamsburg combines a lovely flower garden with peach and apple orchards. Photo by Colonial Williamsburg Foundation. Courtesy, Virginia Tourism Corporation

Right: Brick and stone homes mingle with clapboard row houses, lining the streets in the residential section of Olde Towne in Portsmouth. Courtesy, Virginia Tourism Corporation

Shenandoah National Park is located in the middle of the Appalachian Mountains. These east coast mountains are about 300 million years old. Photo by Richard Nowitz. Courtesy, Virginia Tourism Corporation

Right: Fredericksburg has a colorful history, and is a popular tourist attraction in Virginia. Many of the more than 350 original eighteenth and nineteenth century buildings in Fredericksburg's 40-block National Historic District are open to visitors. Photo by Audrey Gibson

Below: The old and the new Richmond are depicted in this photograph of some historic buildings reflected in the glass of a modern structure. Photo by John Salmon

Left: The University of Virginia is the chief center for graduate and graduate-professional studies in the state, and is one of the top 100 research universities in the country. The original buildings were designed by Thomas Jefferson, and the campus is widely regarded as one of the most picturesque in the country. Photo by Mark Gibson

Above: The Luray Caverns were discovered by accident in 1878 and studied by the Smithsonian Institution. This natural marvel has been designated a Registered Natural Landmark by the National Park Service and the Department of the Interior. Photo by Jack Hollingsworth.

Right: Overlooking the New River, Shot Tower was built more than 150 years ago to make ammunition for the firearms of the early settlers. Today, the tower is on the National Register of Historic Places. Photo by Tim Thompson. Courtesy, Virginia Tourism Corporation

Facing page: When Edwin Boston Mabry (1867-1936) built his water-powered mill in Virginia's Blue Ridge Mountains, he had no way of knowing it would become one of the most photographed places in the United States. The Mabry Mill, on the Blue Ridge Parkway, is now run by the National Park Service and has several hundred-thousand visitors each year. Photo by Tim Thompson. Courtesy, Virginia Tourism Corporation

Above: Busch Gardens, an amusement park located in Williamsburg, offers rides, live entertainment, food, and shopping in an "international" setting. Photo by Paul Pavlik

Right: A tour boat plies the busy waters of Norfolk. Photo by Audrey Gibson

Facing page: The most extensive parks and forests in Virginia are west of the Piedmont. Shown here is Lewis Falls in Shenandoah National Park, which extends along the Blue Ridge from Front Royal in the north to the vicinity of Waynesboro. Photo by Mark Gibson

Right: Natural Bridge, located in Rockridge County, is one of the seven natural wonders of the world. Called the "Bridge of God" by the Indians, it supports a national highway today. Photo by Carol Cotter

Left: The Blue Ridge Parkway affords travelers some magnificent views, such as this autumn scene. Photo by Mark Gibson

Below: In the Shenandoah Valley, oak, hickory, and yellow poplar are the dominant hardwoods while white, Virginia, and shortleaf pine are the major softwoods. Over two-thirds of Virginia's total land area is forested and nearly all the wooded land can produce timber. Photo by Mark Gibson

Above: Civil War reenactments are popular throughout the state. Here, a battle is recreated at the Sully Plantation in Fairfax County. Courtesy, Virginia Tourism Corporation

Right: The Fife and Drum Corps in Colonial Williamsburg consists of boys and girls, ages 10 to 18. Photo by Colonial Williamsburg Foundation. Courtesy, Virginia Tourism Corporation

Facing page: The Iwo Jima Memorial in Arlington National Cemetary commemorating the World War II battle. Photo by Mark Downey. Courtesy, Virginia Tourism Corporation

Right: The Graves Mountain Apple Festival offers locals and tourists a true "taste" of the October harvest. Attendees enjoy food, bluegrass music, clogging, arts and crafts, and homemade apple butter. Photo by Marilyn Ott. Courtesy, Virginia Tourism Corporation

Below: Virginia has evolved from an agriculture-based state into a post-industrial society with one of the country's most diverse economies. Still, farms like this one carry on. Photo by Robert Llewellyn

Above: Felicia Warburg Rogan founded Oakencroft Vineyard and Winery Corporation in 1983, and it is now the oldest winery in Albemarle County. On May 29th, 1986, President Reagan presented a bottle of the vineyard's Seyval Blanc to Premier Mikhail Gorbachev when the two were at a summit meeting in Moscow. Photo by Ann Purcell. Courtesy, Virginia Tourism Corporation

Left: Corn, squash, and beans are grown on this farm in Floyd County. The crops are then transported to the city where they are sold fresh and purchased right off the bed of the truck. Photo by Bob Shell/Shellphoto

Above: Children learn the fine art of wood carving at the Mariner's Museum in Newport News. Photo by the Mariner's Museum. Courtesy, Virginia Tourism Corporation

Right: The General Store, located within the Meadow Run Grist Mill in Nelson County, features a charming old mercantile atmosphere. Photo by Ann Purcell. Courtesy, Virginia Tourism Corporation

Above: The Natural Chimneys State Park includes seven natural limestone towers, nature trails, a swimming pool, and campgrounds. Courtesy, Virginia Tourism Corporation

Left: A train travels over the bridge that crosses the Rappahannock River in Fredericksburg. Photo by Ann Purcell. Courtesy, Virginia Tourism Corporation

Onancock Creek is a birdwatcher's delight and provides haven for boaters who want to avoid storms in nearby Chesapeake Bay. Photo by Len Kaufma. Courtesy, Virginia Tourism Corporation

*A Virginia farm is silhouetted against a
fiery sunset. Photo by Robert Llewellyn*

Right: Situated between the Blue Ridge and Allegheny Mountains, Roanoke is the gateway to the Shenandoah Valley and is therefore the region's commercial center. Pictured here is Market Square in Roanoke. Photo by Audrey Gibson

Below: In the commercial apple orchards of Virginia's Shenandoah Valley, production totaled 455 million pounds in 1983. In recent years Virginia has ranked seventh in the nation in apple production. Photo by Ken Layman. Courtesy, Robert Maust Photography

Colonial Beach is a quaint little resort town and a popular summer destination. Situated along the Potomac River, the community is near the birthplaces of famed historical figures such as George Washington, Robert E. Lee, and James Monroe. Photo by Dwight Dyke. Courtesy, Virginia Tourism Corporation

Above: Celebrating its 77th anniversary in 2004, the Apple Blossom Festival offers parades, band competitions, a 10K run, and the coronation of Queen Shenandoah. Courtesy, Virginia Tourism Corporation

Right: Tourists enjoy a rafting trip on the New River in the Blue Ridge Highlands. Photo by Tim Thompson. Courtesy, Virginia Tourism Corporation

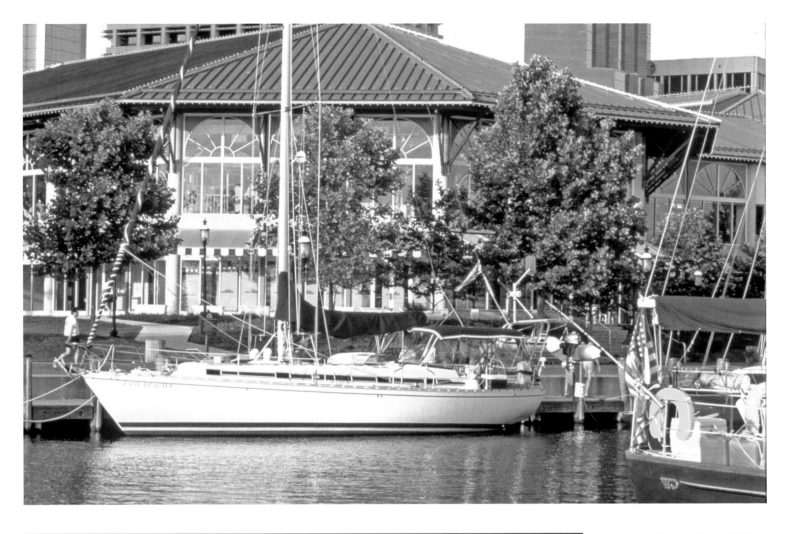

Above: The Waterside Festival Market Place was the catalyst for downtown Norfolk's revitalization. The Elizabeth River ferry and harbor cruises leave from the pavilion on a regular basis, although "The Waterside" is primarily an after-dark dining and entertainment area. Photo by Norfolk Convention and Visitor's Bureau. Courtesy, Virginia Tourism Corporation

Left: Potomac Mills Outlet Mall in Prince William County features over 220 stores, selling brand name merchandise at a fraction of the cost. Photo by Potomac Mills. Courtesy, Virginia Tourism Corporation

Right: Snowboarding is a popular pastime at the Massanutten Mountains in Harrisonburg. Courtesy, Virginia Tourism Corporation

Facing page: A spectacular view of the Roanoke Valley skyline as the sun sets. Photo by Bob Krist. Courtesy, Virginia Tourism Corporation

Above: Sunset on the James River as seen from the Rice Center, Virginia Commonwealth University's 342-acre life sciences laboratory. Courtesy, Virginia Commonwealth University

Left: The dock is flooded preparatory to docking vessels at this Newport News shipyard. Courtesy, Virginia State Library

Schools overflowed with students as more and more families moved to the area. A two-shift system was adopted to handle the ever-increasing number of students, which rose from 79,000 in 1940 to 98,000 in 1945. Unfortunately, many teachers had been lured away from the profession by the high salaries of war industries, government jobs, and the armed services, leaving an insufficient number to support the system. In Norfolk, 35 percent of the city's teachers held only emergency certificates. The percentage was even higher in the counties.

Government agencies in the various communities of Hampton Roads also proved insufficient to service their war populations. Most had neither the funds nor the staff to effectively carry out their tasks. In 1943 an estimated 2,800 children needed nursery care, yet Norfolk's three-day nurseries had room for only 150 children. The city's Family Welfare Association had such a poor reputation that even the juvenile court refused to send it referrals. Newport News had no private family agency to provide all-around services in the community, so several different public agencies, with little or no coordination, attempted to administer to family and child problems.

Community recreational facilities, scarcely adequate to meet the needs of the normal popula-

tion, were wholly insufficient to care for the inflated numbers of civilian workers and military personnel. Inevitably servicemen gravitated to bars and disreputable dives. Although the army and the navy attempted to remedy the situation with the construction of movie theaters, gymnasiums, and a large army-navy USO auditorium and recreation arena in Norfolk, sailors and soldiers still swarmed the penny arcades of Norfolk's East Main Street. Consequently, the rates for most crimes in the Hampton Roads communities doubled and, in some areas, even tripled.

While the war boom wreaked its own brand of havoc on the area, the soaring demand for goods and services invigorated the civilian economy. Before the war there were 154,000 persons in the labor force of Hampton Roads. Four years later, with the proliferation of women and children in the work force, that number had increased nearly 50 percent. Unemployment had virtually disappeared, not only among white males but also among women and blacks. As employment rose so did total income. Income payments for the last half of 1942 reached $323 million, $231 million higher than the same period in 1939.

The shipbuilding industry provided the greatest boost to employment during the early war years. By 1942, more than 55,000 people

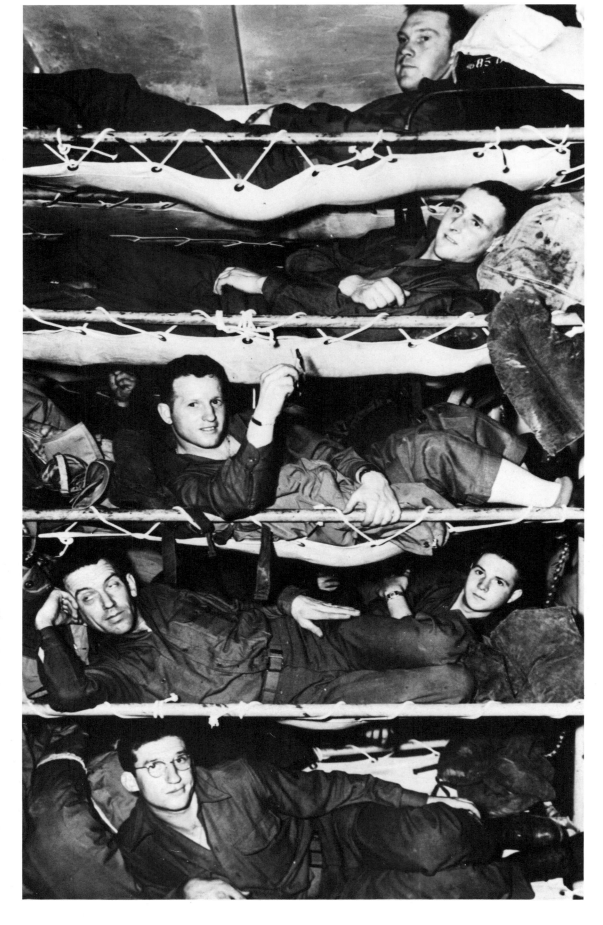

These enlisted men are bedded down in close quarters before sailing overseas from the Hampton Roads Port of Embarkation in April 1944. Courtesy, U.S. Signal Corps, Hampton Roads Port of Embarkation, Virginia State Library

had been added to the shipyards' payrolls as suppliers raced to meet the demand for war vessels. War supply contracts and project orders awarded to Hampton Roads establishments totaled approximately $1.8 billion through November 1944—more than five times the value of the products of the shipbuilding and repair industry in the entire United States in 1939. Nearly all of this business went to the navy yard and to Newport News Shipbuilding. The navy yard's contribution in World War II exceeded its production in all other wars combined. The private company cut out all other business and built itself into the nation's leading designer and producer of aircraft carriers.

As the area's largest employer continued to pad its payrolls, it fed other commerce. The pressure for goods and services combined with sufficiently high incomes fostered new businesses

and bolstered old ones. Shipbuilding employment increased to almost five times its prewar level, while overall business activity expanded threefold during the war years. The additions of new Hampton Roads businesses to the Dun & Bradstreet business reporting service during that period exceeded those of the entire rest of the state.

As residents began buying more, dining out more, and spending more money on higher priced purchases, businesses expanded. By 1943, the number of people employed in all branches of wholesale and retail trade, including eating and drinking establishments, had increased more than 50 percent. Payrolls in these businesses rose from prewar levels of $9.7 million to $21.6 million.

Service industries were likewise affected. The number of hotels, amusements, recreation

This aerial view of the Hampton Roads Port of Embarkation shows the Headquarters Building and Administrative Area, the Chesapeake & Ohio railroad yards, and the Pier Area with ten ships loading. Courtesy, U.S. Signal Corps, Hampton Roads Port of Embarkation, Virginia State Library

Colonna's Shipyard in Norfolk is pictured in 1954. Although the shipyards of Hampton Roads underwent a postwar slump, they maintained a stable economy as they moved into the fifties.

establishments, and personal, domestic, professional, and business services almost doubled by the end of 1943, as did their payrolls. Not surprisingly, more than half the people employed in service industries worked in Norfolk, catering to the navy population. In manufacturing, no industry came close to matching the prosperity of the shipbuilding industry, although makers of clothing, chemicals (mainly fertilizer), and food showed significant expansions. When World War II ended, the boom kept on. The military presence continued to grow as existing military installations were expanded and new ones came to the area. Langley Field underwent considerable expansion under the National Advisory Committee on Aeronautics and the Air Corps. The Army Ground Forces, now the Army Field Forces, moved to Fort Monroe, and the Army Transportation Corps set up headquarters at Fort Eustis. Norfolk's major supply base, the Atlantic Fleet home port, and the new Armed Forces Staff College all contributed to the influx of military personnel.

The civilian population also rose with the return of prewar residents and the immigration of veterans who married Hampton Roads women. Many civilian war workers remained after their jobs ended, further offsetting the postwar outflow of war families and workers. Five years after V-J Day, the population of the Hampton

Roads-Peninsula area exceeded the peak population of the war years.

When shipbuilders were forced to lay off thousands of employees as the navy buildup ceased, unemployment still remained low. Effective buying income in Hampton Roads for 1948 ranged from $4,500 to $4,900 per family, as opposed to a state average of $4,044.

The wholesale, retail, and service industries continued to prosper, fueled by high incomes, low unemployment, and a growing tourist trade. The resort business brought millions of travelers who spent approximately $10 million in the area between May and September.

Spurred by the Peninsula Industrial Committee, the Norfolk Industrial Commission, and the Portsmouth Chamber of Commerce, several businesses established or reestablished operations in the area. U.S. Gypsum Company built a $2 million gypsum plaster and plasterboard plant. Swift and Company established a $700,000 food processing plant. And Ford Motor Company spent $1.5 million reconverting its auto assembly plant to a peacetime operation. Between 1947 and 1948 the value of manufactured goods among Norfolk concerns alone had risen from $250 million to $338 million.

Although momentum inevitably slowed from that of the fevered war pitch, Hampton Roads maintained a stable economy as it moved into the new decade. The world wars had forced the bloating populations of the Hampton Roads cities into a huge, burgeoning metropolis. Construction of the Chesapeake Bay Bridge Tunnel linked the Hampton Roads region with the Eastern Shore, providing more direct motor access to the metropolitan Northeast while bypassing Baltimore and Washington.

Shipbuilding would recover from its postwar slump. By the late sixties, Newport News Shipbuilding and Dry Dock Company was the largest manufacturing employer in the state. Geared up to produce the nuclear aircraft carriers and nuclear attack submarines of a 600-ship navy, the shipyard employed 30,000 workers in 1987.

The shipping industry would be aided by the creation of the Virginia State Ports Authority in 1952. Prior to its inception, outdated facilities at 14 general cargo terminals in the three Hampton Roads port cities were operated by private and government concerns which could not afford to modernize their facilities. Furthermore, civilian business was unevenly distributed among the terminals, clogging piers and slowing operations. Within a decade, the Ports Author-ity would purchase and improve these piers, then lease them back to their former owners to operate them.

Since the opening of the coal mines in Southwest Virginia, coal has consistently led the exports of Hampton Roads. By the early 1900s, three major railroads were funneling trainloads of coal through Hampton Roads for shipment all over the world. After the United States entered World War I, coal remained the principal export as war-torn Europe looked to America for its fuel supply.

When rails through New York could not support the demand of New England's factories for coal, steamers from Hampton Roads hauled the fuel north. In one year Norfolk's domestic coal shipments jumped from 290,000 tons to 5.5 million tons. Coal shipments took a dive in World War II. To protect against German U-boats, shippers moved coal over all-rail routes, causing coastal trade to sink. Dumpings in 1943 were less than half what they had been just two years before. But as the U-boat menace lessened toward the end of the war, coal shipments began to increase, both to domestic ports and to Europe.

This is the interior of the prefabricated sections that were to form the core of the underwater portions of the Chesapeake Bay Bridge Tunnel. Courtesy, Virginia State Library

Exports picked up again after the war, spurred by a revival of the European economies and a demand for high quality metallurgical coal. By 1952, Hampton Roads exports had risen to 23.1 million tons, 22.4 million tons of which were coal. Prospects for coal exports brightened in the seventies when the energy crisis drove up the price of oil and forced countries the world over to substitute coal for oil as a primary fuel in electric power plants. In 1974 some 38 million tons of coal is estimated to have passed through Hampton Roads. By 1980, the figure would reach 100 million tons.

That year labor unrest disrupted shipments from Poland and Australia, America's greatest competitors for European and Asian consumption. Customers from all over the world flocked to Hampton Roads for coal. As many as 160 colliers crowded into the port on a given day, waiting to be loaded. The armada packed the anchorages at Hampton Roads, eventually spilling into Cape Charles on the Eastern Shore. Midyear marked a 40-ship backlog, and coal exporters worried that the lengthy waits, which

cost ships thousands of dollars a day, would discourage coal buyers from returning.

Exports were destined to fall off in any case. With labor problems settled, Poland and Australia reclaimed their market share. South Africa, another coal exporter, expanded its export capacity, while Canada and Colombia crowded into the international market. By the mid-1980s, oil prices collapsed, prompting Europeans to drop plans to switch from oil to coal as a fuel for numerous electric power plants. Despite adversity, Hampton Roads remains the world's largest coal exporting port.

In recent years general cargo shipments have taken up the slack. Launching an aggressive marketing campaign, Hampton Roads began winning business for containerized cargo from other U.S. ports, especially Baltimore. Several major shipping companies have transferred operations to Hampton Roads, distinguishing it as the fastest-growing container-handling port in the U.S. during the mid-1980s. The region's superior ports and railroads also have made it an attractive site for foreign investment.

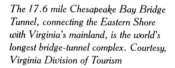

The 17.6 mile Chesapeake Bay Bridge Tunnel, connecting the Eastern Shore with Virginia's mainland, is the world's longest bridge-tunnel complex. Courtesy, Virginia Division of Tourism

Collis P. Huntington

The story goes that Collis P. Huntington was a 16-year-old traveling salesman when he first laid eyes on Hampton Roads in 1837. Even at that time, he would later say, he thought there was no better place in the country for a city to blossom.

Some 40 years later Huntington returned, a railroad baron in search of an eastern terminus for his Chesapeake & Ohio Railway. His Old Dominion Land Company bought up major parcels for the creation of such a town. Huntington, always a man of vision, added coal piers, believing that one day the harbor would be a deepwater port.

In January 1886 Chesapeake Dry Dock & Construction Company was chartered with Huntington as its chairman. Over the next few years the company grew quickly, renowned for its ship repair work. When the surrounding community was insufficient to handle the increasing number of employees, Huntington used his personal funds for the development of a community for his workers, subsidizing the construction of 138 two-story brick houses and a four-room schoolhouse.

In 1890 the company name was changed to Newport News Shipbuilding and Dry Dock Company, and shipbuilding became its emphasis. Although the navy would become the company's primary contractor, that relationship began on shaky ground. As Christmas approached, the news reached Huntington that the Portsmouth Navy Yard had taken in a German steamship for repairs. Huntington protested to U.S. Navy Secretary B.F. Tracy in a telegram:

I was very much surprised and aggrieved to know that the government should have come in and taken this work after the owners of the shipyard at Newport News have been to the great expense they have

incurred in preparing to do just this kind of work.

Collis P. Huntington. From Cirker, Dictionary of American Portraits, Dover, 1967

Within three years the shipyard began a stream of navy work that would keep it afloat for the next century. Huntington died in 1900, but Newport News Shipbuilding and Dry Dock Company kept its lead in the industry as a major supplier through every American war.

After World War II, demand dropped and the shipyard was able to stay in business by converting ships to civilian use. The fifties brought a turnaround when the company entered the nuclear age with the construction of the aircraft carrier *Enterprise*. The shipyard became the only producer capable of constructing all types of navy nuclear vessels.

The company became increasingly dependent on government contract work, as did other yards across the country. In 1968, fearful of a hostile takeover, shipyard officials agreed to merge with the Houston-based Tenneco Corporation, believing that the backing of a major corporation would buffet the company from the fluctuations of the shipbuilding business. At the time of the merger, the shipyard had a backlog of orders totaling nearly $500 million. By 1976 the backlog had grown to nearly $2 billion. Today Newport News Shipbuilding and Dry Dock Company is still the nation's industry leader.

The Dulles Corridor has become one of the country's principal high-tech centers with more than 1,000 businesses, professional firms, and associations. Access to international transportation is just one of the factors which attracts such businesses. As early as 1946, Washington National Airport in Arlington County was serving seven airlines. Courtesy, Richmond Newspapers, Inc.

BEYOND THE SMOKESTACKS

◆

In the nearly four centuries since the founding of Jamestown, Virginia evolved from a fragile agricultural-based colony on the edge of a hostile new world into a community pioneering the frontiers of the post-industrial society. By the end of the twentieth century, Virginia had one of the most balanced, diversified economies of any state in the nation.

Many generations-old industries held their grip on the economy. Railroading, coal mining, forestry, and agriculture remained major contributors to jobs and income. In the mid-'80s Virginia ranked fifth in the nation in tobacco production, sixth in coal production, seventh in apple production, and thirteenth in lumber production.

The smokestacks of old-line industries such as textiles, furniture, transportation equipment, and chemicals still punctuated Virginia's skylines. Among other accomplishments, the state claimed the world's largest privately owned shipyard, the world's largest cigarette-manufacturing plant, the world's largest textile mill under one roof, and the world's largest hot dog production plant. Manufacturing concerns engaged a work force of nearly half a million.

Between 1970 and 1990, new service and technology industries began to blossom. Virginia quickly became one of the nation's centers for telecommunications, software programming, and aerospace. Virginia companies were active in biotechnology, robotics, fiber optics, and many other cutting-edge industries.

Between 1970 and 1980 Virginia's nonagricultural work force grew by 3.4 percent each year, compared to the national average of 2.5 percent. By 1987, Virginia was one of the few states to have shown an increase in manufacturing jobs since the brutal recession of 1980-1981. Throughout the seventies Virginia maintained one of the lowest unemployment rates in the country, and its economy grew faster than the national average.

The increase in jobs was matched by rising incomes. In the mid-1980s—some 120 years after the Civil War—the average income per capita for Virginians finally surpassed the national average. Prosperity concentrated along a swath of extraordinary vitality known as the Golden Crescent. A band of urban-suburban development running from the Northern Virginian suburbs of Washington through Richmond and into Hampton Roads was marked by low unemployment, high incomes, and vigorous industry.

Pockets of deprivation persisted in rural Virginia, where many communities staked their

Smith Mountain Dam is located in a square formed by Roanoke, Rocky Mount, Danville, and Lynchburg. It is 226 feet high and 816 feet long. The dam, along with the Leesville Dam 17 miles downstream, is an Appalachian Power Company hydro-electric project. Courtesy, Virginia Division of Tourism

livelihood on the fortunes of a handful of manufacturing industries. Under the pressure of foreign imports and changing consumer trends, traditional industries such as textiles and tobacco endured prolonged periods of contraction. Although most companies survived intact; it was only through heavy investment in modern equipment and ruthless slashing of jobs. Even then many of these communities showed considerable resilience. Aggressive marketing recruited new manufacturing plants for depressed mill towns.

Lured by moderate taxes, excellent roads and airports, a high quality of life, and modest labor costs, more and more high-tech companies located to Virginia. Not only was the state attracting the gold-collar geniuses responsible for high-tech innovations, it was also producing them. Institutions of higher learning across Virginia began offering curricula geared to advanced technology. Three

universities—the University of Virginia, Virginia Commonwealth University, and Virginia Polytechnic Institute and State University—are among the nation's top 100 research universities in total research and development expenditures. And over the last two decades, George Mason University emerged as a leading research center, having a Nobel laureate in economics on its faculty and a world-class "center of excellence" for software engineering.

High-tech industry entered every corner of the state. The Roanoke Valley, still the leading manufacturing center of Southwest Virginia, became home to a wide range of high-tech companies: ITT's Electro-Optical Products Division manufactures fiber optic components and systems, as well as night vision devices there. Nord Instruments Company began assembling circuit boards, while Keltech produced industrial electronics and computer controls. Almost a dozen medical and commercial laboratories were located in the area. Nearly 20 percent of the area's 21,000 manufacturing employees were involved in the production of electrical and electronic machinery.

Roanoke became an anchor of the emerging I-81 corridor, named for the growth of industry along the interstate highway. The other focal point of development was Blacksburg, home to Virginia Tech. ITT and Virginia Tech seed a number of entrepreneurial firms in the fields of fiber optics, bioengineering, robotics, and electric motors.

Hampton Roads also was showing enormous high-tech potential. Between the National Aeronautics and Space Administration (NASA) research facility at Langley, Newport News Shipbuilding (the only builder of nuclear aircraft carriers in the nation), the Canon copier plant,

the Virginia Institute for Marine Science, and a host of software firms supplying services to the naval establishment, Hampton Roads became one of the largest concentrations of scientific and engineering talent in the country.

Many of the area's high-tech companies provide support services for NASA. Modern Machine & Tool, for example, is active in aerospace research and development, while Wyle Laboratories designs and manufactures electronic and electro-mechanical systems. In Hampton and Newport News, Gambro manufactures dialysis filters and bloodlines for artificial kidney machines. In Norfolk, Dow Corning Opthalmics and Lombart Lenses Division of American Sterilizer Company produce contact lenses. More than two dozen laboratories operated in Hampton Roads in the late '80s.

Virginia Polytechinic Institute, located in Blacksburg, offers programs which are in step with the growth of high tech industry in the state. Courtesy, Virginia State Library

Richmond, historically Virginia's industrial leader, also sprouted a number of high-tech firms. Robertshaw Controls, a manufacturer of control systems, was headquartered there, as was A.H. Robins Company, a diversified multinational pharmaceutical company. The AT&T printed wiring board production facility there was one of the most modern in the world. The Richmond area also had more than two dozen medical and commercial testing labs.

Lynchburg and Charlottesville also claimed a share of the state's high-tech market. In Lynchburg, International Circuit Technology manufactured printed circuit boards, and Paktron, a division of Illinois Tool Works, produced electronic components. Babcock & Wilcox led in the design and maintenance of nuclear power plants. Some 3,600 people were employed by communications companies in the Lynchburg area, while in Charlottesville, headquarters to Comdial Corporation, more than 2,000 people were employed in the manufacture of communications equipment. Charlottesville also is home to the University of Virginia, with its research-oriented medical and

engineering schools, as well as General Electric's factory automation division.

The shift from mills to microchips was most evident in Northern Virginia, where high-technology manufacturing as well as research and development firms play a major role in the local economy. By 1985, Northern Virginia was transformed from a bedroom community into an urban sprawl of high rises and concrete. By the early 1980s, more than 800 high-tech firms and organizations had settled in the region, employing almost 63,000 people. The Dulles corridor, stretching from Tysons Corner to Washington Dulles International Airport, was becoming one of the country's principal high-tech centers, with more than 1,000 businesses, professional firms, and associations. In the software industry alone, the ever-increasing presence of high-tech firms placed the region in the league with California's Silicon Valley and Boston's Route 128.

Economists attributed Northern Virginia's magnetism to several factors, primarily its proximity to Washington. At the turn of the twentieth century, there was little development in the region

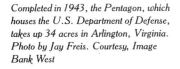

Completed in 1943, the Pentagon, which houses the U.S. Department of Defense, takes up 34 acres in Arlington, Virginia. Photo by Jay Freis. Courtesy, Image Bank West

outside of Alexandria, then a minor river port and commercial center. As the role of the federal government grew, however, so did the size of the federal establishment across the Potomac in Washington. Even so, Arlington and Fairfax counties were little more than bedroom communities for years. One of the greatest boons to regional development was the construction of the Pentagon on the Virginia side of the Potomac.

As the defense department expanded in the decades following World War II, it spilled into the tremendous Crystal City complex. The growing Pentagon also contracted jobs to think tanks, research firms, systems management companies, and a host of other so-called "Beltway Bandits."

Defense spending has not been the only driving force in Northern Virginia's rise to prominence. Many government agencies expanded across the river into the area, and many private organizations followed closely behind. The Washington area attracted thousands of trade associations whose job it is to monitor and lobby legislation, and many settled in Fairfax County, Arlington County, and Alexandria.

The federal bureaucracy also is the nation's largest customer for computer hardware and super-sophisticated systems software. To participate in this lucrative market, virtually every major computer and systems-management company in the country set up operations in the Washington area. Similarly, the telecommunications industry settled in the area in order to keep tabs on the Federal Communications Commission (FCC). For decades telecommunications had been the monopoly of AT&T Communications. With the breakup of Ma Bell, telecommunications firms proliferated, creating the world's most competitive telephone and data-transmission industry, most of which have a major presence in Virginia's suburbs.

Northern Virginia amassed a critical measure of capital, skilled labor, and entrepreneurial talent in a handful of high-tech fields. With one of the largest concentrations of engineers and scientists in the world, George Mason University, a modest branch of the University of Virginia a generation ago, expanded dramatically. Working

closely with the local business community, the university designed a curriculum to supply the trained work force demanded by high-tech industry. In a short time, for example, the university built and staffed an impressive software engineering school.

Access to air transportation is always a primary consideration in economic development. Arlington is the site of Washington National Airport, and Washington Dulles International Airport straddles the Fairfax and Loudoun county lines. The federal government has now relinquished control of both facilities to a regional airport commission.

Alexandria, Arlington, Fairfax, and Prince William enjoy a superior quality of life, with public school systems among the best in the nation, as well as having excellent recreational facilities. Cooperative local governments have enabled development to proceed rapidly, finding creative ways to meet the region's water, sewer, and transportation needs.

Fairfax County is the hub of high-tech in Virginia. Among the growing concentration of firms are the giants of telecommunications, the sovereigns of software, and tomorrow's wizards of aerospace. Fairfax has all the benefits that Virginia can offer. It is 15 minutes from the seat of federal government, and has one of the most highly educated labor pools in the country, with a greater percentage of college graduates than

Because of its moderate taxes, modest labor costs, excellent road systems and airports, and high quality of life, Virginia has attracted major industries to all areas of the state. Expansion of Byrd Airport, now Richmond International Airport, was one outcome of this economic development. In this 1968 photo, construction of a new taxiway and apron is surveyed by an airport aide from the terminal roof. Courtesy, Richmond Newspapers, Inc.

Right: Governor Charles S. Robb organized a Special Task Force on Science and Technology in 1983, and as a result the Center for Innovative Techonology was established. Its goal was to link the capabilities of major research universities in the state to high tech industries. Courtesy, Virginia State Library

Below: On the historic campus of the University of Virginia, important research is ongoing in the medical and engineering schools. Courtesy, Printing Services, Archives, University of Virginia Library

Boston, Chicago, Dallas, Los Angeles, New York, or San Francisco.

Quality of life is also a major drawing card. Companies on the move were pleased to bring their employees to a county where unemployment was nearly half the state's rate and less than half the nation's rate, and where the mean income level for an average household was more than $50,000, fifth highest among U.S. counties. The Fairfax County Public School System, one of the best in the country, offers another plus. Approximately 50 percent of its teachers held master's or doctoral degrees. In 1984, more than 37 percent of Virginia's National Merit Scholarship Exam semifinalists came from Fairfax County.

Educational opportunities in the area matched stride with the evolution of high technology. Three major universities offer programs in the area which address the growth of high-tech: George Mason University, the University

of Virginia's Division of Continuing Education, and Virginia Polytechnic Institute and State University's Dulles Graduate Center.

Washington Dulles International Airport accelerated its pace to meet the growing demand of corporate needs. After Congress turned the airport's operations over to a regional commission, terminal space was added, runway capacity was increased, and more airlines began crowding in. Within three years commercial passenger traffic had doubled.

More and more high-tech companies began cashing in on Fairfax County's available assets. With well over half the state's telecommunication's firms, Fairfax had become a repository for industry giants by the mid-1980s. AT&T Communications, GTE Telenet, Comstat General Telesystems, and Dynalectron Corporation were among those who chose Fairfax, with its access to major markets and its gold-collar workers.

The county became fertile ground for some of the world's leading software technology. Approximately 200 software companies employed one of every seven Fairfax workers. Small firms were numerous, but industry giants took up a lot of turf and hired a multitude of technicians. Both Sperry Corporation in Reston and Systems Development Corporation in Tysons Corner employed 2,000 people, while TRW Federal Systems Group, headquartered in the Fair Lakes area was staffed by 3,000.

Now recognized as a national center for high-tech excellence, Fairfax County grew from strength to strength. As a result of Governor Charles S. Robb's Special Task Force on Science and Technology in 1983, the Center for Innovative Technology (CIT) was established in the county to link the capabilities of the state's major research universities to its technically advanced industries. In its first several years, the CIT—funded by state and industry—backed more than 220 projects involved in the development of technology and its applications to industry.

In 1985, the county opened its Thomas Jefferson Science and Technology High School, a four-year program for students with aptitudes

in science, mathematics, engineering, and computer science. Local technology-oriented companies such as Atlantic Research Corporation, IBM, TRW, and Dynalectron Corporation added funding for specialized, technology-based laboratories for students to actively apply the scientific principles they learn in the classroom. AT&T, for instance, sponsored the school's Telecommunications Laboratory. Satellite Business Systems, Comsat General Telesystems, Sony Corporation, NEC America, and Rolm provided lab equipment, which included a satellite earth

Adjoining the Blues Armory in the 600 block of E. Marshall Street, at the northern end of Richmond's Sixth Street Marketplace, is the Crystal Palace. This 96-foot high, glass-enclosed pavilion houses specialty shops, market booths, open seating areas, and a stage. A glass-enclosed bridge, spanning Broad Street, brings the city's historic past and revitalized present together. Courtesy, Virginia Division of Tourism

Above: Preston Shannon and members of the CSX Corporation, Hays T. Watkins and Prime F. Osborn, III, signed the $7 million merger of Seaboard Coast Line Industries and the Chessie System, Inc., on November 1, 1980. Like Norfolk Southern, CSX is one of the largest railroad systems in the western hemisphere. Courtesy, Richmond Newspapers, Inc.

the region was well on its way to becoming a leading force in the world economy of the twenty-first century.

But Hampton Roads, Richmond, Roanoke-Blacksburg, and Charlottesville followed close behind. Medical research centers in Charlottesville, Richmond, and Norfolk, for example, gave birth to a new biomedical industry. Businesses south of the Occoquan River harnessed technological breakthroughs in the production of goods and services. American consumers still demanded a steady supply of durable and non-durable products, and Virginia's manufacturing centers provided them.

In cities like Danville, Martinsville, and Galax, superautomated textile factories turned out fabrics for apparel, furniture, automobile interiors, and draperies. Factories of the future were found in Philip Morris' cigarette-manufacturing plant in Richmond, and in smaller communities like Marion, Stuart's Draft, and Orange. In Waynesboro, Genicom Corporation designed and manufactured top-of-the-line computer printers.

Of course, there's more to economic development than high tech. The city of Richmond blossomed into a major regional financial center. Two other Richmond firms—Best Products and Circuit City Stores—revolutionized the retailing industry with bold new concepts in discount selling. By the 1980s, James River Corporation had built a continent-wide empire of pulp and paper plants. CSX Corporation and Norfolk Southern had assembled two of the largest railroad systems in the Western Hemisphere.

As the 1990s approached, Virginia was on the move. The shift in economic power to the Commonwealth could be seen in the rapid growth of its largest corporate citizens and in the decisions of several Fortune 500 companies—Mobil Corporation, the multinational oil company, foremost among them—relocated their headquarters to Virginia locales. As long as state government and the spirit of enterprise work hand in hand, Virginia seems destined to regain the mantle of economic leadership it had 200 years ago.

station, a television studio and control room, a weather station, and a radio station. A Life Science and Biotechnology Laboratory for investigation and experimentation in life sciences was sponsored by Hazleton Laboratories, Meloy Laboratories, and FMC Corporation.

Also in 1985, the county was selected as the site for the Software Productivity Consortium, a research center where 15 of the country's top aerospace corporations share research on state-of-the-art software and software development techniques. The technology developed by the consortium was for use by federal defense and intelligence agencies as well as by private industry. The establishment of the research center in Fairfax added significantly to the area's prominence as a leader in high technology.

In 1987, Fairfax became a major landmark in the international effort to expand the frontiers of space when NASA chose Reston as the site for its space station headquarters. The research and development of a manned station in space drew thousands to the county as high-tech professionals, as well as major contractors, line up to bid for jobs.

As the ongoing revolutions in computers, telecommunications, and biotechnology continued to unfold, Northern Virginia businesses were at the vanguard. Blessed by access to the nation's capital, two major airports, a superbly skilled labor force, and Virginia's favorable business climate,

Negotiations between General Robert E. Lee and General Ulysses S. Grant took place in the McLean House in 1865. It was on April 9 that the terms of surrender were agreed upon. This is how the famous house looks today. Photo by Bob Krist. Courtesy, Virginia Tourism Corporation

*Washington, D.C. as seen from the Iwo
Jima Memorial. Photo by Doug Wilson.
Courtesy, Virginia Tourism Corporation*

VIRGINIA'S GLOBAL ECONOMY

◆

By the dawn of the new century, diverse parts of the world had become linked by advanced communications technology that held the promise of commerce at hyperspeed. Globalism became the buzzword of the '90s as free trade organizations reconfigured massive trade flows and import/export patterns.

With the Thatcher-Reagan triumph of capitalism, ownership—of property, corporate stock, and small businesses—was attainable by almost anyone with the foresight and the gumption to bet it all on the belief that globalization would change commerce as we knew it. Free trade organizations, like NAFTA and the World Trade Organization, made it easy to link arms with commercial interests all over the world. Even Gorbachev and Fukuyama agreed: capitalism is good. Not only did the world market open up, broadly expanding import and export opportunities, but outsourcing services to other countries saved some companies and destroyed others.

With its early foothold in the telecom industry, northern Virginia easily slipstreamed into the tide of international commerce. Seeing the future, other industries rushed to fit into the global footprint as it took shape. While NoVa's telecom cluster led the way in worldwide communications, established industries joined the sprint for the future by integrating technological advances to make businesses more efficient, cost effective, and competitive in a worldwide market. Advanced technology in the Old Dominion became

such an integral part of Virginia's plan for the future that, in 1998, Governor Jim Gilmore appointed Donald Upson as the commonwealth's first secretary of technology, charged with managing tech growth and establishing policies that surrounded it.

But as Virginia became swept up in the tide of the global market, local economies in various pockets of the state began to wither, hit hard by the competition of international trade. When manufacturers shopped overseas for low cost parts and products, providers stateside—many with longtime ties to industry—suddenly were forced to compete for lower revenues just to stay in the game. Mill towns like Danville and Martinsville, where local economies were built wholly on textile and furniture manufacturing, saw their output decrease as offshore concerns that produced wares of equal value at lower costs swept the market. Mining communities where coal had been king for generations suffered as well, as other viable energy resources replaced dirty, labor-intensive coal mining.

Compounding the blow, it quickly became apparent that it was as easy to save money in the global market as it was to make it. Finding cheaper labor sources offshore, U.S. companies began outsourcing—essentially exporting—service jobs to other countries like India, where 350 million people still live on less than one dollar a day and wages for service jobs are a fraction of American salaries for the same services. And when China, with its

The single-package integrated switch TDA21201 allows designers of switching power supplies (i.e. PCs and notebooks) to reduce system costs by as much as 50 percent and dramatically reduce the space required. Courtesy, Infineon Technologies

gargantuan, low-cost, labor force, was admitted into the World Trade Organization in the fall of 2001, the bell began to toll for small manufacturing communities and centers everywhere.

Four years into the new century, America had lost 3 million manufacturing jobs to other countries. Virginia, particularly its Southside, felt the shock as its light manufacturing industries fell into wholesale destruction. In the southwest, 13,000 coal miners went to the unemployment line between 1993 and 2003. Things weren't much better to the east, where shipbuilding and the U.S. military—the bedrocks of the local economy for more than a century—had yet to reclaim the breadth of business it lost at the end of the Cold War.

As the end of the century approached, Richmond—the antebellum leader in industry until it was decimated in the Civil War—had come a long way toward reestablishing its preeminence as an East Coast center for commerce. But its hold became tenuous when some of its Fortune 500 companies left, and banking, as well as other major companies, shifted emphases to more accommodating states. As the banking industry evolved, it became obvious that *interstate* banking was inevitable. But Virginia lawmakers were slow to deregulate *intrastate* banking. In the lapse, North Carolina deregulated first. However, by the time interstate banking finally did arrive in Virginia, North Carolina-based banks had outsized their Virginia counterparts and were in a position to

acquire them—not the other way around.

As the global economy ripens, technology continues to drive Virginia's economy. And not just from Northern Virginia. "As university towns, Charlottesville and Blacksburg are positioning themselves as centers of knowledge creation and R&D. Hampton Roads, with its federal labs, is trying to do much the same thing," says James A. Bacon, publisher of *Bacon's Rebellion*, an electronic op-ed page focusing on state economic development issues. "Richmond has begun the process of reinventing itself as a center of the 'creative class,' a place where artistic, scientific, and entrepreneurial innovators are attracted by the quality of life. Meanwhile, Virginia's mill towns are groping for knowledge-intensive strategies like lean manufacturing to compensate for wages which, globally speaking, are very high. The common thread throughout, is that Virginia companies can find competitive advantage only through constant attention to creativity, innovation, and productivity."

In the mid-1980s, while the rest of the world was trying to figure out how to send a fax by computer, Northern Virginia was craftily constructing the onramp to the information highway. Steered by a smart, forward-thinking, economic development division, Fairfax County set about tilling the ground and getting the word out: this is where information technology of the future begins. So when America awakened to the seemingly limitless uses for wireless communications, there sat Fairfax. It was ready and waiting with its highly-educated workforce, its proximity to America's policymakers, one of the best public schools systems in the country, and not without note, exceptional quality of life.

AT&T Communications, GTE Telenet and Comstat General Telesystems were among the first to take advantage of all the county had to offer. As technology became more and more advanced, Northern Virginia became an incubator for every

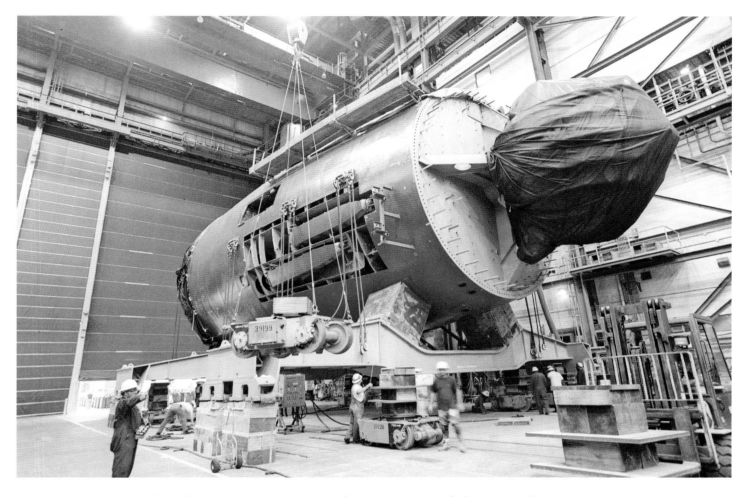

A nuclear submarine being built at the Newport News shipyard. Courtesy, Northrop Grumman

facet of its industry. By the mid-1980s, some 200 software companies had set up shop there.

When the Telecom Act of 1996 broke the chokehold the "Baby Bells" had on the local telephone market, maverick competitive local exchange carriers (CLECs) took on the Bells using advanced technologies and highly-developed business practices. Once again, Northern Virginia was ready with infrastructure in place and user-friendly economic development officials. In just a few years, it had become a hub for global communications.

Just as the new global economy was pumping fresh life into the economy of Northern Virginia, it was simultaneously sucking the lifeblood from the little mining and factory towns of Virginia's southside.

Over the last two centuries, manufacturing had turned whistle stops into towns and then into small cities. Dan River Mills churned out towels and household textiles. Martinsville's Tultex had transformed the sweatshirt from cold-weather,

manual labor-wear, into a fashion item. Henry County's furniture factories were sources for the most notable furniture companies in the mid-Atlantic. But, as the twentieth century was drawing to a close, southside Virginia's factory and mill towns were building unemployment lines.

By the 1990s, the negative effects of globalism were becoming apparent in Virginia's southside. The textile industry was in tatters. Martinsville, once the self-proclaimed T-Shirt Capital of the World, had been stripped naked when the words "third world sweatshop" entered the American lexicon. Close on the heels of the demise of the textile industry, the furniture industry in the southside, once a center for fine furniture manufacturing, went into rapid decline.

Dropping furniture sales and increasing imports swallowed southside Virginia's furniture industry, largely centered in Martinsville. Bassett Furniture Industries, an established business that had survived generations, closed three plants in

*Virginia Biotechnology Research Park.
Courtesy, Virginia Commonwealth
University*

2001, forcing more than 1,000 workers into unemployment. And Bassett was just one of scores of furniture industry casualties that fell to competition from China.

However, the downward trend of the manufacturing industry wasn't felt only in Virginia. As Chinese imports flooded through Hampton Roads, America's manufacturers took it on the chin, losing 3 million jobs in the first four years of this century. Of all the new Chinese products to come through the Virginia port, furniture imports showed the greatest increase. Not only was China's workforce cheap, the country's inspections policy ensured quality that matched American-made products. In 2001, the furniture industry across America suffered through 122 mass layoffs (defined by the U.S. Department of Labor as 50 or more lost jobs).

Although Richmond never regained its antebellum prominence as the South's major industrial center before the Civil War, it made great strides to cement its place as an important center for commerce. At one time, Richmond had boasted of the number of Fortune 500 companies located there. Now the number has fallen to seven, leaving local economic developers to boast the state's number of Fortune 1000 companies in the metro area.

A frantic flurry of bank mergers in the 1990s threatened Richmond's place as the hub of Virginia's commerce. Locally-owned banks morphed into megabanks as outsiders bought and merged them. While Virginia worked hard to protect its financial centers from such a fate, the new monoliths moved their headquarters out of Virginia to states where laws were more liberalized and friendly to big business. But, as large banks got larger, small Virginia banks got busier. Soon, Virginia's big banking industry had been replaced with a new crop of community banks, many with deposits in the hundreds of millions of dollars.

For awhile, it looked like McLean-based Capital One Financial Corp. would help reshape Richmond's new position in the banking industry shift. Using high-tech solutions, through constant experimentation and refining of results, the credit card and financial services company deftly carved out niche markets for its product and services. The company did so well that it hired literally thousands of people each year for five years, until the late '90s when it became the largest non-government employer in the Richmond area.

With more than half of its nearly 17,000 worldwide employees situated in Richmond, the credit card and financial services company generated goodwill and loyalty in the area. However,

Governor Mark R. Warner

Governor Mark Warner. Courtesy, Office of the Governor.

Nineteen-ninety-six was a fortuitous year for Virginians. Both the business community and the telecom industry knew about Mark Warner. Although he came from a working class family in Indiana, Warner seemed destined—or at least determined—to lead Virginia into the twenty-first century, one way or another.

Soon after his graduation from Harvard Law School, young Warner decided to be an entrepreneur. Always a little ahead of the curve, he chose telecommunications as the place to build his empire. He began with a cellular telephone company. He wound up founding Columbia Capital Corporation, a venture capital firm that helped create more than 70 telecommunications and information technology companies—many of which went public.

Warner got his first good taste of Virginia politics managing L. Douglas Wilder's successful bid for governor in 1989. Warner established himself with state democrats and actually headed the state party from 1993 to 1995.

By the time he ran for U.S. senate in 1996, Warner was a self-made multi-millionaire, with plenty of cash to fund a run and the vision to lead the state into the next century. But longtime incumbent republican John W. Warner (no relation) held fast with the voters. The loss didn't dampen the neophyte politician's zeal.

With an estimated net worth of $200 million, Warner built a war chest, largely with his own money, to run for governor in 2001.

Warner handily beat former Attorney General Mark Earley, only to find that he would be hamstrung with the $6 billion revenue shortfall left to him by Governor Jim Gilmore. Since his inauguration in January 2002, Governor Warner has sought to cut the deficit by reforming government services and spending, while making sure that education and economic development continue to thrive.

in April 2004, company officials announced that operating costs—estimated to be 20 percent higher than competitors'—had to be cut. Although the plan was to gradually level the costs by outsourcing, layoffs, and attrition, there was no way the beefy Richmond operation would escape the effects of a 20 percent cut in workforce. Rumors circulated that perhaps as much as 75 percent would be trimmed from the Richmond operation. Hopes that Capital One would be Richmond's silver bullet deflated.

Like Capital One, Motorola's attempt to create a $3 billion plant near Richmond became a cautionary tale of sorts. When an enthusiastic Governor George Allen announced in December 1997 that Motorola—the world's third-largest chipmaker—would be constructing a semiconductor plant with 2,500 new jobs in Goochland County, he was confident that Virginia was well on the way to becoming Silicon Valley East or, as he called it, the Silicon Dominion. With the expectation that it would generate $560 million in tax revenues over 20 years, the company was offered an $85.6 million, five-year incentive package to locate there.

But supply far outstripped demand, and within a year Motorola closed down construction. No jobs were lost. The 25 or so employees onsite had been brought to the area by Motorola. But while Motorola's effort wasn't fulfilled, other semiconductor concerns have fared better. Although its White Oak Semiconductor plant was a disappointment, Infineon Technologies announced in early 2004 that it would expand its Richmond presence. The $1 billion project is expected to be producing 25,000 wafer starts per month in 300mm technology in 2005.

Although its prominence as a center for commerce has diminished, the foresight of local economic development leaders helped lay the groundwork for a new technology platform for the area. Downtown's Virginia Biotechnology Research Park, which provides research facilities for more than 1,000 researchers, has generated spin-offs and entrepreneurial opportunities in such fields as drug development, biomedical engineering, forensics, and environmental analysis. When the park is finally completed, it will house 1.5 million square feet of research space in 20 or so buildings—enough space for 3,000 researchers.

As the coal, textiles, and furniture manufacturing industries of Southwest Virginia fell from prominence into wholesale devastation, everyone—from government officials and politicians to the nearly obsolete Virginia Coalfield Economic Development Authority—joined forces to bring technology jobs to the area. Even the Virginia Employment Commission pitched in, opening a call center in Grundy that employs 70 area residents.

While the trend toward outsourcing leans heavily toward offshore labor, a number of companies have set up call centers in Southwest Virginia. Some, like the Internet travel planner, Travelocity, or the telecom company Nexus Communications, didn't last. But others, like Logisticare and Crutchfield, continue to do well.

In the Tidewater, where generations of shipbuilders have produced ocean-going vessels for hundreds of years, the end of the Cold War signaled a huge drop in the need for defense wares, and high-ticket warships fell off the priority list. Newport News Shipbuilding was forced to shave its workforce by almost half what it had been 10 years earlier. But the company turned out to be as durable as the warships it built. Stringent belt-tightening measures helped it stay the course, even surviving a labor strike in 1999, only to emerge stronger and sounder than any time in its 118-year history.

By spring 2001, Newport News Shipbuilding (NNS) had accumulated orders for submarine and aircraft carriers totaling $7 billion. Nearly 10 years before, NNS visionaries had the foresight to make a long-term commitment of $1 billion to upgrade its information technology. Indeed, in 2001, the company's newest aircraft carrier, the *Ronald Reagan*, went to sea with its own LAN (local area network) and 1,800 computer drops to allow 6,000 crewmembers to stay in touch with home via email.

NNS's eye on the future as well as its track record caught the attention of two giants. The same year that the *Ronald Reagan* was christened, General Dynamics made an all-cash offer to purchase

Philip Morris U.S.A.

Even though smoking is considered a social blight, a health hazard, and just too expensive, Virginians were delighted when Philip Morris USA announced that it would be moving its headquarters to Richmond. Say what you will, Virginia's economy was built on the leaf. From that crisp day when the seeds sown by John Rolfe began to peek above the earth, tobacco farming in Virginia has been revered as an honorable profession. Its related industries are still a cornerstone of Virginia commerce.

Since it began spitting out cigarettes in a factory on the south side of Richmond in 1973, Philip Morris has fed the state's economy in multiple ways. For one, it has supported tobacco farmers, buying from more than 1,500 Virginia growers in 2003. During that time, the company bought half of the state's burley output and approximately 35 percent of its flue cured leaf. Its state-of-the-art manufacturing operations employ hundreds of workers and produces 600 million cigarettes a day.

The company has plumped the area's tax base as well. With 650 employees living in the Richmond area, Philip Morris USA (PMUSA) contributes approximately $638 million annually to the Virginia economy through payroll and benefits. And with a planned $300 million investment in capital infrastructure at the Richmond plant, the numbers are growing. Add to that the $500 million that the state of Virginia has received from PMUSA and other big cig manufacturers under the Tobacco Settlement Agreement, and it's hard to deny: tobacco has been very, very good to Virginia.

Taxes and revenues aside, PMUSA is known for being a good corporate citizen. The company's support of the arts in its local communities has helped transform and even professionalize some arts and culture organizations. For instance, with its own ardent support base and some significant gifts from PMUSA, the Richmond Ballet has gone from a fledgling start-up to a well-regarded regional professional ballet company.

Philip Morris' headquarters. Courtesy, Philip Morris

the company. But with the specter of potential antitrust allegations hovering over the Falls Church-based contractor, Los Angeles-based Northrop Grumman Corporation moved in quickly with an offer of $2.6 billion, making the buy-in the state's largest merger of the year.

Historically, war has economically buffeted Virginia's economy when other areas of the country were stuck with only its harsh realities. And America's war on terrorism is no different. After 9/11, Virginia's defense and telecommunications industries had all the tools in place to get the war on terrorism off the ground. In a state where intelligence, communications, and military are cornerstones of the economy, counter-terrorism became big business almost overnight as

This impressive statue of George Washington which stands in the rotunda of the state capitol in Richmond is a popular tourist attraction. It was sculpted by Jean Antoine Houdon, and is the only such statue of Washington taken from life. Photo by Mark Gibson

Virginia's $30 billion defense industry went into high gear.

In Northern Virginia, where defense contracting has long been big business because of its gold-collar workforce and its proximity to ports and federal government, the effect was profound. Armed with a budget that would only get bigger, the newly formed Homeland Security agency went to work, spending millions on the very products and services that are so plentiful just across the state line from the nation's capital. When defense experts began scouting contractors for the most advanced combat communications and coordination systems, they touched off a NoVa-centric explosion of initial public offerings (IPOs) in defense contracting firms, the biggest surge in years.

As it has for wars past, Hampton Roads, with its multifaceted defense industry, ramped up for engagement, this time with cyber-weapons and war canon. In Newport News, the $58 million Virginia Advanced Shipbuilding and Carrier Integration Center has become the nation's headquarters for developing submarines and aircraft carriers outfitted with the most advanced technological developments usable in modern defense. At the nearby Norfolk Naval Station, the Atlantic fleet mustered firepower and sorted logistics, while the Norfolk Naval Shipyard in Portsmouth set about updating Cold War-era naval weaponry to meet the needs of a new kind of war. Meanwhile, Langley Air Force Base in Hampton prepared its grounds for a new generation of jet fighters.

Tourism has long been the jewel in the Commonwealth's crown. However, after 9/11 airline reservations shrunk and even train travel was viewed with some skepticism as a safe mode of transportation. Not only did tourist attractions suffer, the rest of the tourism industry—from hotels to restaurants to leisure activities—felt the strain. But even when the travel industry struggled nationwide in the aftermath of the disaster, Virginia's commitment to tourism held its own.

Luckily, in Virginia you're never too far from a historical monument or a theme park. The savvy Virginia Tourism Corporation kept

L. Douglas Wilder, America's First African American Governor

Perhaps one of the most ironic moments in modern Virginia history occurred on election day in 1985. That evening, Lt. Governor elect L. Douglas Wilder chose a downtown Richmond landmark, the John Marshall Hotel, to announce the victory that made him the highest-ranking African American state official in the country.

After its opening in 1929, the hotel buzzed with businessmen and politicos, cracking deals while they sipped after-work refreshments. By the time Virginians went to the polls in 1985, it was no longer the grand dame it once had been. But the location wasn't chosen by chance, by price or by bid. It held much greater significance for Wilder, the grandson of slaves. As a college student, he had spent a great deal of time at the John Marshall, earning tuition money by bussing tables.

In 1989, Wilder celebrated a bigger victory in the former capital of the Confederacy when he was elected America's first African American governor. Although he won by the narrowest of margins, his 1 percent edge was enough to consider the victory momentous in a state where at least three-quarters of the population was white. But Wilder's political career was a series of firsts, beginning with his election to the Virginia State Senate in 1969, making him the first African American elected to the post in modern times.

After his graduation in 1951 with a bachelor's degree from Virginia Union University, then a college for blacks, Wilder was drafted into the U.S. Army. After serving in Korea, Wilder returned to his hometown of Richmond, hoping to study law on the GI Bill. But in Virginia,

at the time, blacks were barred from attending law school. Instead, Wilder went to Howard University in Washington, where he was awarded his law degree.

During his service in the Virginia Senate, Democrats zeroed in on Wilder as a candidate who could win much bigger posts, and groomed him to run in 1985 as Gerald L. Baliles' ticket mate for lieutenant governor. Four years later, he was elected governor.

To state democrats, Wilder's political future looked limitless. Halfway through his four-year term as governor, Wilder announced his wishes to be the national party's candidate for the presidency. Although he led the polls in three states with large African American populations, Wilder dropped out of the race. That decision helped Bill Clinton become the Democratic candidate for the presidency in 1992.

Governor Wilder quickly resumed his focus on Virginia's budget deficit and other matters of the state. Reduced defense spending and an unsteady national economy had pitched the state into its worst budget crisis since World War II.

The L. Douglas Wilder Library and Learning Center was constructed at Virginia Union University in 1997. The library facility honors Wilder, a 1951 VUU alumnus and board member. Courtesy, Virginia Union University

But Wilder carved out a plan for reduced spending. Not only did he balance the budget, he maintained the state's AAA bond rating—and did so without raising taxes.

As his gubernatorial reign was coming to a close, Wilder announced he would take on fellow democrat Charles S. Robb for his seat in the U.S. Senate. Robb had preceded Wilder as both lieutenant governor and governor before his election to the U.S. Senate in 1989. Wilder's run as an independent was short-lived. In January 1994, during the last months of his term as governor, he withdrew his bid for the senate.

After leaving office, Governor Wilder became more personality than politician and hosted his own television and radio shows that dealt with current events. Today he spends time lecturing, writing, and serving as a distinguished professor at Virginia Commonwealth University's Center for Public Policy.

tourist destinations jumping by strategically promoting day trips that packed full days of entertainment and leisure into drives not much longer than a Greenwich-NYC commute. It worked. In 2002, while other industries were in emotional and financial recovery, tourism in the Commonwealth rose 1.8 percent to more than $14 billion.

Economic development got a boost in 2003 when Virginia joined 19 other states in enacting a business trust law. The law, which affords greater latitude in businesses' organization and operation practices, has made Virginia even more attractive to investment.

The war in Iraq has not only continued the need for big ships and heavy metal. It also has fueled the urgent need for real-time intelligence, in turn providing even more demand for the already solid defense-contracting industry in Northern Virginia. The number of defense contractors involved in homeland security—companies like ManTech International Corp. of Fairfax and CACI International in Arlington, which assess security and develop technical counter-terrorism solutions—continues to grow.

Virginia ports are poised for their part in the ongoing, ever-growing global economy. The forward-thinking Virginia Port Authority is braced for the flood of imports with a $3 billion 12-year plan to expand and upgrade its facilities in every way, from dredging channels to reinforcing wharves, as well adding larger cranes and container facilities.

In the Southwest, call centers have narrowed the employment gap between that region and the rest of Virginia. Even when internet travel planner Travelocity whittled down its operation in Dickinson County, and Nexus Communications, one of the area's first telecom companies, went bankrupt, other concerns, like AT&T's Relay Center for the hearing-impaired and Verizon's directory-assistance center have trundled along for a decade. Others, such as Crutchfield, Logisticare,

and Sykes Enterprises continue to find the area a good location for their operations. Now the coalfields region, which stretches over seven counties, has 10 call centers employing 2,000 workers.

Manufacturing in Southwest Virginia is on the upswing, too. By early 2004, three major companies announced plans to open facilities there. Globaltex Inc., an international maker of chenille and textured yarn for domestic upholstery, expects to hire 154 workers and invest more than $5 million in its Henry County operation. Master-Brand Cabinets Inc, the second-largest cabinet manufacturer in North America, also announced plans to locate a manufacturing facility in Henry County, promising a multi-million dollar investment in real estate and equipment and 700 new jobs over the next seven years. And Washington-based defense contractor MZM Inc. is moving into Martinsville's Clearview Shell Building to set up a database and information technology operation, creating 150 jobs over three years and representing a $4.4 million investment in the area.

In 2003, Richmond's weakened foothold as an East Coast business center firmed considerably when PMUSA relocated its headquarters to Henrico County, generating 650 jobs and an annual payroll of $83 million. The company added $300 million to its earlier commitment of a $125 million investment in its Richmond cigarette manufacturing operations. Things looked up for the local banking industry, too, when Wachovia Corp. announced that it would locate headquarters for Wachovia Securities and Prudential Securities in Richmond.

The future continues to look bright for the Old Dominion. Early in 2004, Chicago-based Pollina Corporate Real Estate, a site-selection firm, ranked Virginia as the most business-friendly state in America, using benchmarks that included taxes, right-to-work legislation, energy costs, state economic incentive programs, and infrastructure spending.

The skyline behind the James River in
Richmond. Photo by Bob Krist.
Courtesy, Virginia Tourism Corporation

Shipbuilding recovered from its post–
World War II slump with the advent of
the nuclear age. In 1985, the Newport
News Shipbuilding and Dry Dock
Company employed 30,000 workers for
the production of nuclear vessels for the
U.S. Navy. Photo by Robert Llewellyn

CHRONICLES OF LEADERSHIP

◆

A close working relationship between state government and the local business community is a matter of tradition in Virginia. It dates back to the founding of England's "First Colony," and an era when government and its business interests were one and the same.

European adventurers saw the New World embrace a whole new range of economic opportunities. Spanish fleets and French traders had already demonstrated that there were riches to be "taken" from the wilderness. And, although settlers had anticipated traveling down a road paved with gold and silver, their dreams fell short.

By the time the 1600s had begun, tobacco had been imported from the West Indies. It was crossed with a locally grown variety and a new hybrid was born, one that captured the English market. By 1618, Virginia was exporting 25 tons of tobacco each year—the colonists had finally found their gold mine.

Shortly after, land grants were offered to colonists who completed their indentures. This meant that in the New World, any man could become a landowner. Within a decade, tobacco and real estate became the foundation of the Virginia economy.

Eventually the cotton industry gained steam, and plantations sprang up throughout the Old Dominion. However, as time passed, cotton fell by the wayside—and tobacco and real estate regained their power and influence once again.

Today, Virginia has traded its rural roots for a truly global economy. Smokestacks have taken a backseat to science and, although still important, tobacco has been outshined by technology. The Old Dominion has worn many hats, but it is the *people* who have kept the state strong and prosperous.

As the tenth state in the Union, Virginia has always been a trendsetter—government officials, business leaders, and everyday citizens have worked together in a collaborative effort to help shape industries and attitudes. In this chapter you will learn about some of the companies and organizations that have grown along with the state. From major corporations to "mom and pop" businesses and nonprofit agencies, these stories illustrate the gumption and fortitude that has helped set Virginia apart from the rest of the country. Whether a commercial establishment or an educational institution, these local leaders have had a hand in making Virginia the great state it is today.

ALFA LAVAL

Alfa Laval, with its USA headquarters in Richmond, Virginia, is part of an established Swedish company, which returned to the Swedish Stock Exchange in 2002. The global firm specializes in the areas of heat transfer, separation, and fluid handling. Alfa Laval manufactures products that transport, heat, cool, and separate fluids, as well as separate liquids from solids. Many products we use in our everyday lives reach us with the help of Alfa Laval.

The company's products and processes help in the production of every-

thing from beer to salsa, the reuse of fuels, energy reduction, air conditioning, the manufacture of pharmaceuticals, and the treatment of sludge in our municipal wastewater systems. Alfa Laval is also known as an environmentally-friendly company with highly efficient products, which use a minimal amount of energy and consume a minimal amount of the earth's natural resources.

The company dates back to 1877 when employees of Kloster Mill, in Dalecarlia, Sweden were discussing a new German invention for separating cream from milk. One employee, Gustaf de Laval, a young engineer felt he could greatly improve on the German machine. That year, he produced the first continu-

Gustaf de Laval's innovative thinking led to the development of the first continuous separator, Alfa Laval's earliest product.

The Alfa Laval cream separator was important for the dairy farmers in the USA, providing an efficient and fast way of separating cream from milk.

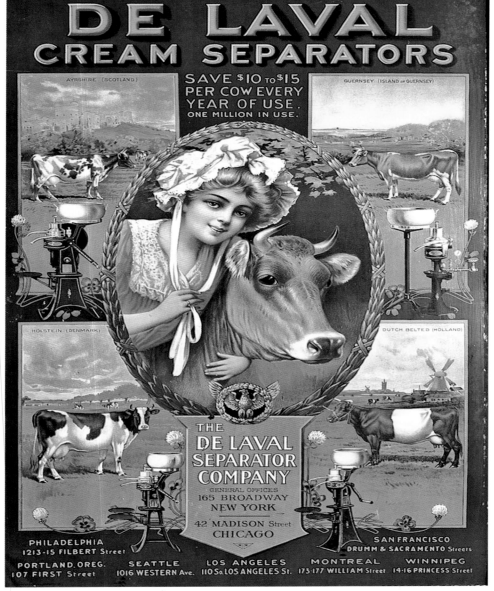

ous separator, which soon became known around the world. In 1878, the de Laval separator was officially introduced.

By 1879, de Laval had perfected his separator to skim 50 churns of milk (more than 35 gallons) an hour and to rotate at 5,000 revolutions per minute—a major feat. The price of the first separator was 450 Swedish Kronor (approximately $60 using current rates). In 1883, de Laval and Oscar Lamm founded AB Separator in Stockholm, the forerunner to what is now known as Alfa Laval.

Alfa Laval was originally founded in the United States in 1883 as the De Laval Cream Separator Company. The demand from dairy farmers for an efficient and fast way of separating cream from milk was growing enormously. The company sold a total of 560 centrifugal separators to dairy farms throughout the northeastern United States that year.

In 1884, Oscar Lamm moved from Sweden to run the U.S. branch of the company and in 1885 the business changed its name to the De Laval Separator Company. By the end of the nineteenth century substantial investments had been made in the new market, but

Kirk Spitzer, president of Alfa Laval in the USA.

with little results. It wasn't until John Bernstrom became head of the parent company in Sweden that the U.S. company prospered.

Bernstrom discovered that their Swedish employees in America were selling the company's trade secrets to American competitors. Among the competitors was a company run by a man named Philip Sharples, who had once been an employee of the De Laval Separator Company. De Laval Separator saw its profits begin to rise substantially once the leak of valuable information had been stopped.

In 1890, De Laval broke ground for its first major U.S. separator manufacturing plant in Poughkeepsie, New York, along the banks of the Hudson River. By 1892, production at the factory was in full swing. Its first manager was a Swedish American by the name of August Almqvist. In 1903, they produced and sold more than 40,000 of De Laval's hand-driven separators.

In 1917, the company expanded its U.S. operations and the following year engineers working for the American com-

pany invented a new milking machine. The design was so innovative that it was immediately marketed throughout the country and became a major success for De Laval. It moved the company in exciting new directions and created a new market for growth. By 1923, Sweden began manufacturing the American machine for sales worldwide.

During the 1920s, the Swedish company's affiliate in Germany started manufacturing plate heat exchangers as pasteurizers. During World War II, manufacturing was moved to Lund, Sweden and the plate pasteurizer was sold to breweries. In the 1950s, it moved into industrial uses such as those in the chemical and processing industries. Since then, Alfa Laval has embraced a broad range of industrial and sanitary industries with its plate heat exchangers.

In 1928, De Laval commissioned a young American artist to celebrate and honor the fiftieth anniversary of the invention of the De Laval separator. The artist was Norman Rockwell. Rockwell's painting depicts a young boy painting a kite while sitting on a milk crate with the name De Laval stenciled on it— a name, which by then, was a household name on most dairy farms.

By the beginning of World War II the U.S. company had increased its workforce to 2,300.

De Laval Separator also reached a major turning point at this time. During the war there was a dangerous shortage of lubricating oil, and the United States Navy approached the company for a solution. De Laval eagerly took on the task of finding a way to recycle used oil, realizing that reclaiming spent oil would be a natural application for a version of its separator. Removing the impurities in the oil meant that it could be used over and over again. This invention brought De Laval into the industrial world, and started the company's productive 60-year relationship with the U.S. Navy.

In the 1960s, the American company began to acquire businesses that would enhance its product and service line. One of these was the acquisition of G&H Products, a fittings company, which

Valve assembly in the newly expanded Richmond manufacturing facility.

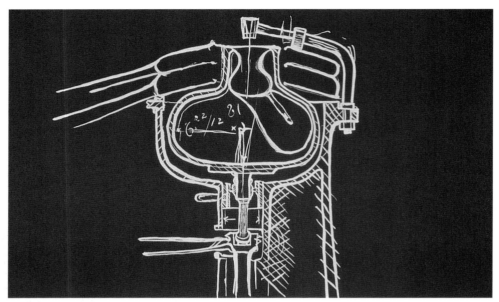

An early sketch of the Alfa Laval separator.

marked De Laval's first foray into the fluid handling business in the USA.

The company continued to expand, and in 1979 De Laval moved its headquarters from Poughkeepsie to Fort Lee, New Jersey. At the same time the company changed its name to Alfa Laval, emphasizing the fact that the company was now moving far beyond its origins as a manufacturer of cream separators. In the 1980s, the company purchased Tri-Clover.

Tri-Clover products are considered the leading sanitary fluid handling equipment in the USA for the food, dairy, beverage, pharmaceutical, and personal care industries. Adding its products to Alfa Laval's helped make the company a leading force in that sector of the market. The product line includes sanitary pumps, filters, strainers, valves, fittings, tubing, and tank equipment.

Today, Alfa Laval is a world leader in the fields of heat transfer, separation and fluid handling, supplying specialized products, and engineered solutions. The equipment, systems, and services are dedicated to assisting customers in optimizing the performance of their processes. From separators and decanters, plate, brazed, spiral and scraped-surface heat exchangers, to pumps, valves, fittings, and tank equipment, Alfa Laval has a diverse product portfolio to offer its customers.

The company's products are found in such diverse areas as the production of oil, desalination of water, wastewater, chemicals, beverages, food, starch, and pharmaceuticals. Its products can also be found on board ships, in air conditioning and heating systems, and in steel and metalworking factories. Alfa Laval backs its products with a parts and service network throughout the United States and the world.

In 2003, Alfa Laval acquired bio-Kinetics, a leader in the engineering and

The Tri-Clover logo represents the leading product range of sanitary fluid handling equipment in the USA.

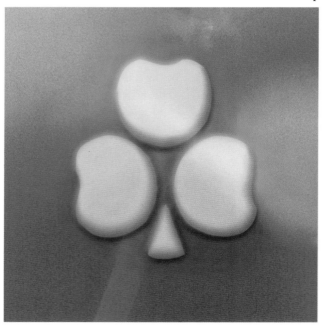

manufacturing of turnkey process systems for the biotech and pharmaceutical industries. The acquisition brought the firm into the earlier stages of pharmaceutical manufacturing.

Kirk Spitzer, a native of Virginia, became president of Alfa Laval Inc. in March 2000. Spitzer joined the company as general manager of Alfa Laval Thermal Division in Fort Lee, New Jersey in 1983 and was named president of that division in 1987. In 1990, he played a leading role in the company's relocation to Richmond from its Fort Lee and Poughkeepsie facilities. Since 2000 he has been the driving force behind the reorganization of Alfa Laval in the U.S. He has also led the expansion of the Richmond facility, which, since 2002, includes the company's USA headquarters. The facility also houses its pump and valve manufacturing areas, in addition to the existing heat exchanger production operations. The Richmond facility now covers approximately 180,000 square feet and employs 250 people.

Under Spitzer's leadership the company has been a major supporter of education. The firm has awarded several scholarships to engineering students and offers one at Virginia Tech, Spitzer's alma mater, and another at Virginia Commonwealth University. The company is also a major supporter of the arts and other nonprofit organizations in the communities where Alfa Laval has a presence.

Alfa Laval in the USA represents about 15 percent of the company's sales and the firm has a presence in more than 100 countries around the world. The company's ambition has not abated since its early days; it is still driven by its founder's desire for innovatation. The same principles that guided Gustaf de Laval to invent new and better products to serve mankind 125 years ago, are still propelling Alfa Laval forward today.

A trainload of pipe, headed from Radford Pipe Works to the Panama Canal, circa 1915. Courtesy, The Library of Virginia

ANSER

In July 1958, the RAND Corporation helped establish ANSER in California as an independent, not-for-profit corporation. The new public service research institution filled the Air Force's need for a technically qualified, objective organization that was close to the Pentagon. Most importantly, it was capable of responding to identified needs for unbiased studies and analyses on a day-to-day basis.

Dr. Stanley J. Lawwill was appointed as ANSER's first president and senior operating officer. He assumed leadership at the institute's temporary office on North Royal Street in Alexandria, Virginia. Lawwill dedicated himself to the principles that were spelled out in his organization's charter. Its mission to serve the public through technical and policy analyses continues to inspire ANSER's ethics and culture, focus its operations, and shape its organization.

A board of trustees with members from business, public service, academia, and military affairs has governed the company from its inception. The board ensures that operations are in the public interest and meet consistently high standards of excellence, objectivity, and utility.

In its early days ANSER served as a Federal Contract Research Center (FCRC). As such, it served a single client —the Air Force. The Air Force's first major document on military space was written at ANSER in 1959. One of

ANSER's office building in 1958.

ANSER's first studies focused on the analysis of short take-off and landing capabilities for military aircraft. Other research projects during the 1960s included the role of the Air Force in anti-submarine warfare and the evaluation of long-range radio navigation accuracy in Southeast Asia.

ANSER dropped its FCRC designation in 1976 and began work for numerous Air Force organizations, along with other Department of Defense components and federal government agencies. Studies conducted during the 1970s helped to put men in space and clarified control issues relating to the third Strategic Arms Limitation Talks (SALT III). In 1982, they

ANSER's four presidents (left to right): Stanley Lawwill, Ruth David, John Fabian, and John Englund.

assisted the White House Office of Science and Technology in its "Report on Contemporary Evolution of U.S. Aeronautical Technology."

Lawwill, ANSER's founding president, retired in 1981. John A. Englund succeeded him as the firm's second president and CEO. By the time ANSER hosted its 25th anniversary party in 1983 at the National Air and Space Museum in Washington, D.C., there were 230 employees. The company's work was used and recognized by the White House, three Department of Defense agencies, seven Air Force directorates, five Air Force Field Commands, U.S. Army Headquarters, NASA, the CIA, and the Arms Control and Disarmament Agency.

On ANSER's 25th anniversary, the Secretary of the Air Force noted that the company's studies and technical approaches had illuminated issues "related to the research, development, and acquisition of almost every major Air Force weapon system over the past quarter of a century." He went on to note that ANSER's work was "marked by quality, responsiveness, and objectivity." President Ronald Reagan remarked on the same occasion that the company's efforts had

"played a valuable role in analyzing our national defense needs and helping maintain American's security."

During the 1980s, ANSER conducted research for almost every major Air Force program and helped to modernize strategic and tactical systems and their supporting communications networks. In 1986, ANSER worked closely with the Air Force, the Department of Defense, and NASA to restore U.S. space launch capability after the *Challenger* space shuttle explosion.

Terrorist activities during the 1980s, including the October 1983 bombing of the U.S. Marine base in Beirut, Lebanon, helped dictate the direction ANSER would take during its third and fourth decades. Regional unrest and instabilities replaced Cold War tensions as the focus for national security issues. In November 1991, Dr. John M. Fabian, a retired Air Force Colonel who had been on board the successful 1983 launch of the space shuttle *Challenger*, became ANSER's third president and CEO. In 1992, ANSER created the Center for International Aerospace Cooperation (CIAC). It became the first U.S. aerospace concern to open an office in Moscow and establish professional contracts within the Russian aerospace industry. By 1995, ANSER had expanded its counter-proliferation and regional security work to encompass several projects for the United Nations—including the U.N. Peacekeeping Organization, High Commission for Refugees, Department for Humanitarian Affairs, and World Food Program.

Dr. Ruth A. David, ANSER's current president and CEO, joined the institute in 1998. David established ANSER as an early leader in homeland security. The firm initiated its Homeland Defense Strategic Thrust in 1999 to address the growing national concern regarding threats from rogue nations, sub-state terrorist groups, and domestic terrorists. Since 2000, the company has focused on providing analytic and technical support to federal agencies in many areas of homeland security, national security, and public safety. Its

Anser Institute for Homeland Securtiy (AIHLS) projects.

work has included security system development and acquisition, information system planning, and foreign technology analyses.

Before the terrorist bombings of September 11, 2001 ANSER had already established its own Institute of Homeland Security (AIHLS) in April 2001. The goal was to enhance public awareness and education in all areas of homeland security. AIHLS, under its founding director, Colonel Randall J. Larsen, initiated electronic publication of the *Weekly Homeland Security Newsletter* and the *Journal of Homeland Security*, both available via www.homelandsecurity.org. By 2004, more than 28,000 decision makers in the education, industry, government, response, and research fields received the newsletter by email subscription. AIHLS addressed a broad range of strategic issues, with particular emphasis on bolstering our nation's ability to counter biological threats. ANSER's AIHLS was subsumed into the Homeland Security Institute, a new federally funded research and development center established by the Depart-

ment of Homeland Security in the spring of 2004.

In June 2002, President Bush appointed David to the Homeland Security Advisory Council. The committee was created to provide the president with recommendations regarding homeland security strategy and policy. In July 2003, David was selected to serve on the Department of Homeland Security's Advisory Council, which provides independent advice to Secretary of Homeland Security Tom Ridge. In December of that year, Ridge appointed David to serve as vice chair of the council's Academe and Policy Research Senior Advisory Committee.

As national security issues have accelerated, so have ANSER's responses to them. Staff members from both ANSER and AIHLS have appeared on national television, from the CBS *News with Dan Rather* to the MSNBC special "Wargame: Iraq." They have discussed issues such as Al Qaeda's use of chemical weapons as well as any U.S. responses to terrorist attacks.

ANSER, now located in Arlington, Virginia, faces research challenges today that are far different from those it faced in 1958. However, the research institute's aim remains the same. Its goal, to promote the public welfare and security of the United States by conducting technical and policy analyses, will guide the company long into the future.

Two analysts at ANSER discuss a project.

ANTONELLI, TERRY, STOUT & KRAUS, LLP

The firm of Antonelli, Terry, Stout & Kraus and its talented intellectual property attorneys have been lauded time and again over the years. They have made a name for themselves due to the number and the quality of patents they have obtained on behalf of their many prestigious clients. Consider the fact that its four namesakes—Donald Antonelli, David Terry, Donald Stout, and Melvin Kraus—have been specializing in patent, trademark, and copyright law since the 1960s. However, their relationships date back even further than that.

Antonelli and Terry met while they were both students in the engineering department at Purdue University in the 1950s. Antonelli was studying electrical engineering, while Terry majored in chemical engineering. After graduation they both came to the Washington D.C. area and began working as patent examiners at the U.S. Patent and Trademark Office (USPTO). In addition to that, the pair also attended law school at night at George Washington University. Antonelli and Terry took and passed the Virginia State Bar together and then went their separate ways. Eventually they started working in different law firms in the Washington D.C. area.

Meanwhile, Kraus came to the area following his graduation from Washington University in St. Louis, Missouri. It was there that he majored in electrical

The firm's founder, Donald R. Antonelli, has had a distinguished career in the practice of law for over 40 years.

engineering. Like Antonelli and Terry, he worked during the day as a patent examiner and studied law at night at George Washington University. In addition to his stint at the USPTO, Kraus also worked as a patent advisor for other agencies including both the Department of the Navy and the Department of the Army.

Stout followed a similar path. He received a degree in electrical engineering from Pennsylvania State University and then headed to Washington D.C. There, he earned his law degree from George Washington University before beginning to practice law as a patent attorney. Over the years, and throughout his employment with other firms, Stout gained considerable experience in litigation and licensing.

The debut of what would eventually become Antonelli, Terry, Stout and Kraus came in 1964 when Antonelli established a firm with another attorney. That attorney ended up leaving and, in 1971, Terry and Kraus joined forces with Antonelli. In the early years of the firm, an emphasis was placed on hiring attorneys who had prior experience as patent examiners. "It is that experience, which allows

you to truly understand the inner workings of the system, that gave us a leg up over our competition in representing our clients," says Antonelli.

In 2003, the USPTO received a whopping 355,418 patent applications and issued a total of 189,597 patents. Of those, 1,423 were issued to clients of Antonelli, Terry, Stout and Kraus, LLP. With that impressive number, this Arlington, Virginia-based law firm specializing in intellectual property was rated thirteenth in the United States in number of patents obtained in 2003.

While the attorneys at this veteran practice are proud of that ranking, they're most proud of another accolade. In 2002 and 2003, Antonelli, Terry, Stout and Kraus was listed as one of the best ten firms in the country in four of six categories (electrical, chemical, mechanical and computer, medical and biotech) and in the top five overall, in terms of obtaining quality patents. In the intellectual property arena, a quality patent is one that provides the broadest scope of protection.

Throughout its long tenure in the patent field, the company has seen its share of excitement. For many years the attorneys occupied the ninth floor of the infamous Watergate building in Washington D.C. They were still in these offices in 1972 when five men were arrested for trying to bug the offices of the Democratic National Party, which was located on the sixth floor. The police and the media flooded the building and the attorneys at Antonelli, Terry, Stout and Kraus watched one of the biggest scandals in U.S. political history unfold before their very eyes.

Years later they got another close-up view of the action as portions of the 1976 film *All the President's Men* were shot on location at the Watergate building. In 1979, the firm left that location and moved into new offices on Pennsylvania Avenue, just three blocks from the White House.

Fifteen years later in 1994, Antonelli, Terry, Stout and Kraus became one of the first of many high-powered businesses to say good-bye to their Wash-

Donald E. Stout (left) and Melvin Kraus (right) in the entrance foyer, adjacent to the main conference room.

ington D.C. offices and move across the Potomac. In its current office space on the eighteenth and the nineteenth floors of one of the tallest buildings in Arlington, Virginia, Antonelli, Terry, Stout and Kraus is said to have one of the best views in the entire Washington D.C. area. The building looks out over the Potomac River, the Washington Monument, the Capitol, the Lincoln Memorial, the Jefferson Memorial, the Iwo Jima Memorial, the Pentagon, Arlington Cemetery, and the Washington National Airport.

Each Fourth of July the firm shares its spectacular view by inviting clients and friends to a party in their offices. From their nineteenth floor perch, they watch the annual fireworks display that routinely attracts hundreds of thousands of people to the Mall. Although many say the real bonus of watching from the office, however, is the cool air conditioning—a welcome relief in the hot, humid summers of the nation's capitol.

The USPTO is only a couple miles away from the new office, and provides easier access to the examiners who have the final word on whether a patent is issued or not. Generally, all communications with the USPTO are done in writing, but thanks to its proximity and its

View of the nation's capitol from the offices of Antonelli, Terry, Stout & Kraus, LLP.

decades of experience, the attorneys at Antonelli, Terry, Stout and Kraus are able to sit down face-to-face with patent examiners. "It's easy for an examiner to say no on the phone. It isn't as easy to do it in person," Kraus says. "When you're sitting across from them, you can explain your case better. It's one of the reasons for our success."

Over the years, the firm has shepherded national and international clients like TRW, Harris, Checkfree, Intel, Hitachi, and Nokia through the extremely complicated patent application process. Antonelli, Terry, Stout and Kraus prepares the patent application, which includes descriptions and drawings of the invention as well as claims which define the scope of protection to be granted. Once

the application is submitted, an examiner is assigned to the file and researches existing U.S. and foreign patents in the same area. The examiner determines if an invention merits a patent or if it is too similar to existing patents. If a patent receives a rejection, the attorneys either make amendments to the claims or attempt to overturn the examiner's decision by showing how the invention actually is different than existing patents.

The firm which has extensive experience in counseling individual and corporate clients in all areas of intellectual property law including licensing, patent enforcement, and defense is especially known for its skill in one particular arena —interference. Interference is when two different inventors say they've come up with the same invention and there's a proceeding before a panel of three judges to determine which inventor came up with the invention first. Everywhere else in the world, the patent would be given to the person who filed the patent application first, regardless of who actually invented it first. Only in the U.S. is the patent granted to the person who can prove he or she was the first to come up with the invention.

Attorneys at Antonelli, Terry, Stout and Kraus recently argued and won just such a case when they represented the Canadian government in a dispute over an invention involving fiber-optic mod-

From left to right: partners, William I. Solomon, Alfred A. Stadnicki, Melvin Kraus, Alan E. Schiavelli, and Gregory E. Montone.

From left to right: partners, Carl I. Brundidge, Hung H. Bui, Donald E. Stout, Frederick D. Bailey, and Paul J. Skwierawski.

From left to right: partner Ronald J. Shore (center) with associate Sterling W. Chandler (left) and patent agent Larry N. Anagnos.

ulations used in communications. The inventor the firm represented wasn't the first to file a patent application, but the client had kept meticulous records about the invention. Thanks to that foresight, the attorneys were able to prove that the person who had filed the application first had actually gotten the idea for the invention from its client. "It's pretty rare to have good evidence like that, though," Kraus says.

The firm's skill in the interference arena is part of why the practice has had continued success in an arena that is currently exploding. The intellectual property law field is experiencing a major boom. In part, that's due to the fact that more people understand how important it is to protect their intellectual property. Whether it's a big firm, a small company, or even an individual, getting a patent, trademark, or copyright is essential in today's business world. "Some individual inventors have been awarded millions of dollars for infringement," Kraus says. "It's expensive to litigate, but the only way to protect yourself is with a patent."

As the number of intellectual property law firms swells, there's no question that Antonelli, Terry, Stout and Kraus will continue to be considered one of the nation's top firms. Even though the company is small in comparison to some of the others in the industry, it expects to continue its tradition of effective representation for its clients in the intellectual property field. However, its commitment is to the area just as much as the industry. "Virginia has been our home base for more than a decade now," Kraus says. "We're here for the long haul."

David T. Terry, counsel to the firm.

Law library adjacent to the entrance foyer and stairway to the 19th floor.

Yorktown Battlefield is the site of the final, major battle of the American Revolutionary War and the symbolic end of Colonial English America. Courtesy, Virginia Tourism Corporation

C&F MORTGAGE

Buying a home is all about the right fit. It's not just finding the real estate that matches a buyer's lifestyle, it's also securing the financing that fits his or her unique needs. That is where the Virginia-based C&F Mortgage Corporation makes all the difference.

C&F Mortgage was established based on the belief that every potential homeowner deserves individual customer care and service. Buyers are often making the biggest financial commitment of their lives, so C&F was created to offer not two or three mortgage options, but two or three dozen in many cases.

It is beyond doubt that for this firm, the tone is set at the top by Bryan McKernon, the company founder. McKernon, who served in the Virginia-area mortgage business for many years, had tired of the industry's rampant mergers and takeovers, which resulted in an impersonal, one-size-fits-all practice.

He began to lay the groundwork in the mid-1980s by assembling a team of top-notch professionals who reflected his work ethic. They also shared his belief that the mortgage business could be a true service industry. Under the leadership of McKernon, the group focused on a

Bryan E. McKernon, president (left) and Mark A. Fox, executive vice president (right).

commitment to local homebuyers, as well as the realtors, brokers, builders, and developers with whom they worked.

In 1995, McKernon joined forces with Citizens and Farmers Bank, a regional bank that had an established reputation as an ethical and customer-oriented institution since 1927. As a result, on September 12, 1995, C&F Mortgage was incorporated.

Serving as president and CEO, McKernon continued to operate the five offices—located in Richmond (2), Fairfax, and Newport News, Virginia and Annapolis, Maryland—that had already been established prior to creating C&F Mortgage. The new name did not change the 60-member team's dedication to its original commitment to provide quality customer service.

Today, the firm thrives while maintaining the personal touch and recognizing its customers by sight and calling them by name. Its growth and success have strengthened the team's resolve to be the best and provide the best.

Just as homebuyers can pick a two-bedroom town home, or a six-bedroom farmhouse, they can pick their financing plan. C&F offers conventional, jumbo, FHA, VA mortgages, ARMs, and several kinds of balloon and niche mortgages, including no-income or asset verification, 103 percent financing, subprime, combination, second-home, bridge loan, lot loan, construction loan, rural development loan, 203 (K) loan, interest-only products, and many more.

If the choices seem staggering, and the benefits of each option more confusing then the next, C&F Mortgage's experienced staff is on hand to give expert advice. The company's experienced loan officers guide first-time homebuyers and clients who have been through multiple real estate transactions with the same care and commitment. They work hard to find the best plan for each customer's particular purchase.

Fundamental to C&F Mortgage's customer satisfaction is what the company calls its one-stop-shopping benefit. Homebuyers can complete the processing, underwriting, and closing all through C&F. The firm also offers its own on-site appraisal and title insurance services, for further convenience.

With no centralized or regional facilities, all transactions are conducted in person in one C&F Mortgage office; therefore, the entire process is monitored and kept on track from beginning to end. In fact, the loan officers provide progress reports to clients ensuring not only that

C&F clients have open door access to the executive management team.

C&F Mortgage's corporate headquarters is located at 1400 Alverser Drive in Midlothian, Virginia.

the buyers get what they want, but it also provides some much needed peace of mind.

Clients also have open-door access to the executive management team, who are active in every customer's transaction. As a result, the person with the authority to make the decision or special waiver is on-site and already involved in the progression of the transaction. Through this policy, C&F guarantees a more efficient, streamlined mortgage processing system.

Each and every team member understands that quality is key to the firm's success. The foundation of the company is built on three quality components: quality service, quality people, and quality work environment. These three principles are not just on paper at C&F, they are part of the everyday culture.

The C&F Mortgage team has created a valued role for the company as a community leader. Employees recognize the importance of giving back to the towns and states which their company calls home. Many local charities and civic groups have benefited from donations given by C&F Mortgage and its employees.

However, the company's commitment to its communities does not stop with financial donations; contributions of time and talent to various organizations is commonplace in day-to-day operations. Many of the company's executives serve on boards for various local organizations including the YMCA, Jaycees, and Workforce Investment. Team members are also very active in Partnership for the Future, a nonprofit alliance of local businesses that support local youth.

C&F Mortgage, with its foundation based on quality and customer service has quickly become recognized as an industry leader. C&F stays ahead of the curve by tracking ever-changing trends and incorporating the latest technological advancements. The industry, which was once predominately paper-based, is rap-idly changing with computer capabilities, and C&F Mortgage remains in step with the evolution.

The company has grown to include 190 employees that work in 16 branches in 12 cities throughout Virginia, Maryland, Delaware, New Jersey, North Carolina, and Pennsylvania. The future holds an unlimited possibility for continued growth in markets that meet the criteria of the organization in relation to its service, people, and environment.

As the firm follows its strategic plan for growth, it will continue to apply its core commitment to values and quality, true to Bryan McKernon's original vision. But no matter the size and scope of C&F Mortgage, the company will continue to remain focused on providing the right fit to every customer, every time.

CHESAPEAKE GENERAL HOSPITAL

Chesapeake General Hospital first opened its doors in 1976, but the quest to open the city's first hospital began long before that January day. It started back in 1966 with an idea by Dr. W. Stanley Jennings, a longtime Chesapeake resident and family practitioner, who had a large family practice in the city and also treated patients at the Norfolk hospitals several miles away. Chesapeake had been incorporated in 1963, and Dr. Jennings felt that it was absurd for a city with a population of 70,000 to not have its own hospital. Several prominent individuals in the community agreed, and the idea moved forward. In March 1966, the Virginia General Assembly established the Chesapeake Hospital Authority with Dr. Jennings as its chairman. The Authority's mission was to "plan, design, construct, remove, enlarge, equip, maintain, and operate hospital and medical facilities," which initiated the planning of Chesapeake's first not-for-profit hospital.

The first meeting of the Authority took place in January of 1967, when the board began investigating various sources of funding. It sent a report to the city's Capital Improvement Budget Committee in 1968 stating the need for a 100-bed hospital and requesting that the city pur-

Chesapeake General Hospital, today.

Considered the father of Chesapeake General Hospital, W. Stanley Jennings, M.D. brought together key leaders in Chesapeake to establish the city's first and only hospital in the early 1970s.

chase a site of approximately 35 acres. In February 1969, the City Council approved a bond referendum for $2.4 million for hospital construction, and that same year purchased the acreage for the new medical facility. The agency also secured a federal Hill-Burton loan in 1971, initially for $561,000, which was eventually changed to a $1 million grant.

That same year the Chesapeake Hospital Authority, through Dr. Jennings, asked Dr. Donald Buckley to serve as a consultant to the project with the intention of him becoming the new hospital's chief executive officer once it was under construction. Dr. Buckley, who was then on the faculty of the University of North Carolina in the department of hospital administration, agreed. By then it had been seven years since the city first began to move toward building a hospital and residents were beginning to doubt that a facility would ever be built. The popular skepticism was evident in a story Dr. Buckley tells of those early days. "I was driving to a meeting one evening when I noticed that the sign on our property, which usually read 'Future Site of Chesa-

peake General Hospital,' had been repainted. It now read 'Future Site of Chesapeake General Woods,' and was indicative of the fact that the residents had waited way too long."

Shortly after that, Dr. Buckley moved from North Carolina to Chesapeake and opened the hospital's first office in a trailer on the wooded site. The trailer had no power, no telephone, no water, nor sewer system. Along with his secretary, Buckley maintained a four-hour electric generator in order to work in the trailer, later replaced with a larger generator.

An architect and engineer were assigned to the project by the Authority; neither of whom had ever built a hospital before, something that would be unheard of today. In the planning of the hospital, the agency gave Buckley two prime directives: create Virginia's first all-private room hospital, and design a structure that could be expanded from its initial 106 beds to a 350-bed facility. Keeping to those parameters Buckley and his team developed a blueprint for an H-shaped facility that would have three patient floors and a fourth floor shell into which they could expand. They also created what is called a "quad pod" on each end of the H, allowing for upward growth.

In 1972, Buckley was officially named CEO of Chesapeake General Hospital (CGH) and by 1973 the hospital was finally under construction. During this time it became apparent that the population of Chesapeake was growing at a steady and rapid rate. Buckley went to the Virginia commissioner of health in order to obtain the state required "Certificate of Public Need," to expand the planned 106-bed hospital to a 141-bed facility. Later another certificate was received allowing the fourth floor shell to be part of the initial construction. CGH opened its doors on January 26, 1976 with 141 beds and 150 employees, finally realizing the community's decade-long dream.

As Chesapeake continued to grow, so did the hospital—expanding to 174 beds by 1981 and 210 beds by 1982. In 1982, CGH put in a request for a "Certificate of Public Need" to create a new obstetrics unit, but the state denied the request. Buckley felt strongly that the denial was unfounded and along with the Chesapeake Hospital Authority filed a lawsuit against the commissioner, and the Virginia courts decided in favor of the new unit and awarded CGH its certificate in 1983. According to Buckley, the commissioner denied their request because it was believed that there was no need for another obstetrics unit in the area.

Today, Chesapeake General's "Birth-Place" delivers more babies than any other community hospital in the South Hampton Roads area. Close to 48,000 babies have been delivered there. The Mother-Baby Unit has 32 private post-partum rooms and features personalized nursing care for parent and child. The unit also includes a Level II nursery for babies that require extra support and care.

With many services being handled on an outpatient basis, in 2000 CGH created a comprehensive outpatient service

Donald S. Buckley, Ph.D, FACHE, became president of Chesapeake General after its founding and has continued at its helm for 32 years.

facility called the W. Stanley Jennings Outpatient Center, named after one of the hospital's founders. CGH saw the new center as a way to make the patient's experience more convenient and streamlined by offering several services in one location. The 19,000-square-foot center is an award-winning design created by the architecture firm of Paul Finch and Associates of Virginia Beach. The first floor contains The Diagnostic Center of Chesa-

peake, a comprehensive diagnostic center which includes mammography, ultrasound, bone density testing, x-ray, EKG, MRI, CT, lab, and general diagnostics. The second floor, The Surgery Center of Chesapeake, is a joint venture with approximately 42 surgeons and anesthesiologists on staff. Part of the strategy behind the Surgery Center was to encourage surgeons to invest their medical skills in the local community, a strategy that has proven quite successful.

The Sidney M. Oman Cancer Treatment Center opened in 1995 and strives to provide the best medical care to patients with cancer. Five radiation oncologists and 14 hematology oncologists operate out of the hospital, which has a 32-bed inpatient cancer unit, treating many types of cancer including breast, prostate, and lung. The center underwent a $5 million expansion in 2004, adding chemotherapy, another linear accelerator, and brachytherapy to its center services. CGH also offers a hospice program through its ComfortCare Home Health Agency.

In 2004, Chesapeake General Hospital officially began its surgical residency program with the Eastern Virginia

The Surgery Center of Chesapeake is designed for patients who have their procedures and return home the same day.

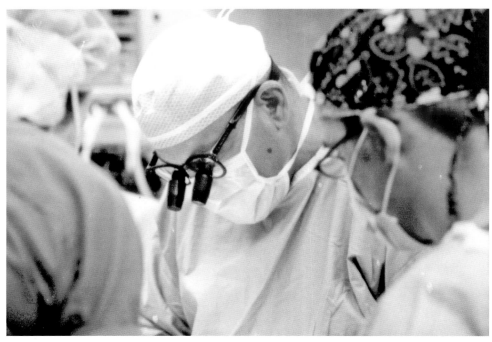

Medical School in Norfolk. The program marked the first significant relationship between CGH and a medical school, including a full team of surgical residents.

Chesapeake Health, the umbrella organization for the family of services, also operates two assisted living facilities nearby. The 82-bed Cedar Manor on Cedar Road includes a 12-bed "memory loss unit," and Georgian Manor has 55 residents. Residents at both facilities must be able to get around on their own or with a walker or wheelchair. Both facilities offer day care for working people with elderly parents who need care or supervision during the workday.

CGH also focuses on preventive care and therapies through its two wellness centers: the Lifestyle Center-CGH and Lifestyle Center-Western Branch. These centers deliver the latest in exercise and wellness services including aerobics, weight-training, monitored exercise, personal training, and health education classes. Additionally, the 45,000-square-foot Lifestyle Center-Western Branch offers an indoor pool for aquatic exercise, as well as tennis courts

and an indoor track. Membership at the two centers now totals more than 3,800. Fees are kept affordable and the facility is open to anyone in the community.

The CGH preventive care program extends even further into the community. In 1980, CGH set up a department of health promotions and health education, one of the first to be established in Virginia. In 1992, CGH discovered that only 10 percent of local students in grades K through 8 were passing the president's physical fitness exam. To remedy the

For over a decade, patients at the Sidney M. Oman Cancer Treatment Center at Chesapeake General Hospital have found the latest technology, compassionate care, and advanced treatment.

situation, CGH searched out and found a California program that had experienced great success introducing Project Fit America, which is an eight-station physical fitness course that can be installed on school playgrounds. Project Fit America also included a curriculum for teachers to instruct students about the dangers of smoking, alcohol, and the importance of good nutrition. CGH went to the local school authorities and agreed to put in these $10,000 units if the school would pay half the costs. Today, the units are in 28 Chesapeake schools and two schools in North Carolina.

CGH also works in partnership with Premier Alliance, a consortium of hospitals that purchase more than $11 billion of medical goods and services annually. This partnership also utilizes a "benchmarking" strategy, allowing CGH to evaluate its operations relative to financial performance and quality of care with peer hospitals that are similar in size and services offered. This allows CGH to more accurately check its own health. A good example of this is the hospital's successful retention of nurses. Where the

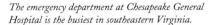

The emergency department at Chesapeake General Hospital is the busiest in southeastern Virginia.

rest of Virginia hospitals and most facilities in the United States deal with a 13 percent vacancy rate, CGH has one that is only 3 to 4 percent. In another strong indicator of health of the hospital, *Money Magazine* recently rated CGH's stroke program as one of the best in the country.

Chesapeake General Hospital has also made a significant contribution to the nearby Dare County area in North Carolina, in the improvement of health care quality and access, since CGH first assumed the management of the Outer Banks Medical Center (OBMC) in 1984. At that time, OBMC was the only medical facility in the area, which consisted of several small communities with a year-round population of about 28,000 and a summer population of nearly 240,000. Before too long Chesapeake Health created 24-hour physician care, enabling OBMC to better meet the urgent and emergency care needs of the area. CGH was also instrumental in changing North Carolina's medical facilities plan to allow for the addition of dialysis services and the building of a hospital.

In 1990, CGH opened the Chesapeake Health Medical Suites in the Marketplace in Southern Shores to attract specialists to the Outer Banks. In 1996, family care services were added to the OBMC. In June 1998, Chesapeake Health joint ventured with Universal Health Systems of Greenville, North Carolina and established the Health East Outer Banks Medical Center. This led to the formation of another joint venture and the creation of the Outer Banks Hospital, a 19-bed facility of which CGH has 40 percent ownership.

To make a lot of these developments and programs possible, CGH relies on its Chesapeake Health Foundation. This is a separate, non-profit entity which was established to raise the necessary funds to enable the hospital and all its ancillary facilities and programs to thrive and grow. The Foundation also involves itself in community outreach as with the recently purchased "Health-

Chesapeake General Hospital, 1976.

Mobile," which travels to under-served areas of the community and businesses to offer flu shots and blood pressure testing, as well as several other educational and diagnostic services.

Today, the approximately 75-acre site of Chesapeake General Hospital's 310-bed facility is caring for the medical needs of a community that has grown to 210,000 residents. There are a total of

2,400 employees in the Chesapeake Health family, plus 550 attending physicians.

It was Dr. Donald Buckley's vision and perseverance that laid the foundation for what is now recognized as one of the foremost medical centers in the state of Virginia. These days, the facility he fought for stands as a testament to his fortitude, and no one in the Hampton Roads area is skeptical anymore.

CT is one of the many diagnostic services offered at Chesapeake General Hospital's full-service radiology department.

THE CHRISTIAN BROADCASTING NETWORK

On April 26, 1607 the first permanent English settlers landed on the shores of what's now called Virginia Beach. Three days later, on April 29, they gathered by the dunes at an area they called Cape Henry. In a ceremony led by Reverend Robert Hunt, the settlers who eventually founded Jamestown planted a large oak cross which they had brought from England and then dedicated the land to God. "That from these very shores," they prayed, "the gospel shall go forth to not only this New World, but the entire world."

Pat Robertson, the founder of the Christian Broadcasting Network (CBN), knew nothing of this ceremony when he held a very similar service more than 300 years later on New Years Eve Day, 1976, only 12 miles away from Cape Henry. Robertson had unknowingly chosen this same area for CBN's new headquarters. Like that ceremony so many years earlier, he dedicated the site to the international propagation of the gospel. The only difference was that Robertson was going to spread the word of the gospel via satellite.

Operation Blessing's medical missions bring medical treatment, surgeries, dental care, and medication to the U.S. and some of the most remote corners of the globe.

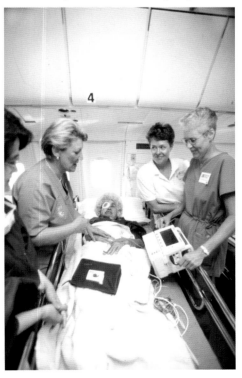

Pat Robertson, founder of CBN Broadcasting Network.

Later that same year, Robertson uncovered the spiritual bond that linked CBN and those first settlers. The discovery finally answered a burning question that had haunted him for some time: Why had God called him to move CBN from its original location in Portsmouth to Virginia Beach? To celebrate the spiritual connection, Robertson led yet another celebration on that very spot at Cape Henry on April 29, 1976, the anniversary of the first settlers prayer. The spiritual leader and his followers dedicated a similar cross and then took it to the future site of the CBN Center. They placed the cross in the ground, where CBN's new headquarters were to be built, and dedicated the land to God and their mission of spreading his gospel to the ends of the earth.

In that time of incredible discovery, the broadcaster learned another bit of information about his personal ties to the state of Virginia. A conversation with a modern-day descendant of the Reverend Robert Hunt revealed that he and Robertson are both decendants of Dr. John Woodson, a surgeon who arrived at Jamestown in 1619. For Robertson, it

was further proof of why God had drawn him to this particular spot.

The evangelist, whose family tree includes kings of England and two American presidents, hadn't always listened to God, though. Born on March 22, 1930, in Lexington, Virginia, Robertson wasn't always the religious icon we know today. The son of a Virginia senator, he graduated with honors from a military prep school, earned a college degree at Washington and Lee University, served in the military in the Korean War, and earned a law degree from Yale. As a young man, Robertson was driven to get on the fast track to success. With some of his Yale buddies, the entrepreneurial law school grad started a business selling electronic components.

Robertson was the picture of success. With a growing business, a beautiful wife named Dede, and a chic residence in New York, he seemed to have it all. But the enterprising fellow couldn't help but feel that something was missing. He kept asking himself, "What is the matter with me?"

After much soul-searching, the up-and-coming business owner realized that his true calling was in the ministry. He sold his portion of the business and entered the seminary. While his spiritual connection with God grew, his income dwindled to almost nothing. One night while praying, he felt he should read Luke 12:33, which says, "Sell all that ye have, and give alms..." He felt as though God was speaking to him through the verse and that until he gave away all of his earthly possessions he couldn't truly know God. So without consulting his wife, Robertson went ahead and sold nearly everything they owned. For many years after that, the couple lived on little more than faith, soybeans, and the kindness of others.

During a visit with his parents in Lexington, his mother handed him a letter she'd received from one of his old classmates—someone Pat hadn't seen in 16 years. The letter had a curious P.S. that read: "There is a television station in Portsmouth, Virginia, that has gone

CBN's studio headquarters building where The 700 Club *is taped daily.*

defunct and is on the market. Would Pat be interested in claiming it for the Lord?" Robertson understood that his destiny was right there before his eyes in that letter.

In November 1959, Robertson left New York with his wife, Dede, and their three children and drove to Tidewater, Virginia, where he planned to buy a bankrupt UHF television station in Portsmouth. Arriving with only $70 in his pocket, Robertson proceeded to raise the funds to purchase the station. CBN was formed January 11, 1960, and on October 1, 1961, CBN went on the air for the first time.

Operating expenses for that first month were only $460. Relying solely on donations, CBN rarely met its monthly budget and was almost constantly operating at a loss. By 1963, the station had a monthly operating budget of $7,000. Unfortunately, that was far more than the contributions that were being received. Robertson refused to increase revenues by selling advertising or by raising capital. Instead, he decided to turn to his viewers for assistance.

In the fall of 1963, CBN went on the air and asked 700 viewers to contribute $10 each per month, enough to cover the monthly budget. The event was a tremendous success and based on that triumph they decided to name the show *The 700 Club*. That night marked the debut of what would eventually become one of

Operation Blessing provides food and relief products to thousands in need each year.

the longest-running daily programs in television history.

Overcoming its financial struggles early on, CBN began to expand. Robertson was incredibly focused and dedicated himself entirely to the ministry, working so many hours that he was always battling exhaustion. His efforts paid off. In addition to the television station, CBN began adding radio stations to its broadcast network—first a radio station in Bogota, Columbia, then five more stations in New York.

By 1973, CBN was reaching 100 million viewers worldwide through its 40 television and radio stations across the U.S., Canada, and overseas. Currently, CBN domestic programs and CBN WorldReach international programs reach nearly 242 million viewers worldwide. By 1981, CBN was reaching 100 million homes—but Robertson still wasn't satisfied. His undeniable drive and determination pushed him to keep expanding CBN as a way to spread the word of God. "By staying in God's will and being obedient to His calling, God continued to bless Robertson and the ministry," says Michael Little, president of CBN.

In the 1970s, Robertson had a vision to establish a graduate-level university that would turn out tomorrow's leaders. That vision materialized in 1977 with the founding of Regent University, the nation's academic center for Christian thought and action. Robertson continues to serve as president and chancellor of the Virginia Beach institution, which offers degrees in business, communications, the arts, divinity, education, government, law, organizational leadership and psychology, and counseling.

Regent also offers a bachelor's degree completion program. Regent University is accredited by the Commission on Colleges of the Southern Association of Colleges and Schools and has an enrollment of nearly 3,000 students. Besides the main campus in Virginia Beach, Regent has a Graduate Center in Northern Virginia/D.C. and offers programs online via its Worldwide Campus.

In addition to broadcasting the gospel message worldwide and creating a graduate-level university, Robertson felt that more needed to be done to help the needy. That inspired him in 1978 to establish Operation Blessing International (OBI), a worldwide relief organization that demonstrates God's love by alleviating human need and suffering in the United States and around the world. The primary goals of OBI are to help break the cycle of suffering by providing hunger relief, medical aid, disaster relief, and other basic necessities of life that will make a significant, long-term impact on those in need. Since its inception, OBI has touched the lives of more than 175 million people in 96 countries and all 50 U.S. states, distributing more than $750 million in goods.

Determined to uphold the rights of people of faith, Robertson also founded the American Center for Law and Justice. This public interest law firm and education group defends the First Amendment rights of people of faith. The agency fo-

Pat and Dede Robertson.

cuses on pro-family, pro-liberty, and pro-life cases nationwide.

Robertson's contribution to the state of Virginia also includes The Founders Inn and Conference Center, a wholly-owned subsidiary of Regent University. Opened in 1991, the facility is located in the greater Norfolk area. It offers 22,000 square feet of meeting space, a

Pat Robertson on the set of The 700 Club.

132-seat theater, 240 guest rooms and suites, two restaurants, and a health club.

Somehow, with all of those activities and organizations, Robertson still managed to find the time to author 16 books. His latest, titled *Courting Disaster*, "addresses the issue of the Supreme Court usurping the power of Congress and the American people." Several of his books have become bestsellers including *The Secret Kingdom*, which hit number three on *Time* magazine's national nonfiction list; and *The New World Order*, which rose to number four on the *New York Times* nonfiction bestseller list.

Today, CBN is a multifaceted nonprofit organization that provides programming by cable, broadcast, and satellite to approximately 200 countries in 71 languages. It also operates a 24-hour telephone prayer line. *The 700 Club* Prayer Counseling Centers (PCC) in Virginia Beach, Virginia and Nashville, Tennessee are departments of The Christian Broadcasting Network (CBN) that provide prayer, scriptural guidance, and literature to people through CBN's telephone prayer line. The center's phone lines are staffed by more than 425 prayer counselors who process nearly 3 million calls a year.

The CBN studios receive over 2.5 million pieces of mail and welcome more than 11,000 visitors annually. A favorite event for CBN visitors is to attend a live taping of *The 700 Club*. The show remains the flagship program of CBN's broadcasting schedule and features Robertson, Terry Meeuswen, Lisa Ryan, Gordon Robertson, Kristi Watts, and Lee Webb. Carried on ABC Family Channel, FamilyNet, Trinity Broadcasting Network, and numerous U.S. television stations, *The 700 Club* presents a lively mix of information, interviews, and inspiration to an average daily audience of approximately one million viewers. On camera, Robertson is just as dynamic and passionate today as he was that first time he went on the air back in 1961.

In the fall of 1995 Robertson launched CBN's international project

Pat and Kristi Watts, one of the hosts of The 700 Club, *tapes a segment for* Pat's Weight Loss Challenge.

has received numerous humanitarian awards. Among the many citations, he was named "Humanitarian of the Year" by Food for the Hungry in 1982 and the Students for America named him "Man of the Year" in 1988. *Newsweek* selected him as one of "America's 100 Cultural Elite." Israel gave him the "Defender of Israel" award in 1994, and the Zionist Organization of America presented him with the "State of Israel Friendship" award in 2002.

Even with all of his accomplishments, Robertson still feels that his work is far from finished. With his wife Dede still by his side after more than 40 years, his four children, and his many grandchildren, the dedicated family man remains determined to find new ways to expand God's reach. Based on his lifetime achievements, it's easy to have faith that he'll succeed in doing just that.

WorldReach in an effort to spread the gospel throughout the world. The goal of CBN WorldReach is to see 500 million people brought to faith in Jesus Christ. In 2002 alone, more than 1,500 various ethnic programs were produced in 41 different languages. WorldReach programs can be seen in more than 200 countries and are accessible by more than 1.5 billion people around the world. Currently, CBN WorldReach international programs and CBN domestic programs reach nearly 242 million viewers worldwide.

Robertson was the founder and co-chairman of International Family Entertainment Inc. (IFE). Formed in 1990, IFE produced and distributed family entertainment and information programming worldwide. IFE's principal business was The Family Channel, a satellite delivered cable-television network with 63 million U.S. subscribers. IFE, a publicly held company listed on the New York Stock Exchange, was sold in 1997 to Fox Kids

Worldwide, Inc. Disney acquired the Fox Family Channel in 2001 and named it ABC Family. After the sale of IFE, Robertson used those finances to fund Regent University and various other charitable organizations.

For a man of his stature, Robertson has never lost the common touch and remains dedicated to helping those in need. Over the years, this compassionate man

"Super Kids Club" in the Ukraine.

DIDLAKE, INC.

Creating opportunities for people with disabilities is the hallmark of Didlake, Inc. As a private, not-for-profit corporation, Didlake has helped individuals find employment and integrate into their communities since 1965. From its origins as a small private school, Didlake, Inc. has evolved into a highly-respected community rehabilitation program, a major regional employer, and an integral part of the Manassas/Prince William County business network. More than 75 percent of Didlake's employees are people with disabilities. But the company is better recognized as a successful business, rather than as a not-for-profit organization that employs the disabled. The people at Didlake wouldn't have it any other way.

Based in Manassas, Virginia, Didlake owns and operates a collection of small businesses and a job placement service. These businesses provide copy and mailroom operations, custodial, grounds keeping, and other administrative services to government agencies and commercial businesses.

Founded in 1965 as a school for the mentally retarded, Didlake was named in honor of a local philanthropic family.

Didlake, Inc. provides a variety of document imaging services for several government agencies ad commercial businesses. Here, Christina Wu-Jian operates equipment at one of Didlake's northern Virginia locations.

Initially located on Sudley Road in Manassas, the institute had an enrollment of 16 children during its first year.

At the time, a new social movement was sweeping across the nation—one that challenged the long-accepted practice of institutionalizing mentally disabled individuals for life. With the congressional passage of the Education for All Handicapped Children Act in 1974, special education programs were implemented in public schools. New ways were also sought for these individuals to make valuable contributions to their communities, when their educations were complete.

When Prince William County adopted an educational program for children with mental retardation in 1975, the Didlake School turned over its buildings and students to the public school system. The organization's board of directors then initiated a new program for former students who were beyond school age. Known as "Step Up," the vocational program was aimed at transitioning young adults from the classroom to the workplace.

In 1977, the Didlake Occupational Center struggled with an annual operating budget of $65,000. Then a mailing business was started, which provided work for 16 adults. Four years later, Didlake opened an electronics assembly business with 20 employees. Then, a competitive job placement service was established.

The company continued to flourish and, in 1988, its name was changed to Didlake, Inc. That same year, a new 12,000-square-foot building was constructed on Breeden Avenue in Manassas. By the time a second building was added on the same street in September 2003, Didlake was managing sites throughout northern Virginia; Washington, D.C.; Columbia, Maryland; and Virginia Beach, Virginia. A new office and service locations in Roanoke, Virginia were soon to follow in 2004.

Much of Didlake's impressive growth is due to contracts it has won through the Javits-Wagner-O'Day (JWOD) program. This federal initiative promotes the purchase of goods and services that are produced by workers with severe

Didlake Inc.'s headquarters in Manassas, Virginia. The company operates sites throughout the state and the Washington, D.C. metropolitan area.

disabilities. Didlake has been selected to do work at many government sites including the Pentagon, the FBI, the Department of Energy, the Army National Guard, and the Peace Corps. In 1996, Didlake received the Performance Excellence Award for its outstanding work on government contracts, presented annually by NISH (formerly National Industries for the Severely Handicapped).

One of the driving forces behind the company's success is Rexford G. Parr, Didlake's president and CEO. Since joining the organization in 1977, Parr has transformed it from a small charity to a fiscally sound and growing business that meets the needs of people with disabilities *and* their employers. Today Didlake's customers include Fortune 500 companies, small businesses, shopping malls, and government agencies. Each year more that 1,400 people with disabilities use Didlake's programs and services to find employment, education, and other opportunities to lead rich, rewarding lives.

"If we want people with disabilities to move into the mainstream of life, then we need to set up employment opportu-

nities," says Parr. "The local business community has been very receptive. They know from experience that people they employ through Didlake are among the most dependable, enthusiastic employees they will ever have."

While the company's primary aim is to place as many people as possible in com-

Didlake employees work at many essential government locations including the FBI, where Tom Lyons works in the mailroom.

petitive employment within the community, some individuals are better served by other options. In 1996, Didlake established the Community Inclusion Program (CIP). This initiative is Didlake's fastest growing program. The goal is to integrate individuals with severe disabilities into the community by offering a variety of daily activities that are tailored to each person's needs and abilities. Participants may choose from art and music therapy, life skills training, and part-time employment options. CIP sites are located throughout northern Virginia and in the Roanoke Valley.

In another recent initiative, The Didlake Foundation was activated to encourage community involvement for the organization's programs and facility needs. The foundation has also begun implementation of the Personal Support Network, a program that provides long-term care services for people with disabilities.

Didlake plans to replicate its services in other parts of Virginia and may eventually start programs in neighboring states. Parr attributes the organization's success to its commitment to customer satisfaction and to broadening the opportunities that are available to those with disabilities. "Our vision all along has been

one of communities in which people with disabilities enjoy valued social roles," says Parr. "When that is achieved, we will all be enriched. We remain committed to that vision and believe that it will guide us into a very promising future."

Since becoming president and CEO in 1977, Rex Parr has transformed Didlake from a small charity to a fiscally sound and thriving organization that meets both the needs of people with disabilities and community businesses.

FIORUCCI FOODS

"If the quality is right, the customers will come." So states Claudio Colmignoli, chief executive officer and president of Fiorucci Foods. Colmignoli should know, as he has been integral in making Fiorucci's authentic Italian meats, a once unknown brand in the United States, into a highly sought after specialty food with national and international distribution. What began as Italian meats prepared from family recipes and sold in a neighborhood store in Norcia, Italy 154 years ago, is now an international specialty product sold worldwide.

Today, under the leadership of Ferruccio Fiorucci, the great-grandson of the founder, the company has experienced its greatest growth to date. They are the largest distributor of Italian meats and have a presence all across Europe. These specialty meats are produced not only in Italy but also in Colonial Heights, Virginia. That is thanks to the visionary foresight of Fiorucci and Claudio Colmignoli, the pioneer who started the Virginia-based plant.

Claudio's father was an engineer in Italy who owned a construction company.

The Fiorucci store in Italy with Ferruccio Fiorucci, as a small boy, standing to the right of his father.

He hoped to see his son come into the business too, but Claudio had other plans. He came to the United States to pursue a degree in economics at Rollins College in Winterpark, Florida. After returning to Italy he went to work for Fiorucci Foods.

The company was founded in the mid-1800s by Innocenzo Fiorucci, whose dream was to provide the finest quality foods to his community in Norcia. Using family recipes and old-world techniques, he produced what has now become the number one selling delicatessen meat in Italy.

However, because of import restrictions on meats at the time, Fiorucci Foods was not able to sell its product in America. Looking to expand, Ferruccio Fiorucci decided to grow the company's operations by opening a plant in the United States. In America he could continue to produce the meat in accordance with their traditional recipes and techniques and sell directly to the U.S. market, thus negating any import restrictions. Claudio Colmignoli was eager to see the expansion happen and because he was fluent in English, had international experience, and had been in production and sales with the company for nine years, Fiorucci looked to him to spearhead the operation.

"In thinking about where to open this plant, we considered different areas in the east," Colmignoli says. "But Virginia was perfectly situated and offered us the best all-around support." So in 1985, construction began on the plant located at 1800 Ruffin Mill Road in Colonial Heights. "I chose this area because of the quality of the people I met, the potential for hiring a very capable workforce, the access to the important northeast and southeast markets, and the number of high quality meat suppliers."

One important aspect of Virginia's economic development package offered the company grants to help facilitate training for the local people who would be working in the plant. Because the company was so committed to maintaining exacting standards, many employees were sent to Italy for training in various techniques, for example, the precise way to debone a prosciutto by hand. This overseas training promoted strong ties between the parent company in Italy and the new company in the United States. Employees enjoyed the opportunity to share ideas and expertise, not to mention the perk of international travel.

Ferruccio Fiorrucci in front of a portrait of his father.

"To come here was a big gamble," Colmignoli admits. "We had no customer base. We spent $30 million to build this plant. We filled it up with hams, waited nearly a year for them to age and then went out and said, 'Does anybody want any hams?'" In the beginning Fiorucci Foods had a plant full of prosciutto, drying, and still did not have one customer. But clearly this gamble paid off as it went from $1.5 million of sales in its first year to nearly $100 million in sales today. Colmignoli laughs, recalling his father's initial concern over the profession his son had chosen. "When I first went into this business, my father used to joke with me about choosing salami and prosciutto over engineering. Today, he is very happy for me and always visits the plant when he is in Virginia."

Ferruccio Fiorucci initially thought his products would be sold primarily through specialty shops and delicatessens. But the market has grown much larger as a wider group of customers have come to demand specialty, ethnic food items. According to John Jack, vice president of sales, "Fiorucci customers now include restaurants, specialty food stores, and many mainstream grocery stores across the country. Shop-Rite, Wegman's, and

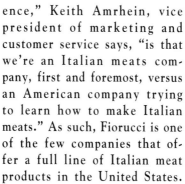

Claudio Colmignoli, CEO and president of Fiorucci Foods, USA.

Ukrop's carry Fiorucci products. Sysco Foods, the #1 food service distributor in the United States, is our biggest restaurant distributor."

From 1995 to the present, the company has experienced profitable growth. The Virginia plant exports a variety of products to Canada, Mexico, and Puerto Rico as well. "What makes the differ-

ence," Keith Amrhein, vice president of marketing and customer service says, "is that we're an Italian meats company, first and foremost, versus an American company trying to learn how to make Italian meats." As such, Fiorucci is one of the few companies that offer a full line of Italian meat products in the United States.

At the plant in Virginia, Fiorucci makes a wide range of dry-cured meats including pancetta, Italian bacon marinated with red wine and rubbed with spices; mortadella, slow-roasted sausage with imported Italian spices; and sopressata, coarse ground salami with red wine and peppercorns. "We are very proud of all of our products" say Elvis Hicks, director of operations. But the heart of the plant is in prosciutto, a high-quality, dry-cured, slow-aged ham with a rich, mellow flavor. Fiorucci offers several styles of prosciutto including prosciutto riserva which is aged for nine to eleven months in the United States and prosciutto di Parma, which is aged at least 14 months before being imported from Fiorucci's Italian production facility.

"Making prosciutto is a 2,000-year-old craft that involves just three ingredients," Colmignoli says. "Meat, salt, and time." United States pork producers have revolutionized pork in recent years to achieve negligible fat contents. While that may be good for pork chops, it's not good for making prosciutto. "You have to look around for the right raw material," Colmignoli says. "We have a very good relationship with our suppliers in Virginia and the Midwest."

The next ingredient is salt, but of course not just any salt will do. It must be sea-salt which is not easy to find in the United States. "The salt we use comes from Canada and has a less bitter flavor than table salt." The balance of salt is part of what separates prosciutto from country or Virginia hams. Prosciutto is made with a minimum of salt, just enough to keep the ham curing.

Authentic recipes, imported spices, and red wine makes Fiorucci salamis "delizioso."

Time is the final ingredient. The prosciutto must lose almost all of its moisture slowly. To accomplish this, the meat must be cured under carefully controlled temperatures. Over 3,500 hams come to the Virginia plant each week. They are hand-trimmed in accordance with rigorous specifications, and then carefully aged for nearly a year in special Italian drying rooms. Mark Bragalone, Fiorucci Foods' director of technical services, says he spends a lot of time in the drying rooms. "I look at the meats every day. At any given time we have nearly 150,000 prosciutto curing."

"When the plant first opened we had 22 employees," says Chris Maze, vice president of finance and human resources. "Today, 280 to 320 people work at the plant depending on the season." The product is produced in the same way as their parent company in Rome with the exception of slight modifications in certain products to accommodate American tastes. "In Italy we eat the meat plain, by itself," Colmignoli says, "In America it is used more for sandwich making and in recipes. These taste profiles change things slightly." Fiorucci takes pride in being innovative, with a focus on making its delicious products easy to use. "By pre-slicing and dicing our most popular items, we help professional chefs and chefs-at-home create their own masterpieces," says Colmignoli. "There have been real changes in consumer behaviors. Now there are customers who want authentic ethnic foods and real quality. And of course we are benefiting greatly from that."

Colmignoli and his team previously thought of their future plans in terms of five year increments, but the growth has been so swift they are now benchmarking every six months. The plant has undergone four expansions and is twice the size it was at its inception. "When I think of starting from scratch here in Virginia

Above: Prosciutto and melon, a popular and delicious appetizer.

when I was 32 years old, and today I look around and see how far we have come, I could not be happier. It is the people, my co-workers, and the relationship of the people working here that make the real difference."

One new worker that Colmignoli is most excited to see coming soon from Italy is his own son, Ollie, who is 26 years old. Ollie has been in the quality control department for Fiorucci in Italy and is scheduled to come to his father's plant in Virginia for an in-depth apprenticeship. Ollie is actually the great-great grandson of the founder, Innocenzo Fiorucci. It's with great pride that the family is now welcoming the sixth generation into the business of producing authentic Italian meats.

Below: Fiorucci produces or imports all styles of prosciutto.

*Right: Overlooking the New River, Shot
Tower was built more than 150 years
ago to make ammunition for the firearms
of the early settlers. Today, the tower is
on the National Register of Historic
Places. Photo by Tim Thompson.
Courtesy, Virginia Tourism Corporation*

THE HOMESTEAD

The Homestead enjoys a history that is unparalleled among American resorts. After all, it traces its beginnings back to 1766, ten years before our nation was even born.

The history of The Homestead is, like all great narratives, a mix of fascinating, documented facts and inspired legend. Its two centuries have been filled with the legends and lore of presidents and princes, war and peace, romance and laughter. And through it all, this spectacular mountain resort is today what it has always been—an oasis of relaxation, a haven for the sports enthusiast, and one of our nation's most magnificent mountain getaways.

The first, and perhaps most inspired, Homestead legend revolves around the discovery of the natural springs that are both the literal and figurative centerpiece for the resort. The area's first settlers told of an Indian brave who came upon the springs on his way to important tribal meetings in the early 1600s. The story says that this brave, exhausted from a long and courageous journey, literally collapsed into the springs for an evening's rest. It is said he awoke reinvigorated

Pictured here shortly after its opening, The Homestead's legendary Cascades Course is a 1923 William S. Flynn design, and consistently ranked among the finest courses in all America. Host to two Senior PGA Championships and seven USGA Championships, the Cascades challenges golfers today just as it did when Sam Snead was its first teaching professional.

with remarkable powers that allowed him to make fantastic time in getting to his destination and gave him knowledge and eloquence he had never before possessed. Such a tale, if true, would certainly be legendary.

The actual founding of the resort came after colonial explorers and settlers

"discovered" the springs and reported about its therapeutic powers. By the early 1740s homesteaders had constructed a number of simple wooden guest cabins near the most desirable springs, and used smooth stones to create deeper and more useful spring-fed spools.

It was Captain Thomas Bullett, an officer in the Virginia militia under George Washington's command, who built the first inn on the property and was thought to have christened it with the Homestead name in 1766. The rustic, one-story, wooden lodge accommodated about 15 people.

Even before this date, in 1761, the springs' medicinal powers were harnessed with the opening of the pools in adjacent Warm Springs. An octagonal, wooden structure still stands today, much as it did then, and houses what are now known as the Jefferson Pools. Taking the water at the Jefferson Pools remains one of the resort's most pleasurable and time-honored traditions.

Thomas Jefferson was one of The Homestead's most legendary visitors. In 1818, he arrived at the resort, where he enjoyed breakfast, dinner, and some sightseeing (an entry in his memorandum book shows that a day at The Homestead set him back a mere $2.12). Jefferson wrote in a letter to his daughter Martha that the springs, in which he sought refuge from rheumatism, were "of the first merit." In fact, The Homestead's presidential pedigree is almost unmatched in the resort world. To date, 22 presidents of the United States have visited the resort.

Many key figures have put their stamp on this Grande Dame resort throughout its glorious history. Dr. Thomas Goode purchased the resort in 1832 and brought with him a great vision for the property and a rare flair for marketing. It was Dr. Goode who introduced many new treatments that remain highlights of the Homestead Spa experience today.

The magical mountain allure of The Homestead has captured the hearts and imaginations of some of the world's most prominent people. One banking giant,

The Homestead's spectacular new outdoor pool has quickly become a new tradition at the historic resort. Families and kids of all ages enjoy the waters, sunshine, and food and beverage service. In addition, the resort's historic indoor pool features naturally warmed spring waters.

J. Pierpont Morgan, was so taken with the Grande Dame that he led a group of 56 investors in purchasing the resort in 1888. He was responsible for much of the development that formed the basis of The Homestead today.

Morgan also brought a remarkable collection of high profile friends to the resort and the project as a whole. Among them was Thomas Edison, who was not only a regular Homestead guest, but supplied the resort's first electric power plant. In fact, The Homestead guest register in this era reads like a who's who of the most prominent families in America: Morgan, Astor, Kellogg, Firestone, Vanderbilt, Carnegie, Rothschild, Wesinghouse, Edison, Guggenheim, Ford, Rockefeller, DuPont, and many others. Among the resorts' most famous guests were the Duke and Duchess of Windsor, who, according to newspaper accounts, arrived at The Homestead with twelve servants and three truckloads of luggage.

The Homestead Spa opened in 1892, helping lay the groundwork for what is today one of America's premier spa experiences. Just as it was during its founding in 1766, and when Thomas Jefferson visited in 1818, today The Homestead Spa

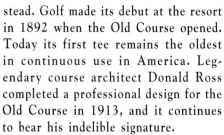

The Homestead's heritage of fine dining is both centuries old and new as today. The renowned 1766 Grille features the finest in American and continental cuisine, a superb wine list, live piano music, and the exceptional experience of classic table-side service.

The Homestead is today, just as it has been for over two centuries, a haven for the sports enthusiast, a home away from home for family vacations, a place set apart for complete relaxation and restoration. Elegant accommodations, superb cuisine, gracious hospitality, attentive service, exceptional golf on three championship courses, mineral baths, hydrotherapy treatments and massage in the historic Spa, skiing and skating in the winter months, and so much more all year long, The Homestead is truly the Grande Dame of the Mountains.

provides the ultimate in relaxation and restoration, using the resorts legendary natural mineral spring waters.

Given the resort's spectacular mountain setting, the sporting life has also been a leading draw to The Home-

stead. Golf made its debut at the resort in 1892 when the Old Course opened. Today its first tee remains the oldest in continuous use in America. Legendary course architect Donald Ross completed a professional design for the Old Course in 1913, and it continues to bear his indelible signature.

In 1924, The Homestead opened its now world-famous Cascades Course. The work of noted designer William S. Flynn, who seamlessly weaved the stunning natural terrain into its design, combined natural beauty with an array of golf challenges. This combination has made it the #1 ranked course in Virginia and one of the finest championship layouts in all the land. In 1963, designer Robert Trent Jones, Sr. completed the resort's terrific trio with the Lower Cascades course.

The Homestead is also one of the earliest pioneers in southern skiing, opening its first slopes in 1959. Today's Homestead ski experience is better than ever, with the addition of state-of-the-art snowmaking equipment. This is a perfect complement to the winter wonderland atmosphere that is provided by the Olympic-sized skating rink, snowboarding, snowmobiling, snow tubing, cross country skiing, and a warm, cozy lodge.

The central section of today's Homestead was completed in 1902, including the Great Hall, the arcade of shops, dining room, and guest rooms. The resort's popularity soared, bringing the completion of the West Wing in 1904, East Wing in 1914, its hallmark Tower in 1929, and Garden Wing in 1973.

One of the most important moments in The Homestead's history came in 1993 when Dallas-based ClubCorp purchased the property and was instrumental in restoring it to the full glory that now has it shining brighter than ever before. ClubCorp brought on one of the hospitality industry's most talented visionaries, Gary K. Rosenberg, as president and CEO. His goal was to lead the resort into the future, and assemble and lead the extraordinary team that has now restored the resort to the Grande Dame status it deserves.

INTELLIGENT DECISION SYSTEMS, INC.

Intelligent Decision Systems, Inc. (IDSI) is a small, woman-owned business dedicated to improving human and organizational performance. IDSI's work reflects an academically disciplined approach that integrates current research, leading edge technologies, and practical experience. For 13 years, IDSI has successfully worked with customers from the United States Navy, Army, Air Force, and Marines to provide performance-related services such as training and education courseware, analyses, evaluation, and studies. IDSI's owner, Marci Murawski, and her team of highly-trained employees understand the impact of each and every one of their assignments.

IDSI's distinctive approach in assisting clients reach their goals is due, primarily, to the uniqueness of its ownership. Dr. Marci Murawski believes learning theory, supported by hard scientific research, can be integrated with performance technology and technical expertise to achieve higher levels of potential than ever thought possible. She hires people who are highly-educated in the disciplines that underlie her company services. Retired military individuals are recruited who have the subject matter expertise that's required to support

Marci Murawski, president and CEO.

the various development efforts. IDSI professionals have a passion for learning and are superbly equipped to ensure complete client satisfaction. "We need to make sure the government gets high-quality solutions," Murawski says.

Her high standards and approach to performance solutions began developing as an undergraduate at the University of Hawaii, where she completed two undergraduate degrees; one in secondary edu-

cation and another in mathematics. She later started a master's in mathematics at the University of Virginia before changing to instructional technology as she pursued her doctoral studies. Typical of her approach to doing business, she researched schools with the best reputations and went there. "I chose UVA because it has a reputation for providing quality education in the fields I was interested in pursuing," Murawski says. Assured of a solid education, she began her studies in mathematics.

Instructional technology, a scientific discipline, was a natural for Murawski, as it integrates instructional design, educational psychology, and analytical methodologies to determine the best learning environment for a given objective and learning audience. The idea of employing psychology and practical analytical skills appealed to her, as she believed appropriate technologies applied in a logical matter could improve learning, and ultimately, workplace performance (versus a "one size fits all" approach to training technology).

Over the next several years, Murawski worked for several consulting companies, where her interest in learning theory, training technology, business and management developed. Her early experiences in her chosen field varied widely from developing training for a U.S. Marine Corps war game, to conducting multiple training evaluation projects and government research projects. She then moved to Washington D.C. to support an extensive intern development program within the Department of Energy. Shortly thereafter, Murawski realized she had built a solid reputation, and had enough experience, to start her own company where she could create a unique work environment for herself and her employees.

Murawski believed that many organizations did not value their highly-trained personnel in the way she believed was appropriate. People who brought in work for the firm, through continued superior performance, were often not shown the respect that was due them. "There needed to be an environment that would allow these highly-creative,

IDSI accepts ISPA award of excellence.

IDSI's annual technical workshop.

very bright people to excel," says Murawski. With that in mind, she decided to build her own company.

In 1994, IDSI was established with only a handful of employees. Today, IDSI has over 100 staff members that support diverse training and education projects that range from Joint Forces simulations in preparation for war to performance management support systems for the Federal Aviation Administration. Most importantly, at least to Dr. Murawski, is that she has successfully established the work environment she had envisioned.

Employees enjoy respect for their expertise. They are rewarded by a flexible schedule when possible and telecommuting is encouraged. A bonus system is in place for all positions within the company. Bonuses are attained by giving back to the "internal culture" of the company. For instance, if one employee is behind on a project and another jumps in to assist, that employee's actions are worthy of positive recognition.

This approach has paid off, as, over the past several years, IDSI has earned an industry-leading reputation for its exceptional work with clients from federal and state government agencies, private industry, and educational institutions. The company has received many awards in recognition of its quality of services including the International Society for

Performance Improvement (ISPI) Award of Excellence for the design, and subsequent development, of the Navy's Division Officer at Sea program. The company designed and completed this very comprehensive program and launched it into practice on naval ships in record time. Its success resulted in saving the Navy millions of dollars.

IDSI's human performance product and services list includes analysis and studies, design and development, modeling and simulating, implementation and evaluation, program support, and strategic planning. In addition to its corporate headquarters in Fairfax, Virginia, IDSI has offices in Pensacola and Orlando, Florida; Fort Leavenworth, Kansas; Norfolk, Virginia; and Pax River, Maryland. To better serve its clients, the firm establishes offices whenever client needs dictate such a presence.

IDSI has a creative, yet technical, approach that sets it apart from its competition. Using the expertise of knowing what is *possible*, and blending it with what is *practical*, the result is inspired solutions for government agencies—and ultimately for the nation.

IDSI demonstrates a joint national training exercise.

C.C. JOHNSON COMPANY

Ann Johnson never expected to find herself at the helm of a business where hard hats are a necessity and bulldozers and backhoes are tools of the trade. However, the blonde-haired president of C.C. Johnson Company is now firmly in the driver's seat of the land-clearing enterprise she and her late husband Charlie started more than 30 years ago. And no one is more surprised than Ann herself.

In the late 1970s, Charlie and Ann began thinking about starting a business that they could eventually hand over to their two teenage sons. "We thought that we'd get it up and running and then bow out and let them take over," says Ann. Deciding what kind of business to start came naturally. Charlie and his eldest son, Chris, had started cutting down trees a few years earlier to clear land for houses to be built. They turned the leftover timber into firewood which they sold on the weekend and during the afternoon. It was this part-time business that eventually developed into the family's full-time venture.

When Charlie retired from his government job and Chris graduated from high school in 1979, it proved to be the perfect opportunity to turn their venture

Ann Johnson.

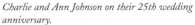

Charlie and Ann Johnson on their 25th wedding anniversary.

into a full-fledged business. That's when the Johnsons incorporated C.C. Johnson Company. To secure a steady source of wood for firewood, they focused on land clearing. The fact that they had minimal experience in this arena didn't stop them. And little did they know at the time that land clearing would eventually become the mainstay of their business.

Their first land clearing job involved a 4.5-mile right-of-way for a water main. To complete the job, they used a rubber tire backhoe and a four-wheel-drive farm tractor. The equipment was purchased with money the Johnsons had earned from their firewood sales. "We took all the money we made from that and put it in a piggy bank in the kitchen," Ann says. "Whenever we saved

up enough money, we'd buy another piece of equipment, like a log splitter. It was very small scale."

With additional equipment, the family decided to expand into excavating and grading. Working mostly on local residences, the firm's new projects included digging basements and drainage tiles, back-filling, and final grading. In those early days, Ann took care of all the administrative tasks associated with the business and Charlie and Chris provided the manpower for the various jobs.

The small business was truly a family affair. Although Charlie and Ann had expected both their sons to participate in the firm, their youngest son opted to take a job elsewhere, leaving Charlie, Ann, and Chris to tackle the business. With the company's office conveniently located in the Johnson's downstairs basement, it was easy to have meetings regarding day-to-day operations and discuss plans for the firm's future. However, there was one thing they hadn't planned on, something that jeopardized the entire future of the company.

In 1988, Charlie was unexpectedly diagnosed with cancer and died three months later. Ann was devastated and wasn't sure what to do about the business. "I didn't think about continuing with it," she admits. "But it really helped me through that time. It was very frightening for me, the worst time of my life. Working from home was kind of like a security blanket for me. And then I got a bookkeeper and that provided some companionship for me."

Working kept Ann going during the trying time and, before she knew it, she found herself leading the company with her son Chris by her side. When she took over, things changed more than she could have imagined. Ann discovered that with her serving as president of C.C. Johnson Company, the business now qualified as a "disadvantaged woman-owned" business. With this new certification, C.C. Johnson Company started bidding on—and landing—state and government jobs.

The entrée into state and government projects is what really propelled the growth of the business. With new jobs clearing land for interstate highways and major housing projects, the company expanded quickly. However, the bigger projects called for bigger equipment.

Today, C.C. Johnson Company's equipment has come a long way since that first rubber backhoe. It now has three grinders that cost more than $500,000 each, excavators, bulldozers, loaders, a chipper, and more than 20 different kinds of trucks.

Since qualifying as a minority business, the company has performed dozens of clearing jobs for the Virginia Department of Transportation. Some of those road projects include work on Interstates 95 and 66, as well as the Dulles Greenway. Although road work now makes up the bulk of its projects, the company also takes on residential work for major developers.

As the company began working on bigger jobs clearing forests, Ann ran into a problem disposing of the debris. Taking it to the dump was out of the question because it was prohibitively expensive, and landfills refused to accept that kind of brush. With a little ingenuity, the folks at C.C. Johnson Company turned that potential obstacle into a profit-maker.

Instead of trying to find somewhere to dump the materials, the firm purchased a 42-acre tract of their own two years ago. While 22 acres are being saved as a "nest egg," the other 20 acres are dedicated to a newly constructed office building, garage, and recycling center. They now use grinders and chippers to create a variety of marketable products, including mulch, firewood, wood chips for playgrounds (tot lot chips), and wood chips for park paths. Charlie, who was a strong proponent of conservation, would have been especially proud of this venture and how C.C. Johnson Company finds new uses for nearly every bit of material that's brought back from a land-clearing job.

Above: Kim Johnson, Ann's daughter-in-law, works in the office.

Above right: Craig Johnson, Ann's youngest son.

Middle right: Caren Haddad, Ann's daughter .

Today, Ann and Chris carry on with the business they launched more than 30 years ago. Since then the company has grown from three employees and two pieces of equipment to 43 employees and dozens of pieces of machinery. As for Ann's original plan to hand over the reins of the business to her son, that hasn't happened yet. She's having too much fun doing it herself.

Chris Johnson working on-site for the C.C. Johnson Company.

KLÖCKNER PENTAPLAST OF AMERICA, INC.

One has only to look in his wallet or medicine cabinet to find packaging enhanced by Klöckner Pentaplast of America. Whether it is the plastic film of a credit card or blister packaging for medications, the company has expertise creating appropriate films for its wide variety of customers. It manufactures films used to preserve and protect products such as pharmaceuticals, medical devices, fresh foods, computer components, stationery supplies, and furniture.

Klöckner Pentaplast of America (kpA) is the largest producer of high-quality rigid films in the United States. Its headquarters is located in central Virginia's Piedmont, in the small town of Gordonsville. This rural setting of rolling hills adjacent to the Blue Ridge Mountains has been a nice fit for the company since its United States beginnings in 1977.

The company originated in 1900 in Germany where it began as a family-owned steel and machinery business. By 1966, the company entered the lucrative world of plastics and built a manufacturing plant in Montabaur, Germany. Soon, the company began exporting its products to the United States. In the mid-1970s, it became evident that an American-based arm of the company was

The kpA Gordonsville production site and headquarters (top left) and the Klöckner Barrier Films plant (lower right).

essential for growth. Harry van Beek, then president of the company, was faced with the decision of where to build in the United States.

Harry van Beek, a family man, not only wanted to choose a place suitable for the American headquarters for the company; he also wanted the location to be agreeable to his wife and children. In central Virginia, he found both. The area was attractive to van Beek, aesthetically. He was also influenced by the state's will-

kpA manufactures high-quality vinyl, polyester, high-impact polystyrene, polypropylene, BAREX®, and barrier films.

ingness to assist financially, helping the company expand and provide jobs in the area. In addition, the land van Beek wanted to build upon ran adjacent to the railroad. Rail cars were essential for receiving raw materials that were necessary for creating product. The decision was made and in 1977 the company put down its American roots. Two years later, the first manufacturing plant was up and running and kpA was open for business.

Harry van Beek was there for the initial growth of the company and continued on until his retirement in the late 1990s. Tom Goeke, who was named president of kpA, soon became COO for the global kp group. In 2001, Klöckner Pentaplast was purchased by two private equity firms. Cinven Limited, based out of the United Kingdom, and J.P. Morgan, based out of the United States, partnered to buy the worldwide corporation which now has over 1,100 employees working in its multiple manufacturing plants located throughout North and South America.

In addition to the head offices, three of kpA's manufacturing plants are located in Virginia along with Intertrans Carrier, the company's award winning trucking operations. There are over 600 employees working out of the Virginia facilities. Michael F. Tubridy, now president of kpA, has been with the company since 1994. He heralds the proficiency of his employees, who meet the variety of needs for the company's expanding number of customers. "Our people provide our customers with technical and manufacturing expertise and unsurpassed service," Tubridy says. "With reliable on-time delivery and continuing technical support after the sale, Klöckner Pentaplast gives the coverage that customers need."

Employees at kpA not only service their worldwide customers, they also manage to serve their community right at home. For more than 20 years, kpA employees have participated in the Walk for Kids. This annual fundraiser benefits the Children's Medical Center at the University of Virginia's hospital, which is located in neighboring Charlottesville. Through their efforts, employees raised $200,000 in 2004, alone.

A local school and university have also been recipients of Klöckner Pentaplast's generosity. Trevilians Elementary School was given books for its library and the University of Virginia received a large donation to build a soccer stadium. The latter honored kpA by naming the facility Klöckner Stadium. Another namesake is a board room built with funds provided by kpA for the Historic Gordonsville Exchange Hotel

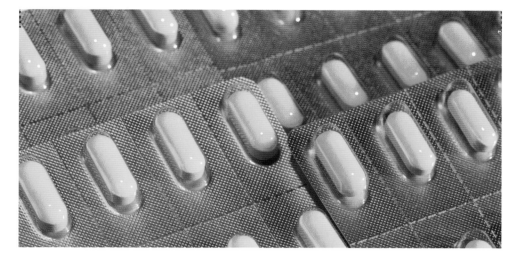

Pharmaceutical blister packs are just one of a wide variety of products packaged in kpA film.

which was used as a hospital during the civil war era. The company also makes yearly contributions to the United Way Foundation, as well as to the local fire department and rescue squad.

The company started out creating films for boxed products. As the industry and product demands became more sophisticated, so did the company's product line. Through the expertise of its engineers, kpA manufactures high-quality vinyl, polyester, high-impact polystyrene, polpropylene, BAREX®, and barrier films to assist in packaging its customers' products. It maintains a broad range of films to provide the most cost-effective solutions for the specific requirements of its customers. The company has been recognized for developing new formulations and films. In 1997, kpA was awarded the ISO 9002 registration for

its quality management system for rigid plastic films produced at its Gordonsville and Rural Retreat facilities. The company was the first rigid vinyl films manufacturer in North America to be registered to the ISO standard.

Klöckner Pentaplast's success has allowed it to make acquisitions of other companies, such as Witt Plastics and VPI Mirrex, therefore broadening its service area and product offerings to more customers. In late 2003, kpA opened its Brazilian production facility located in Cotia, outside of São Paulo. In May of the following year, kpA announced the purchase of the Petco division of the Lavergne Group based in Quebec, Canada. Petco extrudes polyester films that are used for food and general-purpose consumer and industrial packaging applications. The Petco business which has mainly serviced customers in Canada, now allows kpA to increase its polyester product line.

The company is proud to celebrate 25 years of dedication to quality and customers. Each employee's expertise and commitment to client relations is paramount to the company's success. "We partner with our customers to solve problems and exceed expectations," Tubridy says. "Every member of the kpA team takes personal responsibility for a job well done—the first time and every time. Our approach is based on a continued commitment to our customers."

kpA films are specially formulated to meet its customers' packaging, printing, and technical application needs.

LITTLE OIL COMPANY, INC.

"The Little Guardian," a stylized, saluting toy soldier in a red, white, and black uniform, has long been recognized throughout central Virginia as the symbol of The Little Oil Company, Inc. This Richmond-based firm has been providing the region with petroleum products and services since 1921.

Charles Malcolm Little, the founder of Little Oil, was born in Maryland in 1883, the son of John C. and Clara Bacon Little. His family had been Maryland residents for many generations, since James Calder, Charles' great-great-grandfather, first came from the family estate in Scotland to settle in America. Sir Robert Walter Calder, James' younger brother, was captain of the British fleet at Cape St. Vincent in 1797, and later served as first sea lord of the British Admiralty.

A student at The Boys Latin School in Baltimore, Charles Malcolm Little later took courses at a business college before beginning his career with a Baltimore steamship line in 1902. A growing interest in the rapidly evolving new technology soon took him to Pittsburgh,

Charles Malcolm Little, founder of the Little Oil Company.

"The Little Guardian," symbol of the Little Oil Company, stands on guard outside company headquarters.

where he worked with the Westinghouse Electric Company. Two years in the smoke and noise of turn-of-the-century Pittsburgh proved more than sufficient, and Little returned to Baltimore. At that time he accepted a job with the famous Old Bay steamship line, which operated scheduled service between Baltimore and Norfolk, Virginia.

In 1909, Little moved to Richmond and obtained a position with a company that was new to the oil business. At that time kerosene for domestic lighting, and lubricants for machinery and horse-drawn conveyances, represented the primary petroleum products. The automobile had not yet become a leading consumer of gasoline, but that new era was rapidly approaching. Charles Malcolm Little looked ahead to the new era.

In 1921, he started his own oil business and opened The Little Oil Company at Ninth and Dinwiddie streets in Richmond. Facilities initially included a two-room metal building with cold running water for hand washing and an "outside privy." Little's workforce consisted of a bookkeeper. He hired two young brothers as drivers, and they stayed on to serve him up until their retirements.

In the early days, the drivers delivered kerosene from door to door in horse-drawn tank carriages. Moving with the times, Little Oil purchased two Mack tank trucks. Over the years, the firm would establish a fleet of modern trucks for oil delivery. The company initially provided Esso products to its customers, which were produced and distributed by Standard Oil of New Jersey. Standard Oil, created by John D. Rockefeller, held a virtual monopoly on the oil business at that time.

In the early days, Little Oil delivered kerosene in horse-drawn wagons as portrayed in this picture by Lucy Keel.

Little's firm prospered and expanded during the 1930s when the era's large, poorly insulated homes provided a good market for home heating oil. The increase in business brought a need for expanded facilities, which took the form of two additional rooms for office space. The company purchased two new trucks, and drivers were hired for each.

Upon terminating its distributorship program with Esso, Little Oil became area distributor for Mobil Oil. Expanding business again prompted a need for larger facilities, and the firm made the decision to relocate. Little chose a construction site located at Commerce Road (formerly known as Ninth Street Road) and Riverside in Richmond. The road, only a country street at the time of the new construction, grew to become a major thoroughfare paralleling Interstate 95. Drivers on that highway could see Little Oil's distinctively decorated tanks from their cars. The new construction would include a combination office and warehouse building, along with loading facilities. The firm's founder anticipated prosperous times.

Little died tragically in 1950, the victim of an unexpected accident while he was a spectator at the stock car races in Richmond. A sportsman and fox hunter

A growing tank storage capacity and fleet of delivery trucks gave evidence of the post–World War II boom for Little Oil.

This station at Belvedere and Cary streets in Richmond was one of the first opened by Little Oil.

as well as a businessman, he had remained active with the Country Club of Virginia, the Virginia Fox Hunters Association, and the Richmond and Virginia chambers of commerce throughout his life.

Upon his death, his son Charles Malcolm Little Jr. assumed leadership of the company. Under Little Jr.'s direction and leadership, the company would expand into one of the area's leading petroleum distributorships, with new branch openings in Petersburg, Powhatan, and Louisa. In July 1958, increased business again led to expansion and office personnel moved into a new office building directly across the street. All administrative aspects of the business would be handled from this location, with the original site handling only the distribution of petroleum products.

The firm acquired State Oil Company, located in Ashland, in 1975. In 1982 it went on to acquire Dod Oil Company, located in Staunton. Charles Malcolm Little Jr. remained company president until his retirement in October 1985 when he was succeeded by his sister, Anne Little Ward. The firm prospered under her leadership until her retirement in 1991.

Current company president Stratford Ward, Anne's son, represents the firm's third generation of leadership. The company, now affiliated with Exxon, Chevron, Texaco, and Citgo, continues to provide quality branded and unbranded fuels to its customers. It also offers superior motor fuels, fuel oil, and kerosene to service station dealers, convenience store operators, and commercial customers. The firm provides commercial customers with fuel via its automated fueling stations located on the Pacific Pride commercial fueling network. Little Oil Company is moving toward its 85th anniversary and is proud of its continued service to the central Virginia area and the vision of its founder Charles Malcolm Little.

RUTHERFOORD

Since 1794, the Rutherfoord family has been involved with insurance in the Commonwealth of Virginia. It was then that Thomas Rutherfoord, a Glasgow native with significant commercial interests in Richmond, helped finance the Mutual Assurance Society of Virginia. A policy for John Marshall, first chief justice of the Supreme Court, counted as one of the first policies written. Other early policies included an 1803 "declaration" for George Washington's Mount Vernon estate.

Thomas Rutherfoord's son, John, served as the society's chief executive officer from 1837 until his death in 1866. He saw the firm weather the Civil War, with its attendant inflation, currency depreciation, and loss of value from investments due to the fall of the Confederacy. A reserve fund allowed the firm to recover rapidly from the war's effects. The Mutual Assurance Society remains in operation today.

Fire, marine, and life insurance were well established in the United States by 1916, when Thomas Rutherfoord's great-grandson and namesake entered the profession in Roanoke, Virginia. Thomas Rutherfoord initially formed a partnership with Horace Maher. In 1922, Rutherfoord's younger brother Julian joined the firm, which also opened offices in New York City and in Welsh, West Virginia.

Thomas Rutherfoord (1766-1852), lawyer and merchant, Richmond, Virginia.

Railroad and related heavy industries represented clients at that time, including the Virginian Railroad, the Norfolk & Western Railroad, and New York City's transit system. When the growth of state workers' compensation laws presented insurers with new risk valuation challenges in the 1930s, Rutherfoord devised the profession's first retrospectively rated workers' compensation policy, written for Bethlehem Steel.

In 1934, Julian's eldest son, Julian Jr., joined the family business. The younger Julian also spent a good portion of his career with the Virginia legislature. In 1937, Julian Jr.'s younger brother, Thomas D. Rutherfoord, joined the firm's New York office. When Thomas entered the Army Air Corps during World War II, Maher acquired the New York office. Following his military service, Thomas Rutherfoord worked to revitalize the contract surety business, focusing on bonds and insurance for construction contractors. Over the next few decades, the younger Thomas would take on an ever-expanding role within the partnership, driving its future success.

The founder of the Roanoke agency died in 1952. His brother Julian had retired by that time. The firm had grown significantly with the building boom and resulting contract surety and insurance business that followed World War II.

In 1963, Thomas D. Rutherfoord incorporated the present company, succeeding the partnership and initially trading as Thomas Rutherfoord Bonding and Insurance. Thomas D. Rutherfoord Jr., the Rutherfoord organization's current chairman, joined the firm in 1971. Thomas Jr. began his career by editing his father's work in progress, a manual of bond and insurance specifications for construction. His work on this project enabled the younger Rutherfoord to assist the American Institute of Architects with its own insurance specifications published for the construction industry. The collaboration with his father produced a book which became an industry standard for the next decade, with over 10,000 copies distributed.

In 1979, Thomas Rutherfoord Brown, Rutherfoord's current chief executive, began his career with the company at the behest of his godfather, Thomas Sr. The founder's grandson, Brown would go on to open the firm's Richmond office, returning Rutherfoord to the original family seat. Under Brown's leadership, the Richmond operation has grown to promi-

Thomas Downman Rutherfoord (1915-2003).

Thomas Rutherfoord (1879-1952).

Thomas Rutherfoord's Declaration for Assurance No. 2315, dated February 17, 1804, for a new manufacturing mill and counting room on the James River Canal (Henrico County, Virginia). Mutual Assurance Society, Accession 30177, courtesy, the Library of Virginia.

nence in the Richmond business community. He and his second cousin, Thomas Rutherfoord, Jr., represent the family's fifth generation with ties to the insurance profession.

Railroads and related heavy industries continued to represent a large client base for Thomas Rutherfoord, Inc. during the 1970s and 1980s. The company's

fortunes would take a turn in the early 1980s, when the railroads formed their own mutual and reciprocal railroad insurance entities. Together with a recessionary economic environment, which crippled the construction industry, Rutherfoord faced losing a large segment of business at a time when Thomas Sr. was close to retirement. When Thomas Rutherfoord Jr. took over his father's firm in 1986, he faced enormous executive challenges, including a soft market, high interest rates, and a downturn in the firm's business.

Leveraging the organization's strong industry presence in 1985, Thomas Jr.

restructured the firm, building depth throughout the organization. Operating from his office in Alexandria, Virginia, he recruited George (Shad) Steadman early in 1986 to run the large Roanoke office and help direct the return to profitability. Steadman now serves as Rutherfoord's president and chief operating officer.

In 1991, Rutherfoord initiated a stock ownership plan for its employees. This plan, which gave employees an ownership interest in the firm, highlighted the importance of people, both clients and employees, forming the basis of Rutherfoord's corporate culture. Equity participation and a dynamic, entrepreneurial environment that encourages creativity have continued to attract exceptional employees to the firm.

The Rutherfoord organization today is one of the top 50 independently owned insurance brokerage firms in the United States, with clients across the world. The firm counts over 250 people as employees, with corporate headquarters in Roanoke, as well as offices in Atlanta and Philadelphia; Alexandria, Richmond, and Virginia Beach, Virginia; and Charlotte and Raleigh, North Carolina. Flagship Thomas Rutherfoord Inc. offers risk management and insurance expertise to a wide range of industries and professions, including construction, defense, healthcare, maritime, media, real estate, technology and transportation. This expertise extends to insurance issues faced by institutions and organizations, as well as those that accompany corporate public offerings, mergers, acquisitions, and divestitures.

Rutherfoord maintains its preeminence in the construction industry through focused industry practice, providing specialized surety bond credit facilities for construction and commerce. This helps drive high-quality growth in the region while protecting the public interest. In recent years Rutherfoord has again demonstrated its strengths for working within heavy industry, port, and terminal operations.

A number of subsidiary and affiliated companies now fall under the Rutherfoord umbrella. The Rutherfoord

Benefit Services subsidiary offers clients comprehensive employee benefits brokering and consulting to help attract and retain the best talent in a client's industry or profession. Rutherfoord's Assurance Services Corporation, a subsidiary providing risk control and claims management consulting on an independent basis, brought in claims professionals from Fortune 500 companies to take a strong advocacy role for their clients. This staff now handles claims ranging from workers compensation to catastrophic loss, and provides, among its services to clients, cost containment, litigation management, regulatory filings, and loss analysis.

Assurance Capital Corporation helps clients alleviate inconsistency and volatility from insurance markets. This Rutherfoord subsidiary has become a leader in alternative risk strategies, offering captives, self-insurance, re-insurer led plans, risk retention and risk purchasing groups, finite risk, credit enhancement, and loss portfolio transfers. Rutherfoord established its subsidiary Assure-Tech, LLC as an extension of risk management to build secure, customized e-process solutions for insurance applications. This subsidiary, which employs hosting and security models used by the U.S. military and the international banking community, provides business process workflow and compliance automation solutions to mid-size enterprises and corporate business units.

In 2003, Rutherfoord entered the field of environmental consulting with its acquisition of Faulkner & Flynn, an environmental management subsidiary based in Roanoke. By all accounts, the acquisition allowed the firm to bring unique and significant value to an area that commands increasing attention within the insurance industry. Environmental engineers, consultants, and insurance specialists with the independent consulting subsidiary help clients assess and reduce environmental risk. Environmental regulatory compliance, impaired property management, and litigation support are provided, with a focus on prevention as well as compliance.

Northern Virginia and the Washington D.C. area continue to grow as a preferred center for international orga-

From left to right: Thomas R. Brown, Thomas D. Rutherfoord, Jr. and George A. (Shad) Steadman cover photo from the May 2004 issue of Rough Notes *magazine reprinted with permission from the Rough Notes Company.*

nizations and commerce. Rutherfoord International Inc. was formed in the late 1980s to protect clients worldwide with insurance, risk management, employee benefits and crisis management. This affiliated company supports business with the United Nations, the U.S. State Department, the U.S. Agency for International Development, and the Department of Defense, including contracts established during the recent wars in Afghanistan and Iraq.

Through its international connections, Rutherfoord is able to provide its customary innovative solutions wherever its clients do business. In partnership with Assurex Global and as a member of the Council of Insurance Agents and Brokers, Rutherfoord maintains strong relationships with industry leaders worldwide. Through the World Presidents' Organization and Young Presidents' Organization, Rutherfoord executives enjoy access to national and international experts, heads of state and business leaders, enabling them to explore

diverse issues and share expertise on a global level. Regionally, Rutherfoord remains active in local chambers of commerce and boards of trade, and contributes to many civic, cultural, and charitable endeavors.

The leadership that helped Rutherfoord weather the 1980s stands to serve them well into the future. "Rutherfoord will continue to be an important part of the insurance marketplace," the May 2004 issue of *Rough Notes* magazine noted. The insurance journal, which represents America's oldest national insurance journal, characterized Rutherfoord as "a dynamic and creative regional broker." These words aptly describe Rutherfoord's professional culture—a culture driven and maintained by integrity, ingenuity, and leadership.

Above: Civil War reenactments are popular throughout the state. Here, a battle is recreated at the Sully Plantation in Fairfax County. Courtesy, Virginia Tourism Corporation

ST. PAUL'S COLLEGE

In 2001, Dr. John Waddell became only the eighth president in the more than 120-year history of St. Paul's College. Located amid the rolling hills of Lawrenceville, Virginia, the historically black college sits on 183 acres of lushly landscaped grounds and boasts some picturesque historic buildings. For more than a century, it has played host to thousands of students from the local area.

Despite the institution's deep roots in the community, however, it was recently facing difficult times. From academics to financials and from business operations to building maintenance, the institution was in need of an overhaul. It was Waddell's mission to overcome those challenges in an effort to bring the college firmly into the 21st century, and to ensure its future.

Before he could tackle those issues, the new president needed to establish a vision—what the college is now and what it should be five, 10, even 30 years from now. To help create this vision, Waddell enlisted opinions from the very people who knew the college best: faculty, staff, students, alumni, politicians, and the

community. He refused to take any steps forward until he had taken a look back at the college's long history. He traced the college's storied past and when he needed inspiration for his own twenty-first century vision, he turned to the college's founder James Solomon Russell.

Russell was born in Virginia in 1857, just four years before the Civil War divided the nation. The son of slaves, Russell's boyhood was filled with hardship. Once emancipated, his mother vowed that her son would receive a formal education, something she had never had. But financial troubles often interrupted his studies and he was frequently called back home to the family farm to help make ends meet.

A bright student, Russell was selected to attend Hampton Normal and Industrial Institute. He arrived on campus in the fall of 1874 with $22 in the pocket of his first suit. Financial hardship continued to hamper his studies, and he was forced to quit school more than once because he couldn't afford to stay. Russell never let the interruptions

Dr. John K. Waddell, Saint Paul's College president, and United States Senator George Allen (R-Virginia).

dampen his desire to learn, and he never lost sight of his ultimate goal to enter the ministry and serve in the Episcopal Church.

Intrigued by the Episcopal service ever since he was a child in Sunday school, Russell decided to become a priest. Thanks to some forward-thinking bishops in the area, he was given a chance to make that dream come true. On March 9, 1882, Russell was ordained as a deacon. One week later he arrived in Lawrenceville, Virginia where he began his ministry.

The industrious deacon didn't hesitate to get to work and before long he had organized a congregation and moved it into the newly constructed St. Paul Chapel. Soon after, he established a parochial school at the same location. It didn't take long for the school to outgrow its original space and he set out to secure funds for a new building. Russell found a

Brown Hall at Saint Paul's College campus.

donor in the Reverend James Saul of Philadelphia, Pennsylvania and built a three-room frame structure to house the expanding school. That building became known as the Saul Building and is still standing on the campus today.

It was in that very structure that the Saint Paul Normal and Industrial School was started on September 24, 1888. At the time there were fewer than a dozen students, but that didn't last long. Word traveled fast about the school and enrollment increased rapidly. The school soon earned a reputation for training teachers. In 1926 it received accreditation by the Virginia State Board of Education. To this day, a large percentage of the elementary and secondary school teachers in Virginia, North Carolina, and Maryland are graduates of Saint Paul's.

In 1928, Russell, by then an archdeacon in the Diocese of Southern Virginia, retired as president of the college. After a few name changes, the school eventually became St. Paul's College. From the beginning, Russell had a strong belief that a religion-based education was imperative. He was known to say that it was useless to educate the head and train the hand if the heart was neglected.

It's that vision and legacy that St. Paul's current president has embraced and renewed at the college, as part of a stra-

tegic plan to make the college grow and prosper. Saint Paul's College's mission is to provide an intellectual atmosphere that meets the broad range of needs for its students and to provide leadership in an expanding social and technological society. Along with that mission is a renewed relationship with the Episcopal Church, which was so instrumental in the college's founding.

Over the years the college's connection with the Episcopal Church had waned. Waddell has forged renewed ties with the church's bishops to increase its involvement with the college and vise-versa. In his discussions with the bishops, Waddell learned that there are very few African Americans in the Episcopalian ministry. To remedy that, St. Paul's has established the James Solomon Russell Scholarship program for honor students to study in its religion program. Since it began two years ago, the program has expanded to include 15 students. Just as the college will help grow the ministry of the Episcopal Church, the church will reciprocate by helping grow the college with fundraising efforts and outreach to potential new students.

That reconnection with the church is only one part of Waddell's overall strategic plan. Other components include increasing paid enrollment, bolstering

alumni involvement, upgrading the curriculum, improving building maintenance, constructing new facilities, revamping the board of trustees, strengthening community ties, and bringing football back to the college. Many of these efforts are already under way.

Like most historically black colleges, St. Paul's had a long tradition of accepting students, whether they could pay tuition or not. Although the practice is a noble one, it has become increasingly difficult for the college to survive with such a liberal admissions policy. In an effort to not only survive, but thrive, St. Paul's has taken a route several other historically black colleges have chosen and altered its policy to focus on paid enrollment. "It was a very tough and tricky decision because of the sensitivity and the historic mission of the college, but we feel it's the right way," explains Waddell.

Since Waddell's appointment, the college has increased paid enrollment dramatically. In just a few years, the number of paying students has jumped from 300 to 700. While Waddell says the college could easily grow to as many as 3,000 students, a decision has been made to keep the student population down to around 750 to 1,000." Our constituents all felt strongly about keeping the student population down," Waddell says. "They liked the fact that it is a small college."

Keeping the student population low was also very important to the college's alumni, and Waddell understands how important graduates are to a college. In addition to rebuilding ties with the Episcopal Church, the college's new leader is committed to invigorating the relationship with alumni and boosting their involvement in the college. Waddell has initiated a new program in which he travels to various chapters to meet with former students to discuss the exciting changes that are taking place on campus.

Since coming on board, Waddell's emphasis on alumni relations has paid off. This powerful group of graduates contributed more than $200,000 last year, which is the highest amount ever generated by alumni. On top of that accomplishment, alumni chapters are helping recruit talented students and are spreading the word about the college.

One of the most important elements of Waddell's strategic plan is upgrading the curriculum. To ensure that St. Paul's is providing students with an education that is relevant in today's society, Waddell asked the faculty to perform an extensive curriculum review. Based on their input, the college has integrated a strong technology component to the curriculum to make sure students are computer literate. New majors have been added to keep in step with what's needed in the community and the world-at-large. As such, there's a renewed emphasis on

teacher education and business management. To make sure students are ready for the job market, instructors are stressing the importance of critical thinking skills that teach students how to think, ask questions, and reason—as opposed to learning by memorization.

The faculty of St. Paul's is one thing Waddell didn't change after his arrival. Many professors have been teaching on the campus for more than 30 years. Ask Waddell what he finds most inspiring about the faculty and he doesn't hesitate to respond. "There is a loving commitment on the part of the faculty," he says. "They want to teach people, not just teach courses." He says that caring approach is one of the many reasons why the college is such a warm, comfortable place to learn.

Along with revamping the curriculum, Waddell is spearheading renovations and improvements to the existing build-

The Saint Paul's College Child Development Center.

Russell Hall at Saint Paul's College campus.

ings on the expansive campus. Work has already begun on student housing, and plans are in the works for several new facilities. On the wish list are a new library, academic center, science facility, health facility, athletic fields, football stadium, computer lab, and additional residence halls.

The college's makeover doesn't stop there. Waddell pinpointed the board of trustees as another entity that needed some updating. Realizing that the board could have tremendous influence on the college's ability to raise funds, he sought out some high-powered executives to be part of the team. Among the new members are executives from General Motors Corporation and Bank of America, as well as medical doctors and other influential individuals.

However, Waddell's strategic plan doesn't focus solely on ways to benefit St. Paul's. In keeping with the college's long history, Waddell is expanding its efforts to make a contribution to the community. From the beginning, Saint Paul's has played an important part in the life of the

local community. In its early years, the school supplied ice for the Southern Railroad and water and electricity for the town of Lawrenceville. Today the college provides reading courses for the community, which has a high rate of illiteracy. In addition, the school serves the community with its health center and provides services for the elderly.

The community, alumni, and current students are all grateful for another of Waddell's initiatives. After a 15-year hiatus, Waddell brought football back to the school, which is part of the CIAA (Central Intercollegiate Athletic Association) conference. Since the conference is more basketball-oriented, Waddell couldn't have anticipated the impact the return to the gridiron would have. "Football really got the alumni going," he says. "There are homecomings, tailgating, get-togethers, and events all week long."

The return of football has sparked such interest among alumni that new chapters are cropping up throughout the south, including Florida and South Carolina. Thanks to football's return, school

spirit is soaring—not only among alumni, but with current and prospective students as well. Waddell credits the sport for more than just school spirit, though. He believes it has actually played a part in the college's increased enrollment over the past few years, and expects it to continue attracting new students.

The buzz generated by the football team is matched only by the enthusiasm about all the other changes taking place at St. Paul's. Under Waddell's thoughtful direction, the college is building on its historic roots to create a thoroughly modern institution that will be around for many years to come. Although he admits that the college has only accomplished about 25 to 40 percent of his overall strategic plan, he expects to continue making progress. "There are bright days ahead for St. Paul's," Waddell exclaims.

VIRGINIA COMMONWEALTH UNIVERSITY

Colleges and universities may be hotbeds of new ideas, observes Virginia Commonwealth University political scientist Bob Holsworth, but organizationally they are among the most conservative of institutions. Of course, he quickly adds, VCU breaks the mold.

A year ago the Wilder School of Government and Public Affairs, of which he is director, did not exist. At the suggestion of a forward-looking dean, the faculty of four departments—political science, public administration, urban planning, and criminal justice—began thinking about what might be gained by breaking down the walls between them. "We concluded we could do a better job of teaching, recruiting, and developing cross-disciplinary research teams working together than we could with four separate departments," Holsworth says.

By combining resources, the new school now commands the resources to recruit several faculty members in critical fields such as Geographic Information Systems (GIS) and homeland security. The potential for applying GIS technology to traditional fields of study is incredibly exciting, Holsworth says. "Whether we're talking economic development, crime prevention, or transportation, using analytical techniques of GIS is absolutely vital to the future. GIS is a major instrument in the tool box of anyone involved in public policy analysis."

Virginia Commonwealth University's Eugene P. and Lois E. Trani Center for Life Sciences fosters interdisciplinary research and instruction.

The Wilder School is a case study of the new VCU. The university traces elements of its history back to the mid-nineteenth century, but it's not acting like a hoary, ivy-walled institution. VCU is a twenty-first century university whose prime mission is leading the Richmond region—indeed, Virginia—into a knowledge economy built upon new ideas, disciplines, and technologies. "We're reinventing the modern American research university—right here in Richmond, Virginia," says Eugene Trani, VCU president.

As anyone on the VCU campus and in Richmond will quickly acknowledge, Trani is the driving force behind the university's transformation. Fourteen years ago, the former University of Wisconsin vice president for academic affairs

took over an institution little known outside its home town. He proceeded to remold it in line with his vision as a nationally recognized urban university without walls. Today, VCU is the fastest-growing university in Virginia's higher education system, accounting for 31 percent of enrollment growth as measured by incoming freshmen over the past five years.

The catalogue of achievements is impressive.

• Exploiting its location as an urban university, VCU has woven a dense network of ties to the business community, city government, and surrounding neighborhoods. Dr. Trani and the university played a key role in developing the Virginia Biotechnology Research Park.

• Since 1994, VCU has spent $1.1 billion for new facilities, dressing up the Monroe Park campus, and revitalizing a lengthy stretch of the decaying Broad Street corridor. Prominent projects have included the $199-million Monroe Park Campus Addition for the business and engineering schools and a new Brain and Neuroscience Institute at the Medical Center.

• As VCU's national recognition has grown, the number of students from outside the Richmond area has surged. Evolving from a commuter college into a residential university, VCU has brought

Twenty-seven-thousand students attend VCU.

some 6,000 students into downtown apartments, both publicly and privately owned, pumping millions of dollars into the local retail and service economy.

• As part of its broader focus to transform the undergraduate culture, VCU has built a stronger athletics program. With a marquee athletic facility at the Stuart C. Siegel Center, the university now supports 16 varsity teams competing—and winning—at the NCAA Division I level as members of the Colonial Athletic Association.

• With 27,000 students and a growing national reputation in the arts and sciences, VCU supports the ethnic and cultural diversity that attracts to Richmond the creative minds that contribute disproportionately to artistic, scientific, and business innovation.

• VCU has revamped its academic organizational structure, converting MCV Hospitals into a quasi-independent authority, building strong ties between the Monroe Park and MCV campuses, and emphasizing inter-disciplinary study in fast-growing fields. Sponsored research spending, concentrated in the life sciences, reached $185 million in 2004. New technologies provide the basis for a number of promising start-up companies.

In sum, VCU under Gene Trani has emerged as the growth engine—and transformational force—of the Richmond regional economy. "The great thing about Dr. Trani is that no one gets penalized for having an idea," says Holsworth. "He's

Dr. John Fenn, VCU professor and winner of 2002 Nobel Prize for chemistry.

Since arriving in 1990 to become the fourth president of VCU, Dr. Eugene P. Trani has greatly expanded the mission of the university so that it plays a key role in metropolitan and statewide development.

great at taking a good idea and making it happen quickly."

Only a few years ago, the midtown area of Broad Street, one of Richmond's major retail corridors, was a distressed strip of wind-blown parking lots, chain link fences, and seedy, low-rent stores. Then VCU embarked upon a sustained expansion that pumped an estimated $100 million into new facilities, including the highly visible Siegel Athletic Center, along the benighted boulevard. Convinced that the university was committed to the neighborhood, private investors invested another $100 million in the area.

Harper Associates saw the potential early on. At the corner of Broad and Harrison, the company brought in a Lowe's home improvement store, then a

Kroger grocery, and then 15,000 square feet of retail space. Many tenants, from a movie gallery to a Great Wraps restaurant, were eyeing the fast-growing student market nearby. "It was obvious to anyone who toured the market and saw the amount that's been invested, there was real value there," says Tom Kinter, Harper's general manager.

As noted in a recent report by the Initiative for a Competitive Inner City, a Boston-based think tank, urban universities are anchors of inner city economies throughout the U.S. The agency profiled VCU, in one of only two case studies, as an urban university that made a difference.

The figures for the 2003-2004 academic year show the economic impact:
• 26,770 students
• 15,304 employees
• $1.5 billion budget (including the $800 million health care system)
• $34 million annual household spending by students and employees in businesses near VCU's campuses
• $450 million in planned major projects in VCU's proposed six-year capital plan

The impact of VCU on Richmond's downtown is even more pronounced than the bare figures would suggest.

Determined to build a university of national stature, Trani has pushed the university to cast a wider net for students.

Former chief United Nations weapons inspector Hans Blix visited VCU as part of the School of World Studies Crossing Boundaries Lecture Series. VCU President Eugene P. Trani shown here giving Blix a tour of the campus.

Freshman enrollment at VCU has soared 50 percent over the past five years, and the entire increase has come from outside the Richmond region. Five years ago, for instance, the university counted only 189 freshmen from northern Virginia's Fairfax County. In 2003-2004, VCU enrolled 422 freshmen from Fairfax.

With a new student profile, VCU has morphed from a commuter campus into a residential university. Student apartment buildings, both on campus and off, are sprouting all over. Literally thousands of students have moved into Richmond's downtown, reviving the retail sector and attracting loads of private capital.

The changes have been most evident around the Monroe Park campus, especially the Broad Street Corridor and, to a lesser degree, Cary Street. But the Medical Center has gotten a face lift as well, and the adjacent biotechnology research park has converted seemingly endless tracts of disheveled parking lots into a modern office park.

Within a few years, the VCU urban-renewal machine will renovate 10.8 acres east of Belvidere Street to make way for a dazzling new campus for the School of Business and the School of Engineering. There, the key themes of the Trani administration will come together in a single complex: landmark buildings with distinctive architecture, interdisciplinary programs between business and engineering, integration of the residential and learning environments, and a physical plan that embraces the community rather than walls it out. "We're no ivory tower," boasts Trani. "We're square in the middle of the city—that's our great strength."

For Peter Kirkpatrick, organizer of the VCU French Film Festival, the highlight of the 2004 festival came when the French ambassador awarded him and his wife the Honor of Arts and Letters, the highest cultural recognition that France has to bestow. In 12 years the festival has become the largest event highlighting French film outside France itself, becoming something of a Cannes in reverse, where French directors and actors come to talk about their work, test the reac-

In 2003, the VCU French Film Festival was formally recognized by the French government as the largest French film festival in the United States to date.

tion of American audiences, and hobnob with one another.

But Kirkpatrick, the executive director of international education for VCU, is delighted by the recognition that the festival has brought not only to himself but to Richmond. Francophiles and film connoisseurs from around the country make the pilgrimage to VCU to partake in the three-day event. Visitors who think Richmonders are still fighting the Civil War discover another side of the city. At the last event, three different people told Kirkpatrick essentially the same thing: They'd relocated to Richmond because their companies told them to. But after moving away, they missed the festival so much they had to come back!

VCU is ranked nationally by the Carnegie Foundation as a top research institution.

Through events like the French Film Festival, VCU brings cultural, artistic, and ethnic diversity to the Richmond community. According to the cutting-edge theories of Carnegie-Mellon University professor Richard Florida, those are precisely the characteristics that members of the so-called "creative class"—the artistic, scientific, and entrepreneurial innovators who drive economic growth—are looking for.

VCU, the wellspring of so much of Richmond's cultural vitality, creates an ambience of pluralism, tolerance, and experimentation that the "creatives" thrive on. VCU assets include:

• A fine arts program whose sculpture department is ranked number one in the nation, graphic design number four, and painting/drawing tied for number 10.

• The Ad Center, with its nationally renowned curriculum integrating artistic and business creativity in advertising.

• A new School of World Studies that dissolves barriers between traditional disciplines such as religion, foreign languages, anthropology, and archeology.

VCU has long been proud of its diversity, and in fact may be the most ethnically diverse institution in Richmond. Forty percent of entering students are non-white: predominantly African American, but increasingly Asian and Hispanic as VCU has focused in recent years upon recruiting internationally.

VCU also is socio-economically diverse. President Trani describes VCU as a *Flashdance* kind of university, referring to the modest academic background of the main character in the movie by that name. In contrast to institutions which draw heavily from elite high schools, VCU tends to attract highly motivated students from less privileged families. Seventy percent of VCU students work full-time or part-time, he says; 70 percent receive financial aid. "Whether you're talking about art students with green hair or young people studying at the number one sculpture department in the country," says Trani, "we're creating the creative class here at VCU."

Tom Huff will never forget the day in 2002 when the Royal Swedish Academy of Sciences announced that VCU professor John B. Fenn had won the Nobel Prize in chemistry. Fenn sat in Huff's office where the two fielded telephone calls from around the world. It was an exhilarating moment, says Huff, the vice provost for life science. "Fenn's Nobel Prize was a symbol of the new VCU."

Although Fenn won the prize for work he'd conducted at Yale, where he developed analytical methods for studying large, complex molecules like proteins, he had been carrying on his path-breaking research at VCU's department of chemistry for 10 years. The international acclaim for his discoveries validated strategic decisions that VCU had made in establishing the direction of its science programs.

The greatest achievement in modern life sciences was the sequencing of the genome: identifying the order of the 24 amino acids in human genetic material. The next step, says Huff, is to sequence all the proteins in the human body, a field known as proteomics. Fenn won his Nobel Prize for developing methods that made it possible to deconstruct complex organic molecules.

Cracking the molecular structures of enormous protein molecules requires an entirely different way of conducting research. Gone are the days when scientists, like Huff in his younger days, spent a decade scrutinizing a single protein through a series of carefully controlled experiments. The process is just too slow. Instead, says Huff, life science research looks for "patterns of expression," recognizing that the function of a protein can be understood only in terms of its interaction with the others among the thousands of proteins in the human body.

The need to juggle thousands of variables at a time makes life science research incredibly computer intensive. It draws upon disciplines such as mathematics, computer science, and chemistry that are outside of the biological and medical

VCU's School of the Arts is one of the nation's largest arts and design schools.

fields. That's why VCU approaches life science research as a multi-disciplinary activity. The Medical Center, home to the Massey Cancer Center and other research institutes and centers, carries on the proud R&D tradition of the Medical College of Virginia. By pooling scientific talent of the med school with that of the science departments, Huff says, VCU's life science initiative aims to take research on both campuses to a higher level of excellence.

"Many of the most important scientific discoveries fall in between the boundaries of traditional academic disciplines," says Huff. Under the umbrella of "the study of biological complexity," VCU attacks those institutional barriers through a "matrix" form of organization

Founded in 1996, the VCU School of Engineering is a collaboration between the university and industries.

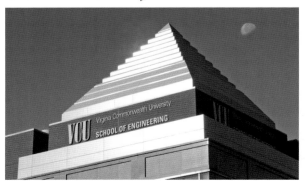

that cuts across departmental silos. Typical of this approach is the Life Sciences 101 class in which top scientists and departmental heads—senior professors not normally known for interacting with undergraduate students—deliver lectures to freshmen, exposing them to cutting-edge thought on topics from robotic surgery to the genetics of schizophrenia.

The life science emphasis helped VCU generate $185 million in sponsored research last year, activity that has yielded a growing portfolio of patents and other intellectual property, some of which has translated into new business activity in the Richmond region. Two dozen or more start-up enterprises coming out of VCU have set up shop in the Virginia Biotechnology Research Park, which is adjacent to the Medical Center. A number, like Discovery Therapeutics, which developed five molecules that have reached late-stage clinical trials, have turned into viable businesses. Now Discovery co-founder Donald A. McAfee has formed a consulting company, McAfee Scientific, to help others through early-stage drug discovery and clinical trials.

"We take our role in economic development seriously," says Trani, VCU president. He hopes to see more companies like Discovery emerge from VCU labs. "That's what VCU does," he says. "We plant seeds. We help them grow."

VIRGINIA RAILWAY EXPRESS

Build it, and they will come. And in Northern Virginia, they will come, and come, and come. That is why, no matter how many highways, overpasses, or bridges are constructed, many of Northern Virginia's most heavily traveled roads were gridlocked by the time the 1980s rolled around. It was, in part, the sad result of a decision to abandon the last remaining vestiges of commuter rail service in Northern Virginia by the mid-1950s—and instead focus on road construction. But with the population exploding far more quickly than roads could be built, and as development shifted from central business districts to the suburbs, reliance on the automobile mushroomed and, with it, the length and difficulty of workers' commutes.

Something had to be done. Thankfully, there were enough far-sighted local and state officials who recognized that fact, and beginning in the mid-1960s, the effort to restore commuter rail service began. Two organizations in particular— the Northern Virginia Transportation Commission (NVTC) and the Potomac and Rappahannock Transportation Commission (PRTC)—spearheaded the effort. With the backing of countless government officials and citizens, the result of their efforts is now known as the Virginia

The reemergence of commuter rail in Virginia provides a welcome alternative to highway traffic.

Railway Express (VRE). As one of the fastest growing commuter rail services in the nation, ridership statistics are increasing four times faster than any other commuter rail system in America (nearly 17 percent per year for each of the last four years).

A transportation partnership of NVTC and PRTC, VRE provides commuter rail service from the Northern Virginia suburbs to Alexandria, Crystal City, and downtown Washington, D.C. It has two lines—Manassas and Fredericksburg—with service approximately every half hour during rush hour. There

are also mid-day options to help get customers home.

Today, VRE provides more than 4 million passenger trips annually—the equivalent of a full lane of traffic from each of Washington's two primary feeder highways, Interstates 66 and 95. But when the first VRE train pulled away from the Manassas, Virginia station on June 22, 1992, with just 825 people onboard, no one could have guessed that VRE would ultimately become what Virginia Governor Mark Warner would one day call "the great success story of the past ten years."

How did it all begin? In short, not easily. Concerted efforts to organize VRE first took off in the 1980s, but doubters undeniably outnumbered believers.

What finally convinced the naysayers? As many of the original organizational team remember it, it was the result of convincing jurisdictions that commuter rail service wouldn't just get cars off the road, but it would also result in faster commutes, additional modes of transportation, and environmental improvements. The train wasn't just going to move people—it was going to clean the air, offer commuters more choices, and provide great economic benefits.

VRE provides a stress-free commute to thousands of Virginians every day.

The fact that a railroad infrastructure for freight and intercity passenger trains already existed, helped matters considerably. More than 10 years after VRE was first organized as a concept it became a reality, with 16 trains and a $20.8 million operating and capital budget.

Since then, steady growth has established VRE's place as an important part of Northern Virginia's transit solution. Originally designed to handle 10,000 daily trips, VRE's ridership grew from a few thousand trips each day in the early 1990s to 7,000 in 1998, and then rose sharply to more than 11,500 trips by 2001. Today, ridership regularly tops 15,500 daily trips. In June 2004, VRE celebrated its 25 millionth passenger with an event at the Alexandria Union Station.

Throughout the years, VRE has promoted—and successfully retained—ridership with a mix of old-fashioned charm and zealous attention to customer service. Constant communication with passengers has long been one of its mainstays. With an e-mail newsletter, weekly newspaper, customer service e-mail service, and extended reception hours, VRE guarantees that no passenger is ever out of touch. An online system also allows passengers to track the exact location of their train via their laptop or desktop computer, thanks to onboard global positioning satellite (GPS) systems. In addition, "Meet the Management" programs give staff members the opportunity to walk station platforms to meet passengers, hand out free refreshments, and field questions.

Treating passengers like friends also goes a long way toward sealing loyalty; VRE's "Security Blanket" program reimburses passengers for daycare late fees if their trains are late. Free Ride Certificates are handed out when trains are 30 minutes or more behind schedule. The Guaranteed Ride Home program provides alternate transportation if a passenger must get home during non-service hours. VRE also participates in several community events throughout the year, providing weekend excursion trains for local festivals and running Independence Day trains.

Attention to the local communities and to customer service has paid large dividends. Year after year, nine out of 10 riders rate VRE's service as good or excellent and would recommend VRE to a friend. As VRE looks forward, it plans to procure more railcars, expand midday storage facilities, and work with host railroads like CSX and Norfolk Southern, so it can increase service frequency and possibly expand into underserved areas further south and west.

Through it all, VRE promises that it will never forget its mission: to make the day-to-day commute safe, dependable, and less stressful than other modes of transportation. Taking care of that core

The Virginia Railway Express has carried millions of passengers to their destinations safely and reliably since its inception in 1992.

service isn't always easy, especially in times of rapid growth. However, VRE knows that its reputation was built on providing a comfortable alternative to the arduous and lengthy automobile commute that has come to define the lives of so many Northern Virginians. It's a reputation that VRE will build upon and make even stronger in the years ahead.

After a long day's work, passengers board VRE for a quiet and relaxing ride home.

VIRGINIA POLYTECHNIC INSTITUTE AND STATE UNIVERSITY

Virginia Polytechnic Institute and State University has been a leader in higher education for more than 130 years—by looking toward the future. With research as a main focus, the university remains ahead of the curve in technology. In fact, Virginia Tech, with its strong focus on undergraduate education, has been ranked by the National Science Foundation as one of the top 50 research institutions in the nation.

Established in 1872 in Blacksburg, Virginia Tech was created as a land-grant institution. The school has evolved over the years by remaining focused on its three missions: instruction, research, and outreach. Every student who enters the school's halls brings the college's founding motto to life, "Ut Prosim—That I May Serve."

Virginia Tech has grown to be respected for its superior reputation in the field of high-technology, such as engineering, architecture, and the sciences. Students can choose from 70 undergraduate majors from seven colleges including the College of Agriculture and Life Sciences, the College of Architecture and Urban Studies, the Pamplin College of Business, the College of Engineering, the College of Liberal Arts and Human Sciences, the College of Natural Resources, and the College of Science. The university also of-

Burruss Hall exemplifies Virginia Tech's unique collegiate gothic architecture.

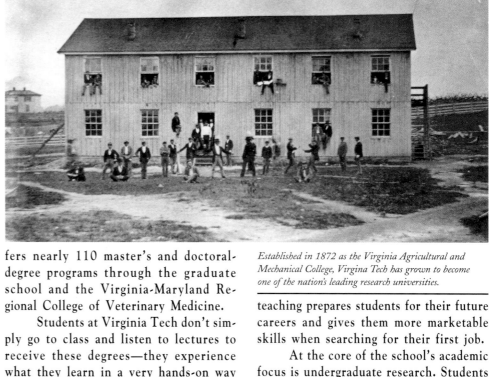

Established in 1872 as the Virginia Agricultural and Mechanical College, Virgina Tech has grown to become one of the nation's leading research universities.

fers nearly 110 master's and doctoral-degree programs through the graduate school and the Virginia-Maryland Regional College of Veterinary Medicine.

Students at Virginia Tech don't simply go to class and listen to lectures to receive these degrees—they experience what they learn in a very hands-on way with the school's unique learning laboratories. This learn-by-doing approach helps students gain a better understanding of their studies through experimentation and research.

These learning laboratories introduce students to a variety of experiences—from food and beverage operations to plant propagation—that can't be found in the pages of a text book. This method of

teaching prepares students for their future careers and gives them more marketable skills when searching for their first job.

At the core of the school's academic focus is undergraduate research. Students can participate in more than 3,700 ongoing research projects, which is one reason why the school is the state's top research university and as well as one of the top in the nation. Virginia Tech has been ranked fifth in the nation among universities without a medical school, according to the number of patents it has received.

Students can also enhance their education through research projects such as language study, cloning experiments, DNA research, and reconstruction of ancient buildings. The research programs allow students to be active in their field of study before they ever enter the work force.

Virginia Tech lives up to its name by operating beyond the cutting edge of technology. It was the first public college in the country to require every student to own a computer, enhancing its technologically enriched learning environment. All residence rooms, laboratories, lecture rooms, and offices are wired and several locations on campus provide wireless LAN. Students can also take quizzes, participate in class chat rooms, review pre-class lecture notes, communicate

with professors, and create their own homepage online.

"That I May Serve" is a motto that is held closely by everyone at Virginia Tech—not just the students, but the faculty too. Being internationally recognized for its success in research, the university is able to attract the top scholars in their respective fields. In fact, 89.5 percent of full-time professors at Virginia Tech hold a Ph.D. or terminal degree. In total, there are 1,300 full-time faculty members at the university—not part-time or graduate students, who teach courses. In addition, the faculty is not separated between undergraduate and graduate classes. This allows undergraduates to learn from the best professors available.

With more than 28,000 students, including 2,000 international students from 110 countries, Virginia Tech provides the full benefits of a diverse and exciting student life. Through the more than 500 on-campus student organizations every interest can be entertained, and it is easy to join in.

Virginia Tech offers activities that serve academic, athletic, religious, arts, sports, and many other interests. For students seeking the quintessential experience of college, the school's Greek life is active and growing. There are more than 31 fraternities for men and 12 sororities for women.

Virginia Tech students, faculty, and administrators are loyal Hokie fans, with 21 men's and women's NCAA Division 1 level sports. Team spirit for the Atlantic Coast Conference school is in the air year-round. Students can also participate in athletic activities such as tennis, volleyball, cricket, bowling, and of course, football. With the 65,000-seat Lane Stadium, the nationally ranked Hokie football team plays to roaring crowds. The team has made 11 consecutive bowl appearances.

There are a lot of varsity sports available as well, including football, basketball, baseball, cross country, and swimming. Students with an athletic edge can also enjoy the McComas Student Health and Fitness Center, which offers three gyms, an elevated track, aerobic

Virginia Tech's 2,600-acre campus is situated between the picturesque Allegheny and Blue Ridge Mountain ranges.

studios, a weight-training area, and an eight-lane swimming pool. There is also a golf course located on the campus.

On its sprawling 2,600-acre campus, the university has approximately 100 buildings, striking an architectural harmony between the old and the new. Many are dedicated to one of the main passions of the institution—research. There are laboratories, the Corporate Research Center, and a 1,700-acre research farm in Montgomery County.

Cassell Coliseum is the home of the Hokies men's and women's basketball teams and exciting Atlantic Coast Conference action.

The Resident Hall Federation oversees on-campus residential life, and plans useful programs such as study skills sessions, movie nights, intramural sports teams, and sessions on cultural diversity and self-defense. The residence halls are overseen by on-staff professionals who provide around-the-clock assistance. With more than 8,700 students living on campus, the facilities are state-of-the-art in terms of technology and culture. All resident hall rooms are equipped with high-tech telecommunications systems that provide voice mail and Ethernet access.

Providing the best there is to offer in academics, faculty, and student life, it is no surprise that Virginia Tech has been recognized and honored on many occasions as a superior university. It has been ranked repeatedly as a top school in several categories by U.S. News and World Report. The faculty has been distinguished with numerous recognitions over the years including seven outstanding faculty awards by the State Council of Higher Education for Virginia. The students also excel annually as recipients of educational awards acknowledging their research work.

With a history of looking forward by discovering new ideas, researching new approaches, and reinventing new standards, Virginia Polytechnic Institute and State University does more than excel at educating its students. Virginia Tech provides an enriched experience that its students will apply throughout their careers and lives.

VIRGINIA UNION UNIVERSITY

As the oldest of the historically black colleges and universities in the South, Virginia Union University holds special distinction. For nearly 140 years it has pioneered a sense of leadership that has inspired students to strive for excellence in the classroom—and the community.

Situated on 93 acres in the capital city of Richmond, this coeducational institution offers a comprehensive undergraduate liberal arts program in the humanities, sciences, business, and education. The Samuel DeWitt Proctor School of Theology offers graduate education in Christian ministries, conferring master of divinity and doctor of ministry degrees.

More than 1,800 students are enrolled in the university, most of which hail from Virginia and other states along the Atlantic Seaboard. The student body also includes internationals from Europe and Africa. Although traditionally known as an African American university, Virginia Union is proud of its cultural and ethnic diversity.

The school's storied history began shortly after the end of the Civil War.

Members of the American Baptist Home Mission Society proposed the establishment of a National Theological Institute to train Freedmen for entrance into the Baptist ministry. Later the institute would expand its offerings to include general curricula at the elementary, high school, and college levels to both men and women. Two branches of the institute opened, the Richmond Theological School for Freedmen, and a sister school in Washington, D.C., called Wayland Seminary.

The first director of the Richmond school, Dr. J. G. Binney, began teaching night classes to about 25 students in November 1865, but left seven months later. He was succeeded by Dr. Nathaniel Colver, an elderly abolitionist who was determined to make higher education a reality for emancipated former slaves. He rented some land and buildings at 15th and Franklin streets, known at that time as "Lumpkin's Jail." The property was so named because it had once been the site of a holding-pen for runaway slaves. Whipping posts were still present on the site. Dr. Colver scheduled a six-hour day of classes in grammar, arithmetic, spell-

ing, reading, geography, and biblical knowledge from 1867 to 1868.

When Colver's health began to fail, he passed the reins of school principal over to Dr. Charles Henry Corey, a former Union Army chaplain. The school was renamed Colver Institute in 1869. The following year the school moved from rented facilities at Lumpkin's Jail into the old United States Hotel building at 19th and Main streets, which was purchased for $10,000. In 1876, the school was incorporated by the Virginia General Assembly under the name "Richmond Institute."

Dr. Corey directed the school for 31 years. The institute was the first school in the South to employ African American teaching assistants and faculty. By this time the school offered curricula which were preparatory (elementary), academic (pre-college), and theological. The school had its first foreign graduate, Samuel Harden of Nigeria, in 1879, and its first female graduate, Maria Anderson, in 1882.

Coburn Hall (in the foreground) is used for chapel, convocations, and other formal university programs. Huntley Hall (in the background) is one of five student residence halls.

With the establishment in 1883 of Hartshorn Memorial College, the first African American women's college in the world, Richmond Institute was once again comprised of an all-male student body. The focus returned to theological studies, and the school was renamed Richmond Theological Seminary in 1886. Facing pressure to merge several American Baptist Home Mission Society schools into one university, in 1899 Richmond Theological Seminary and Wayland Seminary were combined to form Virginia Union University. Land was purchased on Lombardy Street in an area known as "Sheep Hill," and the first classes convened on the new campus in October of that year. Virginia Union became coeducational in 1932 when Hartshorn Memorial College merged with the university. The fourth component of the "Union," Storer College in Harper's Ferry, West Virginia, merged its assets with Virginia Union in 1964.

Nine buildings in the late Victorian Romanesque revival style gave the original campus an aura of dignity and refinement. Pickford Hall served as the first classroom building and now houses the presidential executive offices. The School of Theology is located in Kingsley Hall, site of the first dormitory. In the 1960s, a major building program resulted in the addition of John Malcus Ellison Hall, the major classroom building; the Thomas H. Henderson Center, home of the bookstore, post office, cafeteria, and office of

The L. Douglas Wilder Library & Resource Center houses the university's museum, television studio, and campus bookstore.

Coburn Hall, home of the Allix B. James Chapel.

student affairs; and two dormitories, Storer Hall and MacVicar Hall. The campus currently contains 25 buildings. Renovation projects are planned for the Belgian Tower, Performing Arts Theatre, and the Barco-Stevens Gymnasium.

The most ambitious project was the construction of the L. Douglas Wilder Library and Learning Center in 1997. The library facility honors Wilder, a 1951 alumnus and former board member, who made history when he was elected in 1989 as the first African American governor in Virginia—and the nation.

In November 2003, the university's board of trustees established an art museum showcasing collections from Africa and textiles from Guatemala. The university also has a large collection of folk art.

Athletics are an integral part of student life. The university became a charter member of the Central Intercollegiate Athletic Association (CIAA) in 1912. Competitive programs are offered in football, men's and women's basketball,

baseball, softball, tennis, volleyball, golf, and track and field. The university is especially proud of its 18 CIAA basketball conference championships.

What has distinguished Virginia Union from other universities is its 1 to 15 faculty-student ratio, which allows teachers to take a personal approach in the education of the leaders of tomorrow. The investment of time and caring has paid huge dividends, as evidenced by some of the outstanding alumni the university has produced. In addition to Virginia Governor L. Douglas Wilder, the list of alumni also includes Admiral Samuel Gravely, the first African American admiral in the United States Navy; Henry Marsh, a Virginia State Senator who served as the first African American mayor of Richmond; and Dr. Jean Louise Harris, the first African American to graduate from the Medical College of Virginia.

Eleven individuals have served as president of the university since 1899: Dr. Malcolm MacVicar, 1899-1904; Dr. George Rice Hovey, 1904-1918; Dr. William John Clark, 1919-1941; Dr. John Malcus Ellison, 1941-1955; Dr. Samuel DeWitt Proctor, 1955-1960; Dr. Thomas Howard Henderson, 1960-1970; Dr. Allix Bledsoe James, 1970-1979; Dr. David Thomas Shannon; 1979-1985; Dr. S. Dallas Simmon, 1985-1999; Dr. Bernard Wayne Franklin, 1999-2003; and Dr. Belinda Childress Anderson, 2003-present.

CITY OF WINCHESTER

Few places in the United States are as steeped in history as Winchester, Virginia. George Washington began his military and political career in the city. Revolutionary War General Daniel Morgan; Admiral Richard Byrd; former Senator and Governor Harry F. Byrd; Pulitzer Prize-winning author Willa Cather; Spottswood "Spotsy" Poles, the Black Ty Cobb of baseball; and country music pioneer Patsy Cline are among Winchester's illustrious citizens. Others left the city large financial bequests, adorning it with beautiful architecture and enriching its historical fabric. Resting at the northern end of the Shenandoah Valley, Winchester was such a sought after strategic location in the Civil War that it changed hands between the North and the South more than 70 times. Today, a thriving urbanized area, the City of Winchester has created a well-crafted balance between honoring the past and looking to the future.

Rouss City Hall, at the corner of North Cameron and East Boscawen Streets, was built in 1901 and features a beautiful Gothic/Victorian clock tower. Charles B. Rouss, a successful merchant, donated $30,000 toward the building's construction which still serves as Winchester's city hall.

Original wooden water pipes with cast iron couplings and rings that date back to the early 1800s. Winchester was among the first cities in the U.S. to have a public water system.

Colonel James Wood of the Virginia militia first settled the area in 1744 on lands that were part of the patent of Thomas, the sixth Lord of Fairfax. Of the 26 original half-acre lots that Wood plotted out for the new town of Winchester, he set aside four for public use. Residents were required to possess both an "in-lot" in town and an "out-lot" on the outskirts. The in-lots were generally where the citizen resided, while the out-lots were used for personal livestock and the growing of vegetables. In 1752, the town was officially chartered in the Virginia General Assembly.

One of Winchester's earliest residents was a young 16-year-old land surveyor by the name of George Washington, who first arrived in the town about 1748. Using his earnings from his surveying work, Washington bought a lot in town, as well as several acres on the outskirts of Winchester. The purchase allowed him to run for office and to be elected as Burgess from the Winchester area, a post that he served from 1758 through 1765—his very first political office. During the French and Indian War, Washington commanded the Virginia Regiment as lieutenant colonel from a little log building in town. He also supervised the construction of Fort Loudoun, which was built at the northern end of Winchester. Washington's office during this period has been preserved and is now a museum. It is also believed that Winchester's Washington Street is the earliest ever named for the nation's first president.

The young city was extremely advanced for its time and included one of the first municipal waterworks in the nation. In the early 1800s planners laid out a network of oak pipes eight feet under the streets, which carried 300,000 to 500,000 gallons of water a day from the Old Town Spring downhill to the center of town.

Winchester was of prime strategic importance throughout the Civil War. It was taken and lost and retaken so many times that it has been said that the residents would look toward the courthouse upon waking in the morning to see which flag was flying that day. At different times, Confederate General "Stonewall" Jackson and Union General Philip Sheridan had headquarters in buildings that are still present less than two blocks apart in Winchester. Battles in the area included the First, Second, and Third Winchester, First and Second Kernstown, and the Cedar Creek.

In one of the most famous events in the build-up to the Civil War, Winchester Judge Richard Parker presided over the trial of abolitionist John Brown, who was arrested during the raid of Harper's Ferry Union Arsenal, by abolitionists in 1859. Ironically, the first casualty of the raid was Heywood Shepherd, Harper's Ferry railroad depot baggage master—a freed black man from Winchester.

The Handley Library was built in 1913 at the corner of West Piccadilly and North Braddock Street in Winchester. Considered one of the finest examples of Beaux-Art architecture, it was constructed with funds from a bequest by Pennsylvania Judge John Handley. The facility was completely restored in 2001.

General Stonewall Jackson orchestrated his valley campaign in 1861 and 1862 from a Gothic revival-style house that has been restored as museum in his honor. The Winchester area was also where Jackson suffered his only defeat in the Battle of Kernstown on March 22, 1862. Winchester was the home of Dr. Hunter Holmes McGuire, medical director of General Jackson's brigade. McGuire was known for humanizing the war by originating the custom of immediately releasing all medical officers upon their capture, a custom that is still practiced today as outlined in the Geneva Convention. He was also one of the founders of the American Medical Association.

Winchester is home to some of the finest and oldest architecture in the country. Abram's Delight, a limestone home built in 1754 by Abraham Hollingsworth, endured through the American Revolution, the French and Indian War, and the Civil War —today it is a museum. Glen Burnie, the homestead of Colonel James Wood, is another of

An aerial view of the Winchester Medical Center campus, looking north from Amherst Street along the east side of Route 37. The campus includes the Health Professions building, which has a pharmacy school that is leased to Shenandoah University.

Winchester's historic homes, which today is a museum and contains an impressive collection of antique furniture, paintings, and decorative arts, as well as extraordinary gardens.

Winchester also contains one of the finest examples of Beaux-Arts architecture to be found anywhere. The Handley Library was constructed in 1913 from a bequest by one of Winchester's most ardent benefactors, Judge John Handley.

View of the George Washington Office Museum from South Braddock Street. Washington began his political career serving the people of Winchester in the Virginia House of Burgesses. A bronze statue of Washington, erected in 2004, depicts his time spent in Winchester as a land surveyor before beginning his military and political career.

The library has recently undergone a major renovation, restoring its exterior carving and copper dome, three-story rotunda topped by an interior stained-glass dome, glass stacked floors, iron spiraled staircases, custom woodworking, and Beaux-Arts light fixtures to their original beauty.

Judge Handley, a wealthy Pennsylvania judge who never even lived in Winchester, was nonetheless so fond of the city that he left a bequest worth more than $2 million in 1895, $500,000 of which was to be held in a trust until it doubled in value. Handley's bequest was to be used specifically to build the library and "schools for the education of the poor." In addition to the library, the bequest also financed Handley High School, the "School for Black Students," and an ongoing private endowment for Winchester public schools. He is buried at Mt. Hebron Cemetery in Winchester.

Winchester native Charles Broadway Rouss was another of the city's major benefactors. Rouss got his first job in Winchester as a clerk in a general store, and by the age of 18 had opened his own establishment on South Loudoun Street. He was one of the first businessmen to create a successful catalogue company similar to Sears and Roebuck. In 1866, he moved to New York City and began to buy up real estate on Broadway, which is where he made most of his fortune. He died in 1902, but his love for Winchester never did. He contributed more than half the funding to build a new city hall, which was named in his honor. He also funded the construction of the Charley Rouss Fire Hall and the city's public water works, as well as Rouss Hall at the University of Virginia in Charlottesville. He is also buried at Mt. Hebron Cemetery.

Since the early 1800s, the distinguished Byrd family has played an integral part in Winchester's history. Richard Evelyn Byrd, Jr. moved the family into politics. He was elected to the Virginia House of Delegates and then served as speaker. He served as U.S. district attorney in Virginia and was considered a leader in the national Democratic party.

One of his sons was the world-renowned explorer, Admiral Richard Evelyn Byrd. At the age of 12, he con-

vinced his parents to allow him to go on a solo trip around the world. On May 9, 1926, Byrd made his first flight over the North Pole for which he was awarded the Congressional Medal of Honor. He also made a trans-Atlantic flight with Floyd Bennet the following year, and on November 28, 1929, he completed the first flight over the South Pole. In 1934, he conducted his second Antarctic expedition, which included nearly a six-month solo stay, an experiment that nearly took his life.

Abrams Delight (1754), which is now a museum, provides a delightful backdrop for those enjoying Wilkins Lake in Winchester's Jim Barnett Park.

The late Governor Harry Flood Byrd, another son of Richard, Jr., is one of Virginia's most notable politicians. He became known as the "pay-as-you-go" Virginia senator for his opposition to funding highway improvements with bonds. This pragmatic philosophy propelled him to the Virginia governorship in 1923. His son, Harry F. Byrd, Jr. also served as a Virginia senator and established a scholarship program that has recognized leadership qualities in high school graduates for more than 50 years.

However, it is not only Winchester's past that makes this city of 25,000 worthy of recognition. It also has its feet firmly planted in the 21st century as home to a major medical center and university. The 405-bed, nonprofit Winchester Medical Center (originally known as Winchester Memorial Hospital) employs more than 2,200 people and is one of the largest medical facilities in Virginia. Operated by Valley Health System, which has headquarters in Winchester, the medical center offers diagnostic, medical, surgical, and rehabilitative services, as well as the Shenandoah Valley Cancer Center and The Heart Center.

Sidewalk cafes and specialty retail shops along the Loudoun Street pedestrian mall, created in 1974, are popular destinations for visitors and workers in Old Town Winchester.

John Handley High School opened in 1923 and has served Winchester students ever since. It was constructed with funds donated by Pennsylvania Judge John Handley. In the fall, the Handley Band descends down the front steps into the Handley Bowl (seen in the foreground) before the school's football games.

Shenandoah University (SU), which relocated to Winchester in 1960, dates back to 1875. Today, it offers 60 programs of study to its 2,500 undergraduate and graduate students. SU is a private university, including the Harry F. Byrd School of Business, the School of Arts and Sciences, the Shenandoah Conservatory of Music, the School of Health Professions, and the Bernard S. Dunn School of Pharmacy. Both the medical center and the university play major roles in sustaining the economic health of Winchester through the supply of jobs and the plethora of services they offer to the community.

Winchester also hosts one of the major outdoor events on the east coast. The Shenandoah Apple Blossom Festival has been held each May since 1924 (except during World War II) and has grown to attract more than a quarter million people each year. The festivities include a Friday evening Firefighters Parade and the Grand Feature Parade on Saturday with more than 400 bands and floats, an

apple blossom queen, and a celebrity grand marshal (Mary Tyler Moore, Loni Anderson, Chevy Chase, Bob Hope, and Lucille Ball have all served as past marshals).

Winchester is not only a place to which celebrities come; it is also known as a place where stars come *from*. The late Patsy Cline is one of the world's most revered country western singers and was born in Winchester in 1932. She was posthumously elected to the Country Music Hall of Fame after she died in a

plane crash in 1963. Cline is now buried just outside the city limits. A local group hopes to raise the necessary funds to open a Patsy Cline Museum in the near future to honor her contribution to the world of music.

Winchester is unquestionably a special place: a unique nexus of American history, philanthropy, and a rare respect for the quality of life. For more than 260 years, this small city has continued to be the birthplace of great leaders, the focal point of major battles, and the beneficiary of extraordinary financial bequests. The millions of dollars that its citizens have left to Winchester attest to the powerful magnetism and great love engendered by a city that covers less than 10 square miles. For Americans it is a treasured site that speaks well of our strengths, and only history will tell what noble part this city and its citizens will play in our future.

The Ohrstrom-Bryant Theater, in the Shenandoah University Performing Arts Center (1998), welcomes motorists who enter Winchester along Millwood Avenue (U.S. Route 50) near Interstate 81.

ST. JOSEPH'S VILLA

What does it take to care for a child with special needs? What if that child has a developmental or learning disability, an emotional disorder, or has witnessed domestic violence or been abused himself? What if others have given up on that child, because he's so challenging? St. Joseph's Villa reaches out to children with these kinds of issues each and every day. Located at 8000 Brook Road in Richmond, Virginia, St. Joseph's Villa has been helping children and families meet and overcome some of life's most serious challenges since 1834.

Originally established as an orphanage, today St. Joseph's Villa is a nonprofit, non-sectarian organization that addresses a wide range of needs in the communities it serves. The Villa touches more than 600 children and families each day through a variety of educational, residential, and day support programs. "Our mission has always been to have a positive impact on the quality of life of children and families by helping them become self-reliant and productive in their communities," Ramon Pardue, chief executive officer of St. Joseph's Villa, explains. The scope of services that the Villa offers to facilitate that mission is as vast and grand as the 82-acre campus it occupies.

The Villa's expansive, serene campus is an oasis of help and hope for children and families who have faced some of life's most daunting challenges.

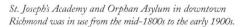

The work began in 1834 in a small church building on the corner of Fourth and Marshall in downtown Richmond. A local priest, Father Timothy O'Brien, had a dream of helping children: the poor, the homeless, the unloved, and the unwanted. With the help of four nuns from the Daughters of Charity, his dream became a reality. Father O'Brien and the Sisters took on the care and education of poor

St. Joseph's Academy and Orphan Asylum in downtown Richmond was in use from the mid-1800s to the early 1900s.

and orphaned girls, and soon thereafter established a day school for paying students as well.

From such humble beginnings the number of students attending the school increased with each passing year. In the 1860s, the Sisters formally organized their efforts as a private nonprofit organization. Amidst the turbulence of the Civil War, St. Joseph's continued to provide care and education while most other schools closed. The population of orphans was also on the rise and by 1868 St. Joseph's Orphan Asylum and Academy was incorporated. In 1874, a five-story building was erected.

For nearly a century St. Joseph's grew at its downtown Richmond location. In 1898, St. Joseph's acquired the Hollybrook Farm, just outside of Richmond and added to it in 1905. In 1922, Major James Dooley, a trustee of St. Joseph's Asylum, generously left a $3 million bequest to help fulfill his vision of a modern, state-of-the-art "home" for these children. As a result, the current campus opened in 1931 with 14 beautiful buildings of buff-colored tapestry brick, trimmed with terracotta and limestone, and roofed with green Spanish tile. The campus included eight cottage-style houses, a beautiful church of Romanesque design, a priest's cottage, a school, an administration building, and a gymnasium complete with a pool. It was the first cottage-plan orphanage on the East Coast and became a model for orphanages across the United States.

For the next 46 years, the Daughters of Charity continued to provide a loving home for children without parents—due to illness or other hardship. However, by 1977, orphanages were largely an institution of the past as the foster care system replaced their function. Simultaneously, other community needs were on the rise and became more urgent.

In keeping with the wisdom and generosity that had guided them for 143 years, the Daughters of Charity decided to step down from their governing role, having fulfilled their original mission. Brother Art Caliman was named the new executive director and Ramon Pardue came on board at that time as a consultant to help formulate St. Joseph's new emerging role in the community. "Since 1834, St. Joseph's Villa has continued to change while essentially staying the same in its goal—serving children with special needs," says Pardue. "From the Daughters of Charity to our current board of trustees, exceptional service for clients has always been the focus." In the first 12 to 18 months of the transition, the executive team worked tirelessly to develop new programs, policies, and budgets—and establish the necessary infrastructure to support human needs in the Richmond community. Today St. Joseph's Villa is comprised of three systems of service that offer a spectrum of educational, residential, and day programs.

Dooley School, a fully accredited education facility that provides alternative and special education services for elementary, middle, and high school students, is the cornerstone of the Villa's educational services. Dooley School offers individualized programs for young people with emotional and behavioral issues, learning disabilities, autism, mental retardation, and other challenges. It serves children across central Virginia and is a past recipient of the United States

Staff members adapt to each child's situation and focus on his or her strengths. At. St. Joseph's Villa each day is a new opportunity.

Department of Education's Excellence in Education Award. "The most important thing I've learned here is to not give in to negativity," says an eighth grade Dooley School student. "I got into a lot of trouble and was suspended from school. I was hanging around the wrong people and I trusted them. I didn't know how to say 'no.' I really like the smaller classes here. There are less distractions and I can learn better that way." This young man is one of hundreds of youths benefiting from the alternatives offered by the Dooley School.

The Villa's Respite Care Center was established in 1979 and provides a range of services to families whose children have mental and/or physical disabilities such as mental retardation, autism, cerebral palsy, and attention deficit disorder. Respite Care services include after-school, summer, and weekend programs and in-home curriculum that give families the support they need to keep their children at home, rather than in institutions. While at the center, the children engage in a variety of recreational, social, and educational activities that build independence, foster community involvement, and enrich their lives. The Respite Care Center is very unique and families with special-needs children repeatedly tell Villa staff that the service is truly life-giving.

In 1989, Mr. and Mrs. Lawrence Lewis approached St. Joseph's Villa to

Children at the Villa always find caring staff and volunteers who believe in them and support their success.

discuss the plight of homeless children in the Richmond area. The Lewises and their daughters, Louise, Janet, and Kenan, were very interested in creating a solution for these children and their mothers. The support and commitment of the Lewis family and the Flagler Foundation was instrumental in creating the Flagler Home at St. Joseph's Villa. According to Ramon Pardue, "The Lewises are the most generous and caring family I have ever met. Theirs has not been only a contribution of financial support, but a gift of total family involvement."

The first service of its kind in the state of Virginia, Flagler Home offers a two-year transitional housing program for homeless women and their children. At Flagler, families are given the opportunity to rebuild their lives and break out of the cycles that led them to homelessness. They prepare for independent living while receiving job-skills training, counseling, childcare assistance, financial planning, and other support services. The program can accommodate up to 26 families at any given time, and has served more than 300 mothers and almost 500 children since its inception.

One shining example of a Flagler success story is Mary Ellen. She participated in a computer-training program offered through Flagler Services. Her hard work, talent, and love for computers so impressed the instructor that he hired her a month after she completed the program. Today she maintains a website for his company. "When I came here I was a victim of domestic violence," Mary Ellen says. "I had no license, no car, and no resources. Now, I am no longer a victim. I am a survivor with a brighter future ahead for my children and myself." Flagler Home was recognized in 1993 by the White House as a model program for combating homelessness.

Additionally, the Villa offers a community-based program, Flagler Family Community Services, which offers similar supportive services to families who are transitioning from homelessness to self-sufficiency. The program also provides continuing assistance to Flagler Home families as they establish their new homes within the community.

As the only 100 percent handicapped accessible housing complex on the East Coast, the Villa's Hollybrook Apartments help adults with disabilities, their families, and the elderly live more rewarding and independent lives. Up to 60 residents reside in barrier-free, specially designed apartments that include

Resources and support for parents are important to a child's growth. St. Joseph's Villa believes that supporting the family is critical to helping children meet their fullest potential.

wheelchair accessible closets, low counters with roll-under spaces, roll-in showers, and other helpful features.

In 1993, the Child and Family Emergency Shelter opened at the Villa. The shelter offers a safe refuge for children in crisis, including those who have been abused or neglected. It provides short-term (up to 120 days) residential

care in a warm, supportive environment, helping children sort out troubling issues in their lives as they await more permanent placement. "When the state found me living away from home, they sent me to St. Joseph's Villa," says John, a recent client. "That made me even madder. My first week I even tried to run away, but I couldn't. The very next day my life changed. It was the staff at the Villa's emergency shelter. At first they listened to me, taught me how to talk and share feelings, and how to control my anger. They made me feel better about myself. They really believed in me."

The Villa's Lewis Children's Center provides affordable, quality childcare for children ages six weeks through 14 years. In addition to caring for those who live at Flagler Home while their mothers attend school or work, the center offers before and after school, full day, and summer programs for children in the surrounding community. Children are encouraged to develop their own unique talents and skills within a safe, nurturing environment. The small class sizes and caring staff at the center help each child feel special.

While the Villa stands as a beacon of tremendous service to the community, the community also gives back through a team of excited volunteers. David Lydiard, who lived at the facility as a child, is now a Villa board member and active volunteer. "Volunteering at the Villa is a great opportunity to help change the direction of someone's life," Lydiard says. "My memories and experiences there are very special and a big part of who I am today. As an alumnus, I feel as though it is my duty and privilege to help carry on this unique legacy."

While the Villa's role in the community has evolved over the years, the agency's mission is still one of helping children thrive and succeed despite the challenges in their lives. "We hold a fundamental belief in the value of *all* children," says Ramon Pardue. "If we can be a part of helping them recognize increments of success in their lives, no matter how great or small, then we will have done our job."

Helping each child find his or her own special talents is a Villa tradition.

*Visitors arrive at the Governor's Palace in Williamsburg
aboard a horse-drawn carriage, circa 1948. Courtesy,
The Library of Virginia*

WOODROW WILSON REHABILITATION CENTER

Surrounded by the Blue Ridge Mountains, the Woodrow Wilson Rehabilitation Center (WWRC) located in Fishersville, Virginia has a rich history in the field of rehabilitation. Spread over 230 acres, WWRC assists approximately 3,000 people a year with a wide variety of rehabilitation services including medical and vocational, in addition to assistive technology services. To understand why and how a facility like WWRC came into existence, it's important to trace the development of rehabilitation itself.

After World War I, thousands of wounded Americans returned home searching for an opportunity to become useful, productive citizens. Congress responded by creating the Veterans' Rehabilitation Service. Their experience resulted in a demand for a similar service to civilians.

The 1920 Virginia General Assembly established a vocational rehabilitation program just a few months prior to the passage of the first Federal Vocational Rehabilitation Act. The new federal law was signed by President Woodrow Wilson and was designed to promote the vocational rehabilitation of disabled persons and their return to employment. Later that same year Virginia's governor issued

Woodrow Wilson General Hospital, erected by the United States Army and acquired by the Commonwealth of Virginia, opened on November 1, 1947.

Woodrow Wilson Rehabilitation Center, pictured today.

a proclamation accepting the provisions of the federal act.

From 1920 to 1928 the program was administered by a special board. In 1928, it was placed as a "division" of the Virginia Department of Education. From 1928 through the early '30s the only rehabilitation staff in the entire state consisted of a director (R.N. Anderson), one secretary, three emergency caseworkers, and one part-time field assistant. W.K. Barnett joined the staff as a special assistant in 1937, just one year before special education and adult education were added to the program.

When war was declared in 1941, speedy production of military essentials became a necessity. As many able-bodied individuals were in the armed forces, a large number of workers had to be recruited from the ranks of those who were disabled. The rehabilitation service organized employment clinics for persons with disabilities in some parts of the state, resulting in more growth in its services.

Amendments to the Vocational Rehabilitation Act (Public Law 113) were passed in 1943. These amendments greatly expanded services to the handicapped, especially in regard to physical restoration. This act was only one of many events that took place over an approximately 20-year period indicating that rehabilitation was answering a definite growing need.

R.N. Anderson attended many crippled children's clinics with Dr. Roy M. Hoover, an orthopedic surgeon from Roanoke. Together they would discuss the possibility of a place that provided service after surgery, where amputees and other orthopedically disabled individuals could live and obtain physical restoration and preparation for employment. It became a dream for Anderson, Barnett, Dr. Hoover and others, notably Corbett Reedy, the state supervisor, to secure such a facility.

In response to the many injuries in World War II, centers emerged that were successfully using new concepts and techniques for the rehabilitation of the severely disabled. In January 1946, Barnett attended classes at one of these new centers which were directed by Colonel John Smith, a native of

Virginia. He was the first to fully develop the idea of combining social, vocational, and medical services to achieve dramatic results with a wide range of people with disabilities. These concepts dramatically pointed to the need for a comprehensive rehabilitation center.

While Barnett was studying and observing the work at the center, the Woodrow Wilson General Hospital located in Fishersville was declared surplus. The War Assets Administration agreed to transfer the property to the state. Governor Tuck asked for a plan that would allow the property to be used for both educational and rehabilitation purposes. Barnett and a representative from the Augusta County School Board developed a project that included a rehabilitation center, vocational school, and secondary school.

This plan was submitted to the War Assets Administration after which a delay ensued. Unable to understand the reason for this delay, Barnett traveled to Washington to discover that this office had "never heard of such a thing as a rehabilitation center." It only took one hour for him to convince the federal medical representative that the idea was a worthy one.

The property was acquired and divided, and the first state-owned and operated comprehensive rehabilitation center in the nation, a far-sighted vision of dedicated men, became a reality. How appropriate that Woodrow Wilson's name had been given to the army hospital and later the rehabilitation center. Not only was he born in nearby Staunton, but more significantly he had signed into law, for the first time in the country's history, a rehabilitation program of national scope.

WWRC opened on November 1, 1947 and Barnett was appointed director of the center. The first student was enrolled November 3, just two days later. In the following years it became generally recognized that rehabilitated individuals were paying back far more in taxes than what was invested in helping them to become self-supporting. Therefore, Congress continued to pass important additional

The center offers physical therapy using the Parastep.

legislation affecting the type of services provided by WWRC.

What is the future for WWRC and for the rehabilitation endeavor? WWRC's location near centers of learning and the recent pattern of congressional appropriations for research and training in such facilities are reasons for expecting growth and progress. Industry, labor, and government are increasing their support of rehabilitation.

As society reaps more benefits from the newer drugs and newer surgical procedures, death has been prevented. However, this has frequently been at the

cost of a disability. Also, there are groups of people with disabilities with growing needs to whom the center must determine its role. Some of these are the aging, individuals with autism, or substance abuse problems. All these factors point out that there will be more people with disabilities in the future. Therefore, the need for the center will increase.

The Woodrow Wilson Rehabilitation Center has two 501(c)3 nonprofit organizations. The WWRC Foundation was established in 1960 and is governed by a 15-member voluntary board of trustees. Its primary mission is to secure and provide funds and other support for comprehensive rehabilitative services. The Council of Organizations, Inc. was established in 1952 and is also governed by a volunteer board of directors. The Council consists of a group of individuals who assist the students and staff of the Woodrow Wilson Rehabilitation Center with gifts, monies, and volunteer services.

Rehabilitation changes lives. When a person enters the Center and is so severely disabled that recovery seems beyond reach, rehabilitative services can teach and retrain people to become not just self-sufficient, but a working member of the community. They leave with a newfound self-esteem, an inner strength to face their lifelong challenges and the skills they need to hold jobs and pursue careers.

Vocational training at the center includes drafting and computer aided design.

GOVERNORS UNDER THE COMMONWEALTH 1776-1852
(CHOSEN BY THE STATE LEGISLATURE)

Patrick Henry, 1776-1779

Thomas Jefferson, 1779-1781

William Fleming, member of the Council of State acting as governor, June 4-June 12, 1781

Thomas Nelson, Jr., June-Nov. 1781

David Jameson, member of the Council of State acting as governor, Nov. 22-30, 1781

Benjamin Harrison, 1781-1784

Patrick Henry, 1784-1786

Edmund Randolph, 1786-1788

Beverley Randolph, 1788-1791

Henry Lee, 1791-1794

Robert Brooke, 1794-1796

James Wood, 1796-1799

Hardin Burnley, member of the Council of State acting as governor, Dec. 7-11, 1799

John Pendleton, member of the Council of State acting as governor, Dec.11-19, 1799

James Monroe, 1799-1802

John Page, 1802-1805

William H. Cabell, 1805-1808

John Tyler, Sr., 1808-1811

George William Smith, member of the Council of State acting as governor, Jan. 15-19, 1811

James Monroe, Jan. 19-April 3, 1811

George William Smith, member of the Council of State acting as governor, April 3-Dec. 6, 1811

George William Smith, Dec. 6-26, 1811

Peyton Randolph, member of the Council of State acting as governor, Dec. 27, 1811-Jan. 4, 1812

James Barbour, 1812-1814

Wilson Cary Nicholas, 1814-1816

James P. Preston, 1816-1819

Thomas Mann Randolph, 1819-1822

James Pleasants, 1822-1825

John Tyler, Jr., 1825-1827

William B. Giles, 1827-1830

John Floyd, 1830-1834

Littleton Waller Tazewell, 1834-1836

Wyndham Robertson, member of the Council of State acting as governor, March 1836-March 1837

David Campbell, 1837-1840

Thomas Walker Gilmer, 1840-1841

John Mercer Patton, member of the Council of State acting as governor, March 20-31, 1841

John Rutherford, member of the Council of State acting as governor, March 1841-March 1842

John M. Gregory, member of the Council of State acting as governor, March 1842-Jan. 1843

James McDowell, 1843-1846

William Smith, 1846-1849

John Buchanan Floyd, 1849-1852

GOVERNORS UNDER THE COMMONWEALTH
(ELECTED BY POPULAR VOTE)

Joseph Johnson, 1852-1856

Henry Alexander Wise, 1856-1860

John Letcher, 1860-1864

William Smith, 1864-1865

Francis Harrison Pierpont (provisional governor), May 1865-April 1868

Henry H. Wells (provisional governor), April 1868-Sept. 1869

Gilber C. Walker (provisional governor), Sept. 1869-Dec. 1869

Gilbert C. Walker, 1870-1874

James Lawson Kemper, 1874-1878

Frederick W. M. Holliday, 1878-1882

William E. Cameron, 1882-1886

Fitzhugh Lee, 1886-1890

Philip W. McKinney, 1890-1894

Charles T. O'Ferrall, 1894-1898

James Hoge Tyler, 1898-1902

Andrew Jackson Montague, 1902-1906

Claude A. Swanson, 1906-1910

William Hodges Mann, 1910-1914

Henry Carter Stuart, 1914-1918

Westmoreland Davis, 1918-1922

E. Lee Trinkle, 1922-1926

Harry F. Byrd, 1926-1930

John Garland Pollard, 1930-1934

George C. Peery, 1934-1938

James H. Price, 1938-1942

Colgate W. Darden, Jr., 1942-1946

William M. Tuck, 1946-1950

John Stewart Battle, 1950-1954

Thomas B. Stanley, 1954-1958

J. Lindsay Almond, Jr., 1958-1962

Albertis S. Harrison, Jr., 1962-1966

Mills E. Godwin, Jr., 1966-1970

A. Linwood Holton, 1970-1974

Mills E. Godwin, Jr., 1974-1978

John N. Dalton, 1978-1982

Charles S. Robb, 1982-1986

Gerald L. Baliles, 1986-1990

Lawrence Douglas Wilder, 1990-1994

George Allen, 1994-1998

James S. Gilmore, III, 1998-2002

Mark R. Warner, 2002-present

VIRGINIA FAST FACTS

Virginia is known as "the birthplace of a nation."

Dulles International Airport is one of the busiest airports in the world.

Virginia was named for England's "Virgin Queen," Elizabeth I.

Eight United States presidents were born in Virginia: George Washington, Thomas Jefferson, James Madison, James Monroe, William Harrison, John Tyler, Zachary Taylor, and Woodrow Wilson.

Patrick Henry gave his "Give me Liberty or Give me Death" speech in St. John's Church in Richmond, Virginia.

The current state capital of Richmond was also the capital of the Confederacy.

Jamestown was the first English settlement in the U.S and was also the first capital of Virginia.

The state song is "Carry me back to Old Virginia."

The first Thanksgiving in North America was held in Virginia in 1619.

Founded in 1693, Williamsburg's own College of William and Mary is the second oldest educational institution in the United States.

Virginia native Booker T. Washington conceived the National Negro Business League.

Wild Ponies have roamed freely on Assateague Island for centuries.

Cotton and coal were the two largest exports to come from the Norfolk area in the 1870s.

Virginia was admitted to the union on June 25, 1788 as the tenth of the 13 original colonies.

Virginia has had three capital cities: Jamestown, Williamsburg, and Richmond.

Of the 4,000 battles fought in the Civil War, more than half were fought in Virginia.

The tomb of the Unknown Soldier is in Arlington National Cemetery.

Robert E. Lee, commanding general of the Army of Northern Virginia, surrendered his soldiers to General Ulysses Grant on April 9, 1865 at the Appomattox Court House.

Martinsville was one of the largest furniture-producing centers in the world in the 1900s.

The state flower isn't really a flower—it is the blossom of the dogwood tree, which is also the state tree.

Six presidents' wives were born in Virginia: Martha Washington, Martha Jefferson, Rachel Jackson, Letitia Tyler, Ellen Arthur, and Edith Wilson.

Yorktown is the site of the final victory of the American Revolution.

Adopted in 1776, the two figures on the state flag are acting out the meaning of the state motto "Sic Semper Tyrannis" (which means "Thus always to tyrants"). Both are dressed as warriors with the woman, Virtue, representing Virginia and the man holding a scourge and chain meant to be a tyrant.

The first peanuts grown in the United States were grown in the state of Virginia.

Mount Vernon, George Washington's home, is located in Virginia.

The Chesapeake Bay Bridge Tunnel is the world's largest bridge-tunnel complex.

Gail Borden's condensed milk, patented in 1856, became an important part of the Union soldier's diets.

The Pentagon building in Arlington is the largest office building in the world.

Lieutenant General Thomas J. "Stonewall" Jackson refused to use pepper on his food, saying it gave him pains in his left leg.

The American Revolution ended with the surrender of Cornwallis in Yorktown.

General Thomas Jackson got his nickname "Stonewall" in Manassass— the site of two major Civil War battles. In the 1870s Norfolk replaced Richmond as the state's commercial center.

President Thomas Jefferson designed his own home and called it Monticello.

The state bird is the cardinal.

Seven U.S. presidents are buried in Virginia: Washington, Jefferson, Madison, Monroe, Tyler, Taft, and Kennedy.

BIBLIOGRAPHY

♦

CHAPTER 1

Billings, Warren M., ed. *The Old Dominion in the Seventeenth Century.* Chapel Hill, N.C.: The University of North Carolina Press, 1975.

Breen, T.H. "Making a Crop." *Virginia Cavalcade* 36 (Autumn 1986): 52-64.

_____ . *Puritans and Adventurers.* New York: Oxford University Press, 1980.

Bruce, Philip Alexander. *Economic History of Virginia in the Seventeenth Century.* New York and London: MacMillan and Co., 1895.

Dowdey, Clifford. *The Golden Age.* Boston and Toronto: Little, Brown and Co., 1970.

Fleming, Daniel B., Paul C. Slayton, and Edgar A. Toppin, eds. *Virginia History and Government.* Morristown, N.J.: Silver Burdett Co., 1986.

Fogel, Robert William, and Stanley L. Engerman. *Time on the Cross: The Economics of American Negro Slavery.* Boston and Toronto: Little, Brown and Co., 1974.

Hemphill, William Edwin, Marvin Wilson Schlegel, and Sadie Ethel Engelberg, eds. *Cavalier Commonwealth.* New York: McGraw-Hill Co., 1957.

Jamestown-Yorktown Foundation. *The Story of John Rolfe.* Jamestown, Va.: Jamestown-Yorktown Foundation, 1962.

Nash, Gerald D., ed. *Issues in American Economic History.* Lexington, Mass.: D.C. Heath & Co., 1972.

Salmon, Emily J., ed. *A Hornbook of Virginia History.* Richmond: Virginia State Library, 1983.

Stewart, Peter Crawford. "The Commercial History of Hampton Roads." Ph.D. diss., University of Virginia, 1967.

Ward, Harry M. *Richmond: An Illustrated History.* Northridge, Ca.: Windsor Publications, 1985.

Wertenbaker, Thomas J. *The Planters of Colonial Virginia.* New York: Russell & Russell, 1959.

Wright, Louis B. *The First Gentlemen of Virginia.* Charlottesville, Va.: Dominion Books, 1964.

CHAPTER 2

Bondurant, Agnes M. *Poe's Richmond.* Richmond: Poe Association, 1978.

Brown, Alexander Crosby. *The Dismal Swamp.* Chesapeake, Va.: Norfolk County History Society of Chesapeake, Va., 1967.

Dabney, Virginius. *Richmond: The Story of a City.* Garden City, N.Y.: Doubleday & Co., 1976.

_____ . *Virginia: The New Dominion.* Charlottesville, Va.: The University Press of Virginia, 1971.

Dickinson, William Penn, Jr. "The Social Saving Generated by the Richmond & Danville Railroad." Master's thesis. University of Virginia, 1975.

Dunaway, Wayland Fuller. *History of the James River and Kanawha Company.* New York: Ames Press, 1922.

Fleming, Daniel B., Paul C. Slayton, and Edgar A. Toppin, eds. *Virginia History and Government.* Morristown, N.J.: Silver Burdett Co., 1986.

Fogel, Robert William, and Stanley L. Engerman. *Time on the Cross: The Economics of American Negro Slavery.* Boston and Toronto: Little, Brown and Co., 1974.

Harwood, Herbert H., Jr. *Rails to the Blue Ridge.* Falls Church, Va.: Pioneer America Society, Inc., 1969.

Havighurst, Walter. *Alexander Spotswood: Portrait of a Governor.* Williamsburg, Va.: Colonial Williamsburg, distributed by Holt, Rinehart and Winston, 1967.

Hemphill, William Edwin, Marvin Wilson Schlegel, and Sadie Ethel Engelberg, eds. *Cavalier Commonwealth.* New York: McGraw-Hill Co., 1957.

Keir, Malcolm. *The March of Commerce.* New Haven, Ct.: Yale University Press, 1927.

Kercheval, Samuel. *A History of the Valley of Virginia.* Woodstock, Va.: W.N. Grabill, Power Press, 1903.

Mordecai, Samuel. *Richmond in By-Gone Days.* 2d ed. 1860. Reprint. Richmond: The Dietz Press, 1946.

Morton, Richard L. *Colonial Virginia.* Vol. 2. Chapel Hill, N.C.: University of North Carolina Press, 1960.

Rice, Otis K. *The Allegheny Frontier.* Lexington, Ky.: The University Press of Kentucky, 1970.

Salmon, Emily J., ed. *A Hornbook of Virginia History.* Richmond: Virginia State Library, 1983.

Simkins, Francis Butler, Hunicutt Jones Spotswood, and Sidman P. Poole. *Virginia: History, Government, Geography.* New York: Charles Scribner's Sons, 1957.

Stewart, Peter C. "The Commercial History of Hampton Roads." Ph.D. diss., University of Virginia, 1967.

———. "Railroads and Urban Rivalries in Antebellum Eastern Virginia." *The Virginia Magazine of History and Biography* 81:1 (January 1973): 3-22.

Striplin, E.F. Pat. *The Norfolk & Western: A History.* Roanoke, Va.: Norfolk & Western Railway Co., 1981.

CHAPTER 3

Anderson, J.H. *American Civil War.* London: Hugh Rees, 1912.

Andrews, Matthew Page. *Virginia: The Old Dominion.* New York: Doubleday, Doran & Co., 1937.

Boney, F.N. *John Letcher of Virginia.* University, Ala.: University of Alabama Press, 1966.

Conrad, Alfred H., and John R. Meyer. "The Economics of Slavery in the Ante-Bellum South." In *Issues in an American Economic History,* edited by Gerald D. Nash. Lexington, Mass.: D.C. Heath & Co., 1972.

Crews, Ed. "Arsenal of the Confederacy Closing Down." *Richmond News Leader* (March 18, 1987).

Dew, Charles B. *Ironmaker to the Confederacy: Joseph R. Anderson and the Tredegar Iron Works.* New Haven, Ct.: Yale University Press, 1966.

Fleming, Daniel B., Paul C. Slayton, Jr., and Edgar A. Toppin, eds. *Virginia History and Government.* Morristown, N.J.: Silver Burdett Co., 1986.

Foote, Shelby. *The Civil War: Fort Sumter to Perryville.* New York: Random House, 1958.

Gates, Paul W. *Agriculture and the Civil War.* New York: Alfred A. Knopf, 1965.

Hemphill, William Edwin, Marvin Wilson Schlegel, and Sadie Ethel Engelberg, eds. *Cavalier Commonwealth.* New York: McGraw-Hill Book Co. 1957.

Hoehling, A.A. and Mary. *The Day Richmond Died.* San Diego, Ca.: A.S. Barnes & Co., 1981.

Jennings, George Wood. *The Fiscal History of Virginia from 1860-1870.* Ph.D. diss., University of Virginia, 1961.

McPherson, James M. *Ordeal by Fire.* New York: Alfred A. Knopf, 1982.

Moore, George Ellis. *A Banner in the Hills.* New York: Appleton-Century-Crofts, 1963.

Paludan, Phillip Shaw. *Victims: A True Story of the Civil War.* Knoxville, Tenn.: University of Tennessee Press, 1981.

Pond, George E. *The Shenandoah Valley in 1864.* New York: Charles Scribner's Sons, 1883.

Rubin, Louis D., Jr. *Virginia: A Bicentennial History.* New York: W.W. Norton and Co., 1977.

Salmon, Emily J., ed. *A Hornbook of Virginia History.* Richmond: Virginia State Library, 1983.

Simkins, Francis Butler, Hunnicutt Jones Spotswood, and Sidman P. Poole. *Virginia: History, Government, Geography.* New York: Charles Scribner's Sons, 1957.

Smith, James D. "Virginia During Reconstruction." Ph.D. diss., University of Virginia, 1960.

CHAPTER 4

Andrews, Matthew Page. *Virginia: The Old Dominion.*Garden City: Doubleday, Doran & Co., 1937.

Chesson, Michael B. *Richmond After the War, 1865-1890.* Richmond: Virginia State Library, 1981.

Dabney, Virginius. *Virginia: The New Dominion.* Garden City, N.J.: Doubleday & Co., 1971.

Fleming, Daniel B., Paul C. Slayton, Jr., and Edgar A. Toppin, eds. *Virginia History and Government.* Morristown, N.J.: Silver Burdett Co., 1986.

Hemphill, William Edwin, Marvin Wilson Schlegel, and Sadie Ethel Engelberg. *Cavalier Commonwealth.* New York: McGraw-Hill Book Company, 1957.

Jennings, G.W. "The Fiscal History of Virginia from 1860 to 1870." Ph.D. diss., University of Virginia, 1961.

Moger, Allen W. *Virginia: Bourbonism to Byrd, 1870-1925.* Charlottesville, Va.: University Press of Virginia, 1968.

Pearson, Charles Chilton. *The Readjuster Movement in Virginia.* Gloucester, Mass.: Peter Smith, 1968.

Ransom, Roger, and Richard Sutch. *One Kind of Freedom.* Cambridge: Cambridge University Press, 1977.

Rubin, Louis D., Jr. *Virginia: A Bicentennial History.* New York: W.W. Norton and Co., 1977.

Salmon, Emily J., ed. *A Hornbook of Virginia History.* Richmond: Virginia State Library, 1983.

Sanford, James K., ed. *A Century of Commerce.* Richmond: Richmond Chamber of Commerce, 1967.

Simkins, Francis Butler, Hunnicutt Jones Spotswood, and Sidman P. Poole. *Virginia: History, Government, Geography.* New York: Charles Scribner's Sons, 1957.

Smith, James D. "Virginia During Reconstruction." Ph.D. diss., University of Virginia, 1960.

Squires, W.H.T. *Unleashed At Last.* Portsmouth, Va.: Printcraft Press, 1939.

Stiles, Robert. "Why the Solid South? or Reconstruction and Its Results." Unpublished manuscript, Baltimore, 1890.

CHAPTER 5

Andrews, Matthew Page. *Virginia: The Old Dominion.* Garden City: Doubleday, Doran & Co., 1937.

Cocke, Karen Hisle, ed. "A Century of Leadership." *Masthead* (Winter 1985): 3-9.

Chesson, Michael B. *Richmond After the War, 1865-1890.* Richmond: Virginia State Library, 1981.

Clark, Victor S. *History of Manufactures in the United States.* Vol. 3. New York: McGraw-Hill Book Co., 1929.

Dabney, Virginius. *Richmond: The Story of a City.* Garden City: Doubleday & Company, Inc., 1976.

———. *Virginia: The New Dominion.* Charlottesville, Va.: University Press of Virginia, 1971.

Fleming, Daniel B., Paul C. Slayton, Jr., and Edgar A. Toppin, eds. *Virginia History and Government.* Morristown, N.J.: Silver Burdett Co., 1986.

Hemphill, William Edwin, Marvin Wilson Schlegel, and Sadie Ethel Engelberg. *Cavalier Commonwealth.* New York: McGraw-Hill Book Co., 1957.

Morton, Richard L. *History of Virginia.* Vol. III. Chicago: The American Historical Society, 1924.

Netherton, Nan, Donald Sweig, Janice Artemel, Patricia Hickin, and Patrick Reed. *Fairfax County, Virginia: A History.* Fairfax, Va.: Fairfax County Board of Supervisors, 1978.

Rubin, Louis D., Jr. *Virginia: A Bicentennial History.* New York: W.W. Norton and Co., 1977.

Salmon, Emily J., ed. *A Hornbook of Virginia History.* Richmond: Virginia State Library, 1983.

Sanford, James K., ed. *A Century of Commerce.* Richmond: Richmond Chamber of Commerce, 1967.

Simkins, Francis Butler, Hunnicutt Jones Spotswood, and Sidman P. Poole. *Virginia: History, Government, Geography.* New York: Charles Scribner's Sons, 1957.

Smith, James D. "Virginia During Reconstruction." Ph.D. diss., University of Virginia, 1960.

Ward, Harry M. *Richmond: An Illustrated History.* Northridge, Ca.: Windsor Publications, 1985.

CHAPTER 6

Addington, Luther F. *A Short History of Extreme Southwest Virginia.* Big Stone Gap, Va.: Chamber of Commerce, 1965.

Bacon, James A., Jr. "Prosperity's Just a Dream at Centennial." *Roanoke Times* (June 12, 1983): A-1.

Barnes, Raymond P. *A History of Roanoke.* Radford, Va.: Commonwealth Press, 1968.

Clark, Victor S. *History of Manufactures in the United States.* Vol. 3. New York: McGraw-Hill Book Co., 1929.

Fleming, Daniel B., Paul C. Slayton, Jr., Edgar A. Toppin, eds. *Virginia History and Government.* Morristown, N.J.: Silver Burdett Co., 1986.

Harmon, John Newton. *Annals of Tazewell County.* Richmond, Va.: W.C. Hill Printing Co., 1925.

"The Historical Pageant of Progress." Program sponsored by Southwestern Virginia, Wytheville, Va., July 4-6, 1934.

Jack, George S., and E.B. Jacobs. *History of Roanoke County.* Roanoke, Va.: Jack and Jacobs, 1912.

Jacobs, E.B. *History of the Norfolk & Western Railway.* Roanoke, Va.: Jack and Jacobs, 1912.

Lewis, Helen M. "The Changing Communities in the Southern Appalachian Coal Fields." Paper presented at the International Seminar on Social Change in the Mining Community, Jackson's Mill, W. Va., Oct. 6, 1967.

Morton, Richard L. *History of Virginia.* Vol. 3. Chicago: The American Historical Society, 1924.

Niemi, Albert W., Jr. *U.S. Economic History.* 2d ed. Chicago: Rand

McNally College Publishing, 1980.

Pendleton, William C. *History of Tazewell County and Southwest Virginia.* Richmond: W.C. Hill Printing Co., 1920.

Prescott, E.J. *The Story of the Virginia Coal and Iron Company, 1882-1945.* Virginia Coal and Iron Co., 1945.

"Roanoke Diamond Jubilee." Program from celebration, Roanoke, Va., June 14-23, 1957.

Rubin, Louis D., Jr. *Virginia: A Bicentennial History.* New York: W.W. Norton and Co., 1977.

Salmon, Emily J., ed. *A Hornbook of Virginia History.* Richmond: Virginia State Library, 1983.

Verrill, A. Hyatt. *Romantic and Historic Virginia.* New York: Dodd, Mead & Co., 1935.

Workers of the Writers' Program of the Work Projects Administration in the State of Virginia. *Roanoke: Story of a County and City.* Roanoke, Va.: Roanoke City School Board, 1942.

CHAPTER 7

Alexander, Will W. "The Negro in the New South." *Southern Workman* 50 (January-December 1921): 145-152.

Barrett, Harris. "The Building and Loan Company of Hampton." *Southern Workman* (July 1890): 79.

Blount, George W. "The Virginia State Negro Business League." *Southern Workman* 48 (January-December 1921): 599-605.

Browning, James B. "Beginnings of Insurance Among Negroes." *Journal of Negro History* 22 (1937): 417-432.

Dabney, Virginius. *Below the Potomac.* New York and London: D. Appleton-Century Co., 1942.

——. *Virginia: The New Dominion.* Garden City, N.Y.: Doubleday & Co., 1971.

Dabney, Wendell P. *Maggie L. Walker and The I.O. of St. Luke.* Cincinnati: The Dabney Publishing Co., 1927.

DuBois, W.E. Burghardt. *The Negro in Business.* New York: AMS Press, 1899.

Engs, Robert Francis. *Freedom's First Generation.* University of Pennsylvania Press, 1879.

Fitzgerald, Ruth Coder. *A Different Story: A Black History of Fredericksburg, Stafford and Spotsylvania, Virginia.*

Unicorn, 1979.

Fleming, Daniel B., Paul C. Slayton, Jr., and Edgar A. Toppin, eds. *Virginia History and Government.* Morristown, N.J.: Silver Burdett Co., 1986.

Fleming, Jesse E. "A History of Consolidated Bank and Trust Company, A Minority Bank." Thesis, The Stonier Graduate School of Banking, conducted by the American Bankers Association at Rutgers, The State University, New Brunswick, N.J., 1972.

Harmon, J.H. "The Negro As a Local Businessman." *Journal of Negro History* 14:2 (April 1929).

Heinemann, Ronald L. *Depression and the New Deal in Virginia.* Ph.D. diss., University of Virginia, 1968.

Katz, William Loren, gen. ed. *Negro Population in the United States, 1790-1915.* New York: Arno Press and The New York Times, 1968.

Lindsay, Arnett G. "The Negro in Banking." *Journal of Negro History* 14:2 (April 1929): 156-192.

Ludlow, Helen W. "The Negro in Business in Hampton and Vicinity." *Southern Workman* 33 (September 1904): 463-501.

McConnell, John Preston. *Negroes and Their Treatment in Virginia From 1865-1867.* Pulaski, Va.: B.D. Smith and Brothers, 1910.

Mordecai, Samuel. *Richmond in Bygone Days.* 2d ed. 1860. Reprint. Richmond: The Dietz Press, 1946.

Morgan, Philip, ed. *Don't Grieve After Me.* Hampton, Va.: Hampton University, 1986.

Pierce, Joseph A. *Negro Business and Business Education: Their Present and Prospective Development.* New York: Harper and Brothers Publishers, 1947.

Rich, William M. "Negro Commercial Activities in Tidewater, Virginia." *Southern Workman* 50 (January-December 1921): 138-144.

Taylor, A.A. "The Negro in the Reconstruction of Virginia." *Journal of Negro History* 11 (1926): 243-537.

U.S. Labor Department. *Bulletin.* Vol. 3. Washington, D.C.: GPO, 1898.

Washington, Booker T. *The Negro in Business.* Boston: Hertel, Jenkins and Co., 1907.

Wheelock, F.D. "A Community Asset: People's Building and Loan Association of Hampton, Virginia." *Southern Workman* 50 (January-December, 1921): 545-546.

Woodson, C.G. "Insurance Business Among Negroes." *Journal of Negro History* 14:2 (April 1929): 202-214.

Woodward, C. Vann. *The Strange Career of Jim Crow.* New York: Oxford University Press, 1955.

Work, Monroe N. "The Negro in Business and the Professions." *Annals of the American Academy* 138-140 (November 1928).

Workers of the Writers' Program of the Work Projects Administration in the State of Virginia. *The Negro in Virginia.* New York: Hastings House, 1940.

CHAPTER 8

Barnes, Raymond P. *A History of Roanoke.* Radford, Va.: Commonwealth Press, 1968.

Bottom, Raymond B. *Virginia's Record of Progress.* Richmond: Virginia State Chamber of Commerce, 1950.

Dabney, Virginius. *Virginius Dabney's Virginia.* Chapel Hill, N.C.: Algonquin Books of Chapel Hill, 1986.

_____ . *Virginia: The New Dominion.* Charlottesville, Va.: University Press of Virginia, 1971.

Fleming, Daniel B., Paul C. Slayton, Jr., Edgar A. Toppin, eds. *Virginia History and Government.* Morristown, N.J.: Silver Burdett Co., 1986.

Gottman, Jean. *Virginia at Mid-Century.* New York: Henry Holt & Co., 1955.

_____ . *Virginia In Our Century.* Charlottesville, Va.: University Press of Virginia, 1969.

Hairston, L. Beatrice W. *A Brief History of Danville, Virginia.* Richmond: The Dietz Press, 1955.

Hartig, Dennis. "Plug Tobacco: A Lucrative Home-Grown Industry." *Martinsville Bulletin* (July 4, 1976).

Heinemann, Ronald L. "Depression and the New Deal in Virginia." Ph.D. diss., University of Virginia, 1968.

Hundley, R.B. "Company Started on Town's Gamble and Founder's Nerve." *Martinsville Bulletin* (July 4, 1976).

_____ . "American Furniture Company Born as Tobacco Declined." *Martinsville Bulletin* (July 4, 1976).

Moger, Allen W. *Virginia: Bourbonism to Byrd, 1870-1925.* Charlottesville, Va.: University Press of Virginia, 1968.

Moore, John Hammond. *Albemarle: Jefferson's County.* Charlottesville, Va.: University Press of Virginia, 1976.

Niemi, Albert W., Jr. *U.S. Economic History.* 2d ed. Chicago: Rand McNally College Publishing, 1980.

Richards, Ginny. "Textiles: Industrialists Developed Natural Resources to Diversify Economy." *Martinsville Bulletin* (July 4, 1976).

_____ . "From Sawmillers to Furniture Giants." *Martinsville Bulletin* (July 4, 1976).

_____ . "Gravely Family Enterprises Date Back 180 Years." *Martinsville Bulletin* (July 4, 1976).

_____ . "Farmer's Son Builds Industrial, Political Career." *Martinsville Bulletin* (July 4, 1976).

_____ . "Fieldcrest: The Firm That Built Its Own Neighbors." *Martinsville Bulletin* (July 4, 1976).

Ritz, Wilfred J. *Industrial Progress in Virginia.* Richmond: Virginia State Chamber of Commerce, 1974.

Rubin, Louis D., Jr. *Virginia, A Bicentennial History.* New York: W.W. Norton & Co., 1977.

Sinclair, Andrew. *Prohibition: the Era of Excess.* Boston: Little, Brown and Co., 1962.

Ward, Harry M. *Richmond: An Illustrated History.* Northridge, Ca.: Windsor Publications, 1985.

Ward, H. Wesley. *The Administration of Liquor Control in Virginia.* Charlottesville, Va.: Division of Publications, Bureau of Public Administration, University of Virginia, 1946.

CHAPTER 9

Bacon, James A., Jr. "Booming Coal Port." *Roanoke Times and World News* (December 28, 1980).

Darnton, Donald C., and Charles O. Meiburg. "The Contributions of the Ports of Virginia to the Economy of the Commonwealth." Report prepared by the Bureau of Population and Economic Research, Graduate School of the Business Administration, University of Virginia, Charlottesville, Va., January 1968.

Department of Research and Statistics, Federal Reserve Bank of Richmond. *Economic Effects of the War on the Hampton Roads Area.* Richmond, Va., 1944.

Fleming, Daniel B., Paul C. Slayton, Jr., and Edgar A. Toppin, eds. *Virginia History and Government.* Morristown, N.J.: Silver Burdett Co., 1986.

Foss, William O. *The United States Navy in Hampton Roads.* Norfolk, Va.: The Donning Co., 1984.

Gottman, Jean. *Virginia In Our Century.* Charlottesville, Va.: University Press of Virginia, 1969.

Kale, Wilford. "Trials of War, Peace Challenge Yard's Creed." *Richmond Times-Dispatch* (January 18, 1987).

Knapp, John L., James Hammond, and Donald P. Haroz. "The Impact of Virginia's Ports on the Economy of the Commonwealth." Charlottesville, Va.: Tayloe Murphy Institute, 1976.

Marsh, Charles F., ed. *The Hampton Roads Communities in World War II.* Chapel Hill, N.C.: University of North Carolina Press, 1951.

Ritz, Wilfred J. *Industrial Progress in Virginia.* Richmond: Virginia State Chamber of Commerce, 1947.

Rubin, Louis D., Jr. *Virginia: A Bicentennial History.* New York: W.W. Norton & Co., 1977.

Tazewell, William L. *Norfolk's Waters.* Northridge, Ca.: Windsor Publications, Inc., 1982.

CHAPTER 10

Burton, Mary T., ed. *Picture Yourself in Fairfax County.* Dunn Loring, Va.: Fairfax County Chamber of Commerce, Spring 1987.

Center for Innovative Technology. *The Institutes.* Herndon, Va.: Center for Innovative Technology, 1985.

_____ . *Annual Report,* 1986.

Cosin, Elizabeth. "Reston Lands Space Station." *The Connection* (April 8, 1987).

Deschamps, Elizabeth M. "Reston in Space Windfall." *The Connection* (July 8, 1987).

_____ . "Space." *The Connection* (August 5, 1987).

Fairfax County Economic Development Authority, *Business Report: Construction Activity.* Vienna, Va.,

June 1987.

_____ . *Business Report: Association Report.* Vienna, Va., April 1986.

_____ . *Business Report: International Business, Fairfax County.* Vienna, Va., January 1986.

_____ . *Business Report: Real Estate Market Review.* Vienna, Va., Winter, 1986.

Fairfax Economic Development Authority. *Fairfax Prospectus.* Vienna, Va., September 1985.

_____ . *Fairfax Prospectus.* Vienna, Va., May 1985.

_____ . *Fairfax Prospectus.* Vienna, Va., May 1984.

_____ . *Economic Overview.* Vienna, Va., 1986.

_____ . *Population and Demographics.* Vienna, Va., nd.

_____ . *Labor Market.* Vienna, Va., 1986.

_____ . *Fairfax Prospectus.* Vienna, Va., April 1986.

_____ . *Fairfax Prospectus.* Vienna, Va., December 1985.

Fleming, Daniel B., Paul C. Slayton, Jr., and Edgar A. Toppin, eds. *Virginia History and Government.* Morristown, N.J.: Silver Burdett Co., 1986.

Gottman, Jean. *Virginia In Our Century.* Charlottesville, Va.: University Press of Virginia, 1969.

Governor's Task Force on Science and Technology in Virginia. *The Report of the Governor's Task Force on Science and Technology in Virginia.* Vol. 1. Richmond: 1983.

Kelly, Brian, ed. *Regardie's Regional Report: Fairfax County.* Washington, D.C.: Regardie's, 1986.

Malone, Roger. "Engineers Orbit Reston." *Alexandria Journal* (September 1, 1987).

Miller, Bill. "'Area Second to None' For High-Tech Firm." *Richmond Times-Dispatch* (July 24, 1983).

_____ . "Northern Virginia." *Richmond Times-Dispatch* (July 24, 1983).

Rhodes, Karl. "Make-Do Dulles." *Virginia Business Magazine* (April 1986): 32-44.

Rubin, Louis D., Jr. *Virginia: A Bicentennial History.* New York: W.W. Norton & Co., 1977.

Ruehrman, James C. *High Technology and Electronics.* Richmond: Commonwealth of Virginia, Department of Industrial Development, 1982.

_____ . *Virginia Facts and Figures.* Richmond: Commonwealth of Virginia, Department of Economic Development, 1987.

_____ . *High Technology, Biomedical and Related Industries.* Richmond: Commonwealth of Virginia, Department of Economic Development.

Williams, Bob. "Putting the Byte on Uncle Sam." *Virginia Business Magazine* (November 1986): 53-56.

_____ . "From Rats to Riches." *Virginia Business Magazine* (October 1986): 19-24.

CHAPTER 11

Editorial "Travelocity: A Warning For Region?" *Bristol Herald Courier* (Feb 13, 2004)

Galuszka, Peter "Building the Behemoths." *Virginia Business* (May 2001).

_____ . "Defense in Virginia." *Virginia Business* (August 2002).

Hazard, Carol "Cuts to Hit Area Hard." *Richmond Times-Dispatch* (April 28, 2004).

_____ . "Capital One Shifts Focus." *Richmond Times-Dispatch* (April 29, 2004).

Martinsville-Henry County Chamber of Commerce Competitive Assessment http://www.mhcchamber.com/userdocs/11dec03_compet_assess_final.pdf

Moritsugu, Ken "Foreign Trade Deprives Textile Towns of Hope Factory Workers Suffer, Retrain For the Unknown." *Detroit Free Press* Washington Staff (March 22, 2004).

Peters, John "Furniture Under Fire." *Virginia Business* (August 2002).

Rubino, John "Teligent Rising." *Virginia Business* (November 2002).

Shean, Tom "Banks Turn to Branches to Help Drive Expansion." *The Virginian-Pilot* (April 7, 2004).

Still, Kathy "Note: Answering the Phone is Not a Technology Job!!!" *Bristol Herald Courier* (February 22, 2004).

_____ . "Call Centers 'A Global Business in a Competitive Market.'" *Bristol Herald Courier* (September 28, 2003)

Still, Kathy "Economic Efforts Detailed at Summit." *Bristol Herald Courier* (October 24, 2003).

Virginia Business "Special Publisher's Profile: Banking." *Virginia Business* (May 2003).

Waldman, Amy "What India's Upset Vote Reveals." *New York Times* (May 15, 2004).

INDEX

Y